ABSOLUTELY FOXED

ABSOLUTELY FOXED

Graeme Fowler

with John Woodhouse

SIMON & SCHUSTER

London · New York · Sydney · Toronto · New Delhi

A CBS COMPANY

First published in Great Britain by Simon & Schuster UK Ltd, 2016
A CBS COMPANY

1 3 5 7 9 10 8 6 4 2

Simon & Schuster UK Ltd
1st Floor
222 Gray's Inn Road
London WC1X 8HB

www.simonandschuster.co.uk

Simon & Schuster Australia, Sydney
Simon & Schuster India, New Delhi

A CIP catalogue record for this book is available from the British Library.

ISBN: 978-1-4711-4229-1
Ebook ISBN: 978-1-4711-4233-8

Typeset and designed in the UK by M Rules
Printed and bound by CPI Group (UK) Ltd, Croydon, CR0 4YY

For

Sarah Louise

Katherine Elizabeth

Georgina Ruby

Alexa-Rae Evie

Without their love, support and humour I would be lost.

I love you and am proud of you.

CONTENTS

FOREWORD

by Sir Ian Botham

My first night out with Graeme Fowler, the man we all call Foxy, came after the Ashes touring party of 1982-83 was announced. During the evening, as you do, I got him in a headlock, the idea being to persuade him to drink a glass of whisky – all quite natural at the time, an everyday part of an evening out – but I couldn't change his mind. He still doesn't like whisky, and I'm still trying to get him to drink it now.

I mention this because it shows a determination. As a player, Foxy was one of the gutsiest I ever encountered. When he went out to the middle, he always showed bottle and fight. We, as an England dressing room, always loved having him at the top of the order. We knew he was going to give his all. Never did you question his commitment to the cause. But his wasn't a game built solely on grit. Foxy was incredibly skilful, too. You only have to look at the double century he made in Madras to know he was a really good player. I was at the other end when he made a century against the West Indies at Lord's, too. As a batsman, you don't get to three figures against that kind of attack unless you know what you're doing.

In his last two Tests, Foxy scored 201 and 69, and then he didn't play again for England. How that happened, I'm not quite sure. He should undoubtedly have played more Test cricket than he did. He had many more good years in him, and it was England's loss that at Test level we didn't see them.

Alongside his skill came his personality. You need all sorts to make a dressing room, it is vital to have a balance, and Foxy was an integral part of that. He made a dressing room tick. His humour and wit were legendary – and he's still got that now – at least he thinks he has! Not only that but, like me, he knew you have to switch off. When you step off the field, you can't take the game with you. If you do, it starts affecting those around you as well. Foxy was one of those, and we understood each other from that point of view.

We also shared a similarity in that if he felt something was unnecessary or unjust, he'd say so. As he was coming up through the system, if he saw something he disagreed with or felt was unfair, he'd stand his ground, and I respected him for that.

Over the years, we have remained close. We still live near to one another, and we always enjoy catching up for what we call our 'board meetings'. We click, not just as former players, but as people. Foxy is as good a friend as I have ever made in the game. He's useful to have around when it comes to talking about the games we played, because I don't remember any of it!

We were together for the latter end of our careers at Durham CCC and you could see the way he was going to go. He always had time for the young players and I wasn't surprised when he went down the route of coaching. What he achieved in setting up and running the centre of excellence at Durham University, a system expanded across the country, was incredible. He is directly responsible for a large number of very good players making it into first-class cricket and beyond. The coaching system he put in place produced amazing results, and it's a great loss to the game in this country that it no longer exists. I can't understand quite why anyone would feel the need to change something that had so much success. It's something I, and a lot of other people, can't work out.

In recent years, Foxy has been affected by depression. When I first found out, I didn't know how to take it. I don't claim to understand about depression, I don't understand the problems people have mentally, everyone's different in different ways, but I wanted him to know he has a friend if ever he needs one. These days he's got his issues under control, but he knows he's got that cushion there – people who care about him – and hopefully that in itself is some kind of help.

The fact he is no longer coaching doesn't mean the end for Foxy. He's not in the wilderness. He is a man with an immense amount of knowledge and I am sure he will put it to good use. The game of cricket owes a lot to Graeme Fowler. It needs people like him. There are many good years in him yet. You can't keep a man like Foxy out the game for long.

CHAPTER 1

THIS IS A LOW

I am lying in a tent in my back garden. It is late – the early hours in fact – and the family are all inside asleep. I find that particular escape elusive. It's why I'm here, outside. It's where I spend the nights, May to September, each year. Tonight, I lie with my head by the opening. It means I can look up and see the stars. Wonderful. And then a light rain starts falling. It feels beautiful, absolute paradise. And it is in this state, I consider my life.

I was 47. I'm very lucky: I have a good constitution, I'm hardly ever ill, rarely get colds, don't have headaches, it's impossible for me to throw up. But every winter I get a cough, and this particular winter I couldn't get rid of it. I went to the doctor's, had four sets of antibiotics, steroids, and it was still there. It was that bad I'd have coughing fits and wake everybody up. So I slept downstairs, so I didn't disturb my wife Sarah and the kids.

I remember it clearly. One day I was sitting on the settee, and Sarah was standing next to me: 'You need to go back to the doctors,' she told me.

'I'm still on antibiotics.'

'No, not for that.'

'Well, what for?'

'You're depressed.'

'What?'

'Graeme,' she said, 'you haven't spoken to any of us for weeks.'

It was true. I just hadn't realised it – unlike my daughter, Georgina. 'Dad,' she said, 'you just sit in the conservatory with your Land Rover magazine – and it's the same magazine.'

At no point was I aware that this was what I'd become, and that this was the space I was in. I hadn't noticed that I'd stopped talking, stopped communicating. I hadn't realised I'd lost interest in everything. And that really is how it was. Nothing mattered, I didn't care about anything – family, my life, nothing. And when I thought about it, I realised I didn't really want to be alive. Everything was hopeless, pointless, worthless.

I'd been feeling like that, but hadn't stopped, sat up, and worked it out. For the first time in my life, I hadn't analysed anything. It was as if my head had just stopped working. All I felt was like I was at the bottom of a well.

I'm going to cry now, but I'll carry on.

Once I realised I hadn't thought about it, I knew there was something massively wrong. So when Sarah told me to go to the doctor, because I was depressed, I didn't question it. I didn't say anything or deny it, I simply agreed to go. When I got there, the doctor asked me how I felt, and I replied: 'I feel terrible. I can't sleep, I'm not interested in anything, everything's pointless, I've no appetite.'

He asked if I'd thought of suicide? 'No, because I know I have a nice life. I have a great job, great family, lovely wife. I know all that exists, but I can't get to it. It's over there, and I can't get there. So am I going to kill myself? The answer is no. But do I wish I was dead? Yes.'

We sat and talked. He told me I was clinically depressed, although on the sick note he gave me it said 'moderate depressive episode'. And I quite liked that, because when I read the word 'moderate', I didn't think 'that's terrible', I thought 'thank fuck, there are people in a worse state'. That's always been my way, flipping things. I looked on the bright side of being moderately depressed.

The doctor explained the situation to me: 'Look, this is not going to turn around in two weeks. This is going to take a long time. It'll be a slow process, so you'll have to be patient.'

I started on medication, but after three weeks I felt just the same and still wasn't talking to anybody. At one point I didn't leave the house for six weeks – this from a man who has lived outside all his life. I can't stand being inside. I was shut down so much I couldn't even go into the back garden. I was sleeping downstairs and lived on the sofa. Sarah would go to work, the kids would go to school, I would want a cup of tea – and I couldn't get up off the settee to make it. I was almost paralysed. It was incredibly horrible. It's just bewildering to think there's nothing happening. There were no synapses at all working in my brain.

So the first pills hadn't worked. I was then faced with a

fortnight of waiting for them to leave my system so I could start again. By this point I'd had five weeks, but the difference was now I was aware I was depressed. There was no reason for it. I'd got the centre of excellence at Durham University going, and had been there ten years, but all of a sudden I couldn't analyse it because my head wouldn't work and I couldn't think. I was physically immobile, but I was mentally incapable with it. Sometimes I'd get up, and Sarah would ask where I was going, and I didn't know, so I'd sit back down again. I was just not functioning at all.

They put me on Citalopram. I felt like it was starting to work, but not much. The dose increased and increased until eventually I was on about 150ml a day, which is a massive amount. It made me feel numb, like I was looking at life through five-inch-thick glass, but that was better than wanting to be dead. It was better than feeling worthless and pointless, and after a few weeks I started to function just a little bit.

It was then that I came up with 'the scale', out of 20, to describe how I was feeling. Ten is neutral, and anything above that number I'm OK and can communicate. Anything below, I'm not and I'm struggling. When you've got young children – Kate was nine, Georgina was eight, and Alexa-Rae was just two (so she didn't know what was going on) – you need a way to get things across simply.

They'd ask how I was, but I couldn't talk to them or vocalise how I felt. I didn't know how to approach it with kids that age, so it was great when that flash of inspiration came along to give me the scale. I told Sarah about it, and she asked where I was. I thought for a moment and told her I was five, which was probably as bad as I've ever been. The best I've ever been is 16.

Sarah told the girls about the system, and so they'd come up to me: 'Hi Daddy, what number are you?'

'About a seven.'

Kate or George would ask: 'Do you want me to sit with you, Daddy? Or do you want to be on your own?' And whatever I said, they didn't take offence.

George told me years later that she thought at the time that I didn't like her. And that's a horrible thing, but thankfully we'd said to the girls: 'We'll always love you. We might not always like what you're doing. But we'll always love you.' She kept that close, realising: 'Daddy doesn't like me, but I know he loves me.' She always had that.

I thought of my depression as a chemical imbalance in my brain, and told myself this was not permanent, and once the chemicals were balanced again it would be OK. Once I'd worked that out, it was obvious my brain had started to work a little bit because I could start to think again. I began to realise I must have come out of the worst bit. Even though I still felt dreadful, I knew I must be making progress.

I had three months off work, went back, and struggled like mad. I didn't mention it to any of the lads at the centre of excellence because I wasn't well enough to tell them. I could manage to deal with the pre-match stuff, but when the game started I needed to be on my own. A lot of the time I'd sit in my Land Rover next to the pavilion and pretend I was watching. I wasn't really. I was just staring at the ground. I was literally just existing, and I was using energy I didn't have, so every time I came home my numbers were going down, so I was actually worse when I was in the house.

I worked out that when I coached, I acted. When I spoke at

dinners, it was acting. Broadcasting – acting. Every day I'd be acting, acting, acting, and then all of a sudden, when I'd come home, I couldn't act anymore. When it got to the end of the season, I fell in a heap again, but at least it was summer, the nights were bright. I was starting to spend more time outside and to engage with people again.

Without telling anybody, I wanted to look at life through less glass, so I started to reduce my medication. I didn't tell the doctor or Sarah – nobody. I did it very slowly, but it was going OK – I'd got to numbers above ten and we were starting to do things again. When the kids knew I was above ten, they understood they could ask if we could do something that day. But even that had parameters. If we went shopping and there were too many people in the shop, or it was too busy, too warm, I'd say: 'I can't handle this, Sarah. I'll be outside.' Even now when we go shopping, 90 per cent of the time I don't go in the store as I can't stand being inside for too long. And that's one of the reasons I started sleeping in the garden between May and September.

One day Sarah looked at me and realised I wasn't having a good day, so she asked if I needed to up my medication. 'Sarah,' I said, 'I haven't been taking any for six months.'

'Wow! You're doing fantastic then.'

'Yes, I'm just having a wobble today.' And she almost cried.

When I was first diagnosed with depression, it was Sarah's brother, Mark, who at the time was a psycho-geriatric nurse, who gave me a wonderful piece of advice – 'Do what you must, avoid what you can.' I took that with me from day one. I also listened to what the doctor said, which was to be patient. It meant I could allow each day to have its own pattern.

As time went on – and remember I was still wishing I was dead at this point – if I had a good ten minutes that was great. If I had a bad ten minutes, I didn't care. I just let it go. It's almost like trying to get rid of mental food poisoning – you have to let it work its way through. I was patient, took each day as it came, recognised it wasn't going to be a short thing. I came to the conclusion that, for me, this was probably going to be like being an alcoholic. Once you are, you are. Even if you're not drinking, even if you've not had a drink for years, you still are. I thought: 'Well, if that's the way it is, get on and deal with it.'

That meant I had to modify my behaviour. I've never had a good memory – things in the distant past, yes, what happened yesterday, no. If someone tells me something, in two hours I won't know what they've said as I'll forget it. I know a lot of people say that, but I genuinely will, so I started writing things down. I also began to talk about what was happening to me, although not in counselling. When I first went to see the GP, he'd asked if I wanted to go to a therapy group or talk with a psychiatrist, but it was the last thing I wanted to do.

That's just me, everybody's different; some people need that sort of interaction, desire it, and it helps them enormously, but I'd always made all my own decisions in my life by going inside my own head. I never wanted to talk to people about my depression when I was depressed; I would internalise it, but as time went on I found that by talking about it other people would gain comfort and reassurance, and that's when I realised being open about it was actually helping some people. I didn't need to know why, but decided to keep on doing it. Once I was well enough, and found I was able to talk about it,

I'd tell people my story and see if they could make any sense of it, because no one's the same. I'm more than happy talking about my mental health. I've never felt it's something I should keep back. It doesn't define me, but it's part of who I am.

I've also found humour is very important in that conversation. At home, for instance, I'm the 'house lunatic' – that's what my family call me. Some people might think that's a bit bizarre, but I actually think it helps break down the nastiness and seriousness of it. If you can take the piss sometimes, it's therapeutic. But perhaps that's because humour has always been very therapeutic to me. The same way as David Lloyd and I used humour to discuss serious points, I do the same with mental health. If I talk to somebody about my mental-health issues and make them laugh, initially they feel uncomfortable, but I encourage them to laugh if they find it funny. Because although it's a serious topic, finding humour in it is, to me, essential. It's a 'fuck you'.

Talking to others, I'd find some people could attribute a direct trigger to the onset of their depression, but for me it came totally out of the blue. I've no idea why it happened and I've given up trying to work out why. I can only think I'd been a dynamo for 40 years and my head has said: 'I've had enough, I'm going on holiday. You've mistreated me for all these years. Some of the stuff you've done you should never have got away with. I've had enough. Bollocks. I'm off. Going. Bye!'

Maybe I was predisposed to it, but if I was it took a long time to kick in. I mean, I've been on tour, as happened in New Zealand, when I was not getting picked, pig sick of being there for weeks on end, wishing I was at home. But that's not depression – that's emotionally down, not mentally down.

There's a massive difference between emotions and mental health. Emotions happen for a reason, they ebb and flow, there's a cause. Mental health isn't like that. There doesn't have to be a cause. There doesn't have to be a trigger.

The only possible indication was during my playing career when, at the end of the season, I'd go home, draw the curtains, unplug the phone, and lie on the settee for a week, not talk to anyone and just watch videos. You could call that the blues. Alternatively, you could look at it as a way of mentally recharging the batteries after playing non-stop all season. I needed that, no matter how I was feeling, physically or mentally, as my reserves of mental energy were depleted by September. Similarly, when I talk about my depression, I pay an emotional price, not a depressive price. I need to recharge, but that's OK because it's only emotions.

I'm not sure the same thing would happen now, as the game is different. Players these days might see a specialist for help. There may very well be one available at their club, or in the set-up, as with the England team. But it wasn't like that during my career. If I'd asked my club if I could see a sports psychologist, first of all they'd almost certainly not have known what one was, and second they'd have wanted to know why I'd wanted to see one and wondered what was wrong with me. These days it's different, as attitudes have changed. Players will often see one simply to make them better at their sport, not because they have an issue.

That's not to say the acknowledgement of mental-health issues isn't lagging behind in sport – as it is in society as a whole. It's only in the last five years or so that people have started to acknowledge it as a problem in our game. With

Marcus Trescothick, people didn't think it was a widespread issue and he was the most iconic sufferer. They thought 'that's just him'. But it's not just the odd person, such as Trescothick and Michael Yardy; it's far more of a problem.

The good news is the game is learning to cope. The Professional Cricketers' Association (PCA) has been excellent and very proactive with mental illness. They asked me to put together a checklist to help players keep a note on their mental health, which is useful, but I think what's more important is to provide a checklist of indicators for team-mates. It's more likely they'll notice something's wrong, just as Sarah did with me – I wasn't aware.

If I was in a dressing room with someone who was a fun, lively bloke and a good cricketer, and all of a sudden he decided he was not coming out at night and he'd gone really quiet in the dressing room, I might start thinking 'hang on, something's not right here'. It could be a domestic issue, his child being ill, all sorts of reasons, but if I was the coach I'd gently take him into the office, tell him what I'd observed and ask him: 'Are you aware of this? Is there anything you want to discuss with me? Anything I can do to help?'

If he didn't want to engage, all you can do is make it clear that you are not happy to see him like that, and remind him that you are there if he changes his mind and decides he needs to talk. Sometimes, two days later, he'll be back and admit that he'd not been feeling great, which gives you a chance to offer him someone to talk to or some time off.

I don't know why it's taken so long for there to be a discussion about mental health in cricket. I've played with three people who killed themselves, but few people have a concept of what it's like. Ian Botham has little idea about depression, which is fine, because he doesn't know. Why would he? He's never had it, and probably never will, and I'm thrilled to bits for him. I'm not angry; I'm pleased that he doesn't understand, just as I didn't when it came to David Bairstow, Mark Saxelby and Danny Kelleher, players who all committed suicide.

I'm fortunate in that I don't have the 'suicide gene'. I simply wanted the pain to end: I didn't want to be in the situation I was in and feel that bad, and recognised that if I was dead it would end. If people have the suicide gene, it's my suspicion it's at that point they do it. But I didn't want to be out of it through killing myself, as I knew somehow, somewhere, I had a good life, and all that came with it.

In the deepest darkest moments it's almost like I'm wading through a river of crap, but at the far shore, down the river, everything will become clear and it will be lovely – but I've got to go through all that to get there. I have got to go through a process and, once I've worked that out, I have no option but to go through it, because I'm not going to kill myself. Even if I didn't have all I have around me I wouldn't commit suicide, because I have a memory of how good life can be. It's not just about my wife and three kids – it's the whole of life.

Perhaps it helps that I'm a complete and utter atheist. I have no belief in a higher power. I don't think I'm going to go to heaven, I'm just going to go. Being an atheist means there's nothing after this, there's no 'I can do it in the next life'. I don't believe that. For me, you've got to make the most of this life, because you're here only once. So even though you're going through all this turmoil, you've got to keep going because this is your only chance, this isn't a dress rehearsal. I'm not going to go to heaven and have another life or be reincarnated as a budgie that talks. Thinking like this almost frees you up to have a little bit of strength, because this is it – make the most of it. Nowadays, I can also look at it and be pragmatic and know it will go away. Experience does count for something.

I've always had two reactions when people have found out I suffer from depression. The first is: 'How can you have mental-health issues? You've always been bright and bubbly.' And the other one is: 'I've always known you were a lunatic.' But the reality is it's just a thing, a chemical imbalance. It doesn't make me a bad person. I haven't thrown a brick through your window or nicked your car.

But most of all, I'm still here. I'll live my life to the full. That, after all, is what I've always tried to do.

CHAPTER 2

THIS IS A HIGH

Cricket is a game based on failure. Statistically, the best batsman was Don Bradman, who scored a hundred every three innings, therefore two-thirds of his career was a failure. As a batsman, you always have to deal with not being the player you want to be and find a way of coping with that. You have to find a way to ensure that when you do get in, you make runs and capitalise on it. You also have to deal with the fact that nine times out of ten you never do your job. Even if you get 140, you should have got 180. It never ends. This being the case, if you can't switch off, cricket is a game that can consume you. You need an escape or else it can eat you up inside. You can't let it define you as a person.

I was quite good at switching off. I was very good at switching off! But I did that by telling myself 'cricket is what I do, it's not who I am'. That's not to say I wasn't totally committed to the game, because I was. It's more of a reflection of the fact I was more than willing to embrace other areas of life that came with it. I knew that being good at cricket took me into areas I'd never have got near in a million years – meeting musicians, going to brilliant places, parties, all sorts of stuff. So while getting hit in the box by Joel Garner is the downside of playing international cricket, the upside is you meet some very interesting people, some of whom are famous.

The first time that really kicked in for me was during the Ashes tour of 1982-83. We were in Sydney and Ian Botham asked me what I was doing that night. I didn't have any plans, so he said: 'You're with me.' It was Beefy; you didn't question anything. A bit later, Vic Marks chirped up: 'Foxy, are you coming tonight?'

'Yeah. Where are we going?'

'We're having dinner with Elton John.'

'Fuck off.'

I had loads of Elton John records, loved his music right from the start. So off we went, Bob Willis, Beefy, Vic Marks and me. We met Elton in a restaurant. Naturally, he had an entourage. Beefy, who knew Elton, said hello and then we filed off into a private room, cricketers down one side of the table, Elton's group the other. Directly opposite me was the man himself. Inside I was churning: 'Oh my God!'

He was wearing an earring, a big hoop with a jewelled parrot sitting on the bottom. All I could do was sit there thinking: 'That's Elton John! That's Elton John!' But I was also wondering what I was going to say to him. Obviously, I was nervous. I'd not really been in this situation before. If anything, I was socially clumsy. I was trying to come up with something to say when, all of a sudden, Elton leant across to me. 'Do you know,' he confided, 'I've been nervous about this all day.'

'Why?'

'Meeting you lot. You're international cricketers.'

It instantly dawned on me. You're only famous if someone thinks you are. He thinks we're famous because we're sportsmen, I think he's famous because he's a musician. But the truth is he's just a bloke and I'm just a bloke. We both wore nappies when we were kids. Yes, he's had a slightly more extravagant life, made a little bit more money, and he's a bit more famous – well, more than a bit – but essentially all he wants to do is talk about sport, about cricket.

I couldn't believe how warm and funny he was. I had a brilliant night, and after that I realised: 'It doesn't matter who they are, they're just people; they're just the same.' I say this now to my kids: 'What a person can do may be extraordinary, but it doesn't make them extraordinary.'

The following winter was the 1983-84 tour of Fiji, New Zealand and Pakistan. Again Elton was around. He'd become big friends with the England team and we with him. We had a party with him in Auckland, and it is here that to say I misbehaved would be an understatement.

During that tour I made friends with quite a few locals and we had a great time. One particular occasion, I'd been out with them during the day to a music festival. You weren't allowed to take any drink, but we took Tequila and orange in a Fanta bottle. That night, Elton was having a party at the hotel. By the time I got there it's safe to say I was plastered. At one point I saw a glass of water. I was thirsty, so I just downed it, and it was only as I finished I realised it was gin. It didn't improve my situation, something which became clear when I fell backwards through a glass-topped coffee table, which was smashed to pieces, including the framework.

As everybody was cleaning up, I found myself positioned between Elton and his then wife Renate. I don't know why, but I just turned sideways and bit her on her upper arm. I've no idea why I did it – up until that point, the only person I'd routinely bitten was Paul Allott – but she wasn't very happy. 'Get him out of here!' she screamed as she ran off. Everyone turned to look. There was all sorts of kerfuffle going on. John Reid, Elton's manager, tried to push me out the way, so I took a swing at him, missed and hit the wall. Next thing I know, Beefy was dragging me out of the room.

He put me to bed, but I didn't want to go to bed. So I got up, went back to the party, and took another swing at John Reid. It was down to Beefy once again to drag me off. 'Make sure he stays in his room,' he ordered a nurse at the party. I didn't want to stay in my room. So off I went outside, furious I couldn't go back and join the fun. There was a derelict building next door. I was so angry that, like a lunatic, I put my hand straight through a window. Backhand – the scar on my knuckle is still there. The nurse had a little white car – white body, wheels, mirrors, bumpers – and I was leaning against it. She was trying to talk sense into me, but I wasn't having any of it. When I looked down, the blood from my hand had run down the wing and filled up the alloy wheel. I was, put simply, bleeding like a stuck pig. Being a nurse, she could see I needed stitches. She went upstairs and fetched Beefy. He came down, put me in a headlock, and took me to hospital.

'Do you want anaesthetic?' It was a reasonable question, but I just came out with a mouthful. Beefy put his forearm across my throat and started squeezing. 'Foxy,' he whispered, 'keep quiet, or I'll break your neck.' So the doctor stitched me up, I went back to the hotel, and next thing I knew I was waking up in the morning with a bandage on my arm down to my hand. I was feeling terrible, but starting to piece things together. I noticed that my face was sore. It was then it came back to me: I'd bitten Elton John's missus and I'd taken a swing at John Reid – and I was a man who'd never had a fight in his life.

I knew that day Elton was having a barbecue on his hotel balcony. He'd sent out, bought half a lamb, the works. I, however, wasn't really in the barbecue mood. I was feeling terrible, embarrassed and ashamed. I thought I had to go and apologise, not least because the following day we were leaving for Pakistan. Eventually, I wandered up to Elton's room and knocked on the door. Fair to say I wasn't expecting the best of receptions. Elton's PA answered: 'Hey, Foxy!' He beckoned me in. I was feeling, to put it mildly, a little sheepish. Then something unexpected happened. Everyone got up, cheered, and gave me a round of applause. I got a standing ovation. Elton was sitting on the bed in a pair of faux zebra-skin boots and white towelling dressing gown. All I could do was apologise. 'Foxy, come on,' he said. 'It's all right. Stay! Stay!' But I couldn't, I was just too embarrassed.

I didn't see Elton again until 1986 when I had possibly the best winter any England cricketer has ever had. I was working for a company in Perth which made scissor lifts, owned by two Scouse brothers. They offered me a salary to play for North Perth, and they told me they wanted to buy Lancashire

County Cricket Club, but as it's a private members' club that was never going to be possible. So they gave me a good wage and a nice little car. Together we lived in a four-bed detached house with its own swimming pool, gardener and cleaner – it was absolutely stunning.

'Whatever you buy, wherever you go,' I was told, 'get a receipt.'

'Whatever I do? Whatever I buy? Case of beer? Champagne? You're just going to give me the money back?'

They had an executive box at the WACA, the cricket ground in Perth, to entertain clients, through which I took the England team, the Australia team, and Elton John and his band. And they had a 44ft yacht on which to watch the America's Cup, which was taking place off the Fremantle coast at the time. Now that's not a bad job is it? And that's how it was. The whole winter was an extravagance. We used to drink champagne out by the pool and throw the corks on the roof. Before I came home, I thought I should clean out the gutter. I filled two cardboard boxes.

I was out of the England team by then, but in Perth I'd gone to watch them net and they were going to an Elton John concert. They offered to take me along, and I was eventually persuaded that it would be all right to go with them. When I got there, Elton spotted me. 'Foxeye [that's what he used to call me], what are you doing here?'

'I'm living in Perth, in Scarborough, near the beach.'

'Come and see me tomorrow,' he said.

I met him at his penthouse suite. He asked if my house had a barbecue, and when I told him it did, he suggested having a barbecue there that afternoon. A few hours later, two gold stretch limousines drew up outside my house, with me behind them in my little Ford Fiesta. His people got out, checked everything was secure and that the garden was walled so no one could see in. Then he said we should go and get some food. There was a supermarket nearby so he jumped in my Fiesta, stretch limos following behind, and I took him inside. There was this promotional woman selling chipolata sausages, and she had no idea who Elton John was. 'Excuse me, sir, would you care to try . . . ?' Before she could get any further, this huge bodyguard picked the whole lot up and ate them.

Elton filled three shopping trolleys. He was like a kid. Well, when was the last time he'd been in a supermarket? He was running around, just chucking stuff in. When we got to the till, I told him we wouldn't need it all. 'Yes,' he looked at me, 'but darling, you won't need to go shopping for a few days, will you?'

That Christmastime, Elton rang me up: 'Foxeye, what are you doing for New Year's Eve?'

'I don't know, why?'

'Can I have a party at your house?'

It was the usual subtle little affair. Elton got his hotel to decorate the property, had lobsters, oysters and champagne flown in, there was a DJ, two chefs, three waiters, three bouncers – the whole thing must have cost tens of thousands. The England team came, as well as some of the Aussies. Word, unsurprisingly, got out. All of a sudden there were 150 people outside queuing to get in. The whole thing was just phenomenal. You didn't have a chance to step back and think 'this is ridiculous!' because it all was.

Elton called me up a couple of days later: 'I wanted to say thank you for letting me have a party at your house.' He flew me first class to Adelaide where, naturally, I was picked up by a bloke with a peaked cap in a stretch limousine. I was taken to a hotel, put up in a suite, same again in Sydney, where we went on to the harbour on a yacht he'd hired. So there I was, on this beautiful boat, single, having the time of my life, an absolute hoot. But I ran out of Taittinger Rosé. Disaster, I know.

It was like a military operation, as messages were sent out left, right and centre, and next thing we saw was a courier, driving round the foreshore on a motorbike with a huge case of Taittinger on the back. He got in a little boat, came out to ours, and there it was, chilled Taittinger. All I could think was: 'This is a different life.'

We moved on to Melbourne. He wanted to go clothes shopping, so we went to this incredibly trendy shop, which they opened just for him. He tried on all these clothes – and they were turning the arms and legs up to make them fit. After a while I went to get a coffee, and when I came back Elton threw a package at me. It was a $300 shirt, shall we say distinctive. In total he spent way over $10,000. I looked at his mound of purchases.

'You can't possibly wear all that.'

'I know, but my fun is in buying them. If I never wear them it doesn't matter, I've had a great morning.' I thought that as he'd earned the money, he deserved to spend it how he wanted.

Later we went to the MCG where we bumped into the former England fast bowler Frank Tyson. He said something Elton didn't like and a massive argument erupted. It was a sporting matter. Elton was on the side of the sportsman, how much he has to give, how little he earns, and Frank was saying they earn far too much. Elton was really passionate about this kind of thing. He looked at Patti Mostyn, his tour manager. 'Pateye,' he said, 'let's buy Foxeye out of his contract. How much will it cost us?'

I was on one of the best contracts anyone has ever had to play club cricket, in the region of $10,000. Elton considered this: 'I wouldn't sing two bars of fucking "Rocket Man" for ten thousand dollars!' He genuinely thought that people like Ian Botham – and he was probably right with Beefy – should earn as much money as him. He actually viewed his talent as just being able to write little songs. Real talent was what Beefy did, or George Best and Ivan Lendl. In his mind, he simply wrote happy little tunes.

Eventually, we got past the partying and used to sit down and have a chat. One day he took the whole Australia team to a seafront restaurant in Perth. He had one stretch limousine, I had another, and afterwards we went to the White Horse Yacht Club, the British America's Cup challenge headquarters. But before all that we had a couple of hours to kill and just hung around, two blokes, like any others, having a chat. It was at that point I asked him, 'How come I'm here?'

He pondered this. 'I thought cricketers were quite boring until I came across you in Auckland. You were the best entertainment we've ever had.' He'd never wanted me to leave that party. He loved the chaos I was creating.

I also found out years later the true reason behind my sore jaw in Auckland. I was messing about with Beefy, the usual knockabout stuff. 'Pack it in!' I said to him.

'You pack it in,' he replied, 'or I'll knock you out.'

'You wouldn't knock me out.'

'I've done it before.' The penny dropped. 'You bastard! Did you knock me out in Auckland?'

'How do you think I got you to sleep?'

Looking back, I should be grateful.

CHAPTER 3

THE WAY UP

'You need to calm down.' That's what people used to say to me when I played for Lancashire. And I'd say, 'Hang on a minute. Do you think I'd jeopardise my career by being an idiot? I might be daft but I'm not stupid. I don't do half the things you think I'm doing.'

Lancashire manager Jack Bond once pushed me against a wall and told me to stop sleeping with a committee member's wife. I got him round the throat: 'Two things, Bondy. One, I'm not. And two, that sort of gossip could get me the sack. So pack it in.'

People underestimated the kind of person I was. In fact, it was only when I started writing for the *Sunday Telegraph* and working on *Test Match Special* they realised I had a brain. 'He's jack the lad, joker in the dressing room.' It even says that on Wikipedia. And I was, a bit, but it doesn't mean that's all there was to me.

It was partly what barred me from being considered for captaincy, even though I was more than capable of doing the on-field stuff. In fact, I captained eight matches and won three, bearing in mind that for me to be doing it meant that neither captain Clive Lloyd nor vice-captain Jack Simmons was playing, so we obviously had a depleted team. These days I'd have been a good captain, but back then you had to organise all the transport, all the admin side of things, and I couldn't have done that as I'm not sure I had the organisational skills. And I'd probably have spoken my mind too much when it came to the powers that be, a group of people who rarely appeared to occupy the same planet, though they were somehow in the same pavilion.

This is how ridiculous it was. I was picked for my first Test match and got called into a meeting in the Lancashire committee room with former international Cyril Washbrook. He was a committee member, but I'd never spoken to him. I'd been playing since 1973, a pro since 1978, and this was 1982, and in all that time we'd never said a word. Bear in mind this was a guy who gave me a contract. I did the right thing, put my blazer and tie on, and went and sat down – no tea, no coffee, just two chairs.

'I've been speaking to Peter May [the chairman of selectors],' he told me. 'The selectors are more than happy with your ability to open the batting, but they are a little bit concerned about your fielding.' I didn't know what he was on about. 'I don't know whether it's because you're slow to the ball or your arm isn't very good, but I just want to tell you to commit one hundred per cent to your fielding. Best of luck. Thank you very much for coming in.'

What? What just happened there? Richie Benaud once described me as the greatest cover fielder in the world, and I could run 100m in under 11 seconds. Cyril used to sit right at the top of the pavilion – we used to call it the pigeons' loft, where all the committee perched – and watch me, and yet he didn't know I could field. But that's how it was. There was a massive 'us and them'. The committee didn't like us, and we didn't like them. I overheard two committee members once – it was the end of the season and we'd finished in the bottom four. 'Well, at least we didn't lose to Yorkshire,' said one. 'That's all that matters.' And he meant it.

Lancashire was like a private members' club with a cricket field at the side. The committee was just a gentlemen's drinking club where they could take friends – 'I'm on the committee, would you care to come and watch?' They didn't appear to care about the members or about the results. It was simply a jolly little place to take their pals and have a glass of wine on Sunday.

When Cedric Rhoades was chairman, I got 120-odd and that night went into the committee room. It was a stinking hot day so we were allowed to take our blazers off. I had on a pair of silver trousers, white shoes, white belt, green checked shirt and a white leather tie (it was the 1980s). Nobody said anything. The following day, Peter Lever, the coach, came up to me: 'The chairman wants me to tell you that you're not to come dressed like that again.'

'If the chairman wants talk to me about my dress, tell him to come to see me, not send a monkey.'

'I'll have to fine you if you do it again.'

'Tell him, if he doesn't like how I dress, I don't particularly like how he dresses, but I'm not going to say anything. And if he wants to say anything, tell him to come to talk to me.'

Next Saturday, we were at home again. Five minutes before stumps, I chipped one to long-on. I should have had the biggest bollocking of my career for getting out at such a time in such a way. I went to the committee room again, only this time in my England tour uniform. The jacket was miles too small, the trousers way too big around the waist and too short, my shirt collar was all over the place and I had my touring tie on and my tour shoes. I looked a shambles, like a tramp, but the reaction of the committee was totally different. The chairman came over, shook my hand, 'How lovely to see you.'

And it's at that point you just go: 'Fuck off. You're not in it for the right reasons. You're not in it for the cricket, you're concerned about your image, your little club, and how you want to run things.'

They didn't know what they were doing. Joel Garner played for Milnrow in the Central Lancashire League before he played for Somerset. He had a couple of games for Lancashire's second team, but the view came back from the committee that he was too tall to be a fast bowler, so they didn't sign him. Every time he came back, how fast do you think he bowled then? They told Clive Rice he was just an average league professional and didn't sign him either, so every time he came back it was the same. I began to wonder how many people they could get wrong?

When they did bring in a quality player, it was more by luck than judgement. They signed Colin Croft thinking he was left-arm over. He was right. And these people were actually voting for whether I get a job or not? It was just preposterous. So later, when I turned to coaching, would I want to have gone and coached Lancashire's first team? You must be joking.

Things weren't always better in the dressing room. When I started playing in the first team we had a poor side. There was this inevitability, especially in the Sunday League, that batsmen couldn't get enough runs and bowlers couldn't keep it tight enough. So we decided to have a team meeting over a meal, which you should never do, because if it goes wrong you're stuck there. Whereas if you have a normal meeting and it goes wrong, you can all separate.

Jack Simmons kicked off the meeting. Now I love Jack, but God he enjoyed an argument. People thought of him as everyone's friend, but someone once described him as a street fighter with a friendly smile, and I think that summed him up. He and I fell out every day, and then we'd go home and start again the next. It was never serious, but it was how he operated. Some people didn't bother, but I answered him back.

On this occasion, Jack complained that we'd often be 30 without loss after ten overs, and that this wasn't a good enough start. David Lloyd felt he was having a go at the openers, him and me, and ended up by telling him to do it – and Jack said he would. The following week we were at Old Trafford, with Simmo opening the batting. At the end of 40 overs, he was 60-odd not out. 'Well?' Bumble asked. Simmo thought about it: 'It's not that easy, you know!' And that was it. Bumble just looked at me, incredulous.

Dressing-room culture isn't something you slip into. It takes time, especially as a youngster, to get used to it and the various different characters, the set ways of doing things, the hierarchies, both real and imagined, and other people's conceptions of you and where you fit into their world.

At that time in the 1970s and 1980s, dressing rooms were hard. This was the era when you got told. Early on, I had to whiten senior pro Barry Wood's pads and clean his boots. Similarly, when I started out, the second team used to change in a separate dressing room downstairs. It was referred to by various names – the dogs' home, the stiffs. To start with, when I got a game in the first team, I still had to use that dressing room. After fielding practice, the next time I'd see the rest of the side was when I heard them coming down the stairs, and then I'd follow them out. At lunchtime, all the first teamers would go upstairs, I'd go into my dressing room, wait for the sound of them coming downstairs, and follow them out again. If there had been a team meeting in the break, I certainly hadn't been party to it. But half the time there weren't any team meetings anyway. 'Right, come on! Everybody ready? Simmo, put your jumper on!' That was it.

One day after I was out, I thought I'd better go upstairs and sit with the rest of the side. I walked into the dressing room and Barry Wood, who wasn't even playing, was sitting there. 'Did you knock?' he asked.

'I'm playing in the game!'

'I didn't ask that. Did you knock?'

'No.'

'Well, fuck off out then.' And he threw me out. I had to come back and knock. That was the culture at that time.

For a senior player to have a massive go at you was not unusual. If it came from someone like Bumble, who I respected so much, I took it. He didn't do it for nothing or for a laugh; he did it because he felt he needed to. And if I learnt from it, which I did, it worked. But what did I learn from someone telling me to knock on the door?

A lot of the juniors hated Barry Wood because he had a go at them so often, and he used to have a go at me as well. One day he was tearing a strip off me and I decided to answer him back: 'I'm a better player than you.'

As soon as I said it I thought: 'Oh my god, what are you saying? He's an England player, and you're saying this?' It didn't stop me, though. 'I've more talent than you,' I continued. 'You're manmade, you are. You're just clockwork.' I looked at him and thought: 'Christ, I'm going to get sacked.'

'Brilliant!' he shouted. 'That's the spirit!' All along, all he'd wanted me to do was stand up to him. After I confronted him that day, we became really good mates. It was a bit of a weird way to do it, but that was the culture, the way that things were done.

People like Paul Allott and I tried to change that petty culture of knocking on doors, which is why I felt the committee didn't like us. We even managed to persuade them to change the sweaters. At the time, if you were an uncapped second XI player, you'd wear a plain white sweater; if you were a capped second XI player, you'd have a plain white sweater with a rosebud in the middle; and the first-team players had one with green, red and blue stripes with no rose. It didn't make any sense, so we asked that everyone could take to the field in a sweater with stripes. Uncapped second XI players would have stripes only; second XI capped would have stripes with a rosebud on the left breast, and first XI capped would have stripes with a rose in the same place. At least we then looked similar, like we were a team.

We sorted out the dressing-room situation as well. We

pointed out that it was bloody stupid having one dressing room downstairs and one upstairs, while the opposition were upstairs as well. It made much more sense to put them downstairs and for us to have both rooms upstairs. Despite what a lot of people have said, I don't kick against establishments. I only rebel against nonsense. If a tradition is worth keeping, I'm happy to be traditional. But if it doesn't make sense, I'll challenge it and I'll question it. And if it's nonsense, I'll rail against it.

As my career progressed, I tried to make sure I didn't become one of those people I'd encountered along my way. I can't say there were never some of the young lads that my tongue didn't lash out at, but not to the same extent as happened to me, or Paul Allott for that matter. I remember one senior batsman saying to him when he was only 19: 'You'll never be a bowler as long as you have a hole in your arse.' How was that supposed to help a young team-mate to develop? Also, I'd never ask anybody to whiten my pads, or do other menial tasks. I remembered how, when I was twelfth man, the senior players used to tell me to wash their car, but I told them I wouldn't do that.

In any team, there will always be an element of senior speaking to junior, and 99 times out of 100 they are trying to help them be a better player, but it doesn't always come across in a positive way. Occasionally, when I became a senior pro, I know that I overstepped the mark. All you need to do afterwards is say: 'Sorry, I shouldn't have said that. I know you were trying your best.' And if they're man enough, they'll reply: 'Yes, OK. I know you were frustrated.'

Inevitably, in any dressing room, there are some people you get on with better than others, even if it's something as simple as wanting to do the same thing in the evening. Some people like Chinese, some people like Indian, some people like a pint before eating, some like to eat early. So you fit in with people who like to do the same as you, which is why I've never understood this talk of cliques. I'm not sure what a clique is. I think it's something that's only noticed by someone who thinks they're outside, but if they made an effort to get to know those people they'd quickly realise they're just friends, not a clique. The best thing to do is go along and join in.

It's like all this talk about bullying cultures. Have these people never been in a dressing room? Even the best in the world can be acidic. At Lancashire we had a dressing room full of people who liked arguing and shouting at each other, but that's part of what the whole experience is about. People get shouted at and have strips torn off them, then you get up next day and start again.

The weird thing was, while there'd be occasional flare-ups, when we were playing badly we'd generally get on like a house on fire; we had a good social life and great meals at night. However, the more successful we became – we won the Benson & Hedges Cup in 1984, were runners-up in the NatWest Trophy in 1986 and runners-up in the Championship in 1987 – playing really well and becoming a good team, the more arguments we had. We would even argue about how we could have won better than we did, or we'd have batsmen v bowlers rows; none of it was productive at all.

When we were rubbish, we had to rely on each other. We rallied round on the social side with friendships and camaraderie, but when we became a good team we rallied round on the pitch and went our separate ways off it. When we were winning, at night I'd just want a couple of pints, something to eat, and then I was keen to get back on the field. My life was on that pitch. When I walked on to that grass, the rest of my life didn't exist – it was all I lived for, all I wanted.

But that's what I'd always taken from cricket, right from the start. Life at home wasn't easy. My mum and I never spoke civilly to one another, ever. She was always having a go at me and I had a go back. At home my mum would hit me, then at school I'd get hit by the teachers. It seemed as though there was no escape from it – except at the cricket club where I got blokes telling me I'd done well.

What happened with my mum gave me resilience; I learned to bounce back. Whatever she did to me, I just got up again. I did a psychology test once, developed for the Swedish air force, which straight away identified that the situation with my mum was at the centre of my personality. It gave me the ability to focus on what was important, ignore the rest of it, and to do what I want. I developed that through combat with her. It gave me a skill to look after myself and deal with things. Between the age of 15 until I left home, I went out every night – to a friend's, for a walk, to the pub in later years – because I couldn't sit in the house. I was pestered relentlessly. I had to go out just to get away. I am pleased to say that in recent times we have made our peace.

That's not to say everything was straightforward at cricket. I soon learned you can't just wander into a dressing room at 16, like I did at Lancashire, and start saying things. But sometimes it just comes out. I've got the ability to answer back quickly and have a sharp mouth, and I haven't met many people who can out-respond me, so there were times when people said something to me in the dressing room and I'd answer straight back. My mouth could get me in trouble, the same as it could get me out of it.

I also found out that in second XI cricket the atmosphere is often, though not always, horrible. When I was 16, I'd made three 60s in three days, and in the dressing room somebody wanted shampoo. I offered him mine. Andrew Kennedy, who usually opened in the first team, piped up: 'It's a good job the ammy [amateur] has turned up.'

'It is this week,' I said. That went round the first-team dressing room very quickly. Andrew hadn't liked what I'd said, and he let everybody know I'd said it. Perhaps he felt a little bit threatened at seeing a young kid coming up through the ranks, scoring runs, and he was down in the second team not getting many.

When I was young, I played with a lot of cricketers who had come down to the seconds and obviously wanted to get back into the first team. They saw you as competition and didn't want you to do well. There were others who knew they were going to get sacked at the end of the year, so they didn't care and were out every night; and there were some who just weren't good enough for first-team cricket. Unsurprisingly, it was an awful atmosphere at times. I learned to keep my head down and do my job. The only thing you want to do with second XI cricket is get out of it. And the best way to get out of it is to learn, to deliver, and not look sideways. Don't compare yourself to anybody else, forget all that, it's about you, how you perform, and if you perform well enough for long enough you'll get picked for the senior side.

The first time I played for the second XI was against

Northamptonshire in June 1973. Colin Milburn, the ex-England opener, was making a comeback with one eye after a road accident. It was just five years since I'd first picked up a bat. We'd gone to Westward Ho! on holiday and the beach there had miles of rock-hard sand. Dad and I played football, got fed up, and so went to a little seaside shop where we bought a set of stumps and a bat. 'Put it on the sand,' he told me. I laid it flat. 'Pick it up as if you're chopping down a tree.' I picked it up. 'Where's the tree?' he asked. I motioned to my right. 'OK. You're left-handed.' And that was how it was decided. As usual, he was right, although I'm completely right-handed otherwise – the only other thing I do left-handed is use chopsticks.

Every summer holiday he'd give me some money to buy myself a present. The next year I decided I wanted to buy a new cricket bat. I didn't know that my dad was secretly thrilled to bits, as he never said anything. The one I wanted was 150 shillings, which was a lot of money, so instead we got a little Wisden bat, size three, no stickers, just branded with a hot iron. That was my first bat, and I've still got it in the attic. My dad gave it to one of his friends who knew Garry Sobers so it could be signed by the touring West Indies team. This is how weird cricket can be; among the signatures are Michael Holding, Clive Lloyd and Viv Richards. I played with two of them and against the other. Clive would have been in his mid-20s at the time, while Mikey and Viv weren't much more than kids.

When we got home, Dad asked: 'Right, what do you want to do? Do you want to just play and enjoy yourself, mess about with your mates? You'll get to a certain level and then you'll never get any better. Or do you want to learn to play properly? It'll take a long time, but eventually you'll be as good as you can be.'

I knew it was the second option. My dad taught me the basics in the back garden. He never played the game, but he loved it and he knew what to do. There were some nights he just used to shout commands; 'Forward defence offside! Forward defence straight!' There was no ball so I had to shadow play, but I didn't mind. I remember one night my mum came out and had a go at my dad to such an extent I ended up crying. I realised how much I was enjoying this, and I didn't want it to stop.

By this time I was running home from school to watch the Test match on the BBC. Often it was Boycott and Edrich opening, and I loved watching Edrich because he was left-handed. When Boycott was on strike, I'd look at the screen through the mirror above the sideboard to make him left-handed. It didn't work, as it made the angles all wrong, but I never sat in front of the Test match on TV and thought I want to play for England. It never entered my head. I was never this stereotypical kid with posters on my walls. I didn't have cricketing heroes. I liked Garry Sobers and John Edrich, but nothing beyond that. For me, it was more about doing it, living life, getting involved. I used to spend hours throwing a ball at the wall, making up little games, catching one-handed or whatever. I didn't realise it, but riding a bike meant I was learning timing, when things are going to intersect; playing football I was learning movement; badminton helped my fielding, learning to change direction. I was picking up all sorts of transferrable skills.

In Gordon Leach I had a great PE teacher, too. He was only little, but he wouldn't stand for any nonsense if you got out of hand. When I look back, he was an incredibly good teacher. Hard but fair, he was dedicated to his students and to teaching. His love of sport was infectious; he broke down techniques and explained them. I loved him. I can still remember things he taught me about basketball and volleyball after all these years. It was the first time I'd encountered someone explaining sports techniques to me, which was the seed of me breaking things down myself.

We also had an English teacher, who was a ginger-haired, artistic lunatic of a bloke. He loved racket sports and took me under his wing and taught me how to play squash. 'Everything you do,' he told me, 'you do it your way. I call it Fowler-esque.' Fowler-esque – I've always liked that.

The day I got my O-level results, they were put up on a board. Everyone was standing around looking nervous; Gordon Leach was at the back. He wasn't a bloke who displayed any affection, but I got mine, turned round, and he was there in front of me. 'How many have you got?' He threw his arms around me when I told him I'd got seven. I found out that a lot of members of staff had been giving him a hard time because of me playing so much sport. By getting seven O-levels, I'd made his life a bit easier.

At the same time I started going down to Accrington Cricket Club. I had two mates and we used to play out down there. The third XI were short one day, and needed two players and a scorer. Two of us played and the other lad ended up with the scoring book. We didn't realise it at the time, but all three of us would end up playing for Lancashire seconds.

We had no idea we were good for our age, but we must have been.

By the time I was 15, I was opening the batting for the Accrington first team in the Lancashire League. The format was 32 eight-ball overs, and the plan was to let me bat the first ten as I wanted. If I was scoring runs and getting on with it, fine. If I wasn't, I either had to get a move on or get out.

Early on, I played against Neil Hawke, an Australian Test match opening bowler – I couldn't lay a bat on it. At the start of the next season, I played against a bloke called Bob Leatherbarrow, who was Colne's professional. He started shouting and cursing at me, sledging me. I was only a kid, and it was the first time I'd ever come across this kind of thing. I got really upset while I was still batting, but carried on. Afterwards, I was in the little bar, having a lime and lemonade as I always did, and in he walked. He came straight up to me. I was quivering. He stuck his hand out. 'Well played, son. Would you like a drink? Listen, all that on the pitch, it was because I couldn't get you out and I was just trying to wind you up a little bit. But always remember, that doesn't mean I don't like you. What happens on the pitch is one thing, what happens off the pitch is another. Off the pitch, we're friends.'

As I progressed, I never thought I didn't want to go to training, or that I'd rather do something else or go to a party. I never felt any peer pressure to do other things, I just decided that cricket was what I wanted to do. It didn't matter who for or what level a game, it always took priority. I missed loads of stuff as a result. People would tell me there was a wedding I needed to go to, and that surely that took priority over a club game – but it didn't. I don't think I understood when they said, 'It's only a club game,' and I don't think they understood when I said, 'I've got a game.' To me, I didn't need to say anything more to explain things.

That's why I say cricket found me, rather than the other way round. I had no ambition as a young kid, I simply fell into it. Initially, I liked it because I got compliments off people I didn't know, and I enjoyed it. When I got asked to play for Lancashire's second XI, I didn't even know you could be a professional cricketer. I didn't think Lancashire even had a second team. I'd never thought about it. I'd never thought beyond playing for Accrington.

When I realised there was an opportunity to do this for a living, I merely noted the fact; there wasn't a light that went on and I didn't decide I was going to be a cricketer. I just carried on playing, went to school, ended up playing quite a lot for Lancashire, and loved it to pieces. But I didn't have a goal in mind, I just wanted to play. Even when Lancashire asked me what I was doing the following year, I told them I was going to university. They explained they were going to offer me a contract, but I still went off to university anyway.

When I did eventually start my full-time professional career at Lancashire, my wage was £50 a week. The money really didn't matter. People of my era never went into cricket because of the money. There was none. OK, playing for England against the West Indies in 1984 we got £175 for a one-day game, which I suppose is all right – but I could have got killed. You did it because you wanted to play cricket, and you loved playing cricket. And let's face it, if you get to do that for a living, you're a lucky bloke.

My dad died in 2009. He didn't know it, but he had a beautiful philosophy. He taught me virtually everything, but when I played for Lancashire seconds, I said to him: 'This isn't how you do it at this level. You do things differently.' And he backed off. Most dads wouldn't have done that.

'Can I come and watch?' he asked. 'Not really, Dad. No parents come and watch.' When I got picked for the first team, it was different and I told him he could come along.

The first time I made a hundred for Lancashire was against Nottinghamshire, and I got it at about 6.25. I drove home thrilled to bits, and my mum was standing there grinning. I was baffled how she already knew, as I was pretty sure it wouldn't have made *Look North*. 'Your dad's been there all day,' she told me. I had no idea. The smile on his face was amazing. But that's what he did, he'd turn up and watch, and then when I was out he'd go back to work.

As a kid I remember once asking my dad to carry my bag, but he replied: 'I'll carry your bag when you're playing for England.' When I got picked for my first Test match, my bedroom was so small I had to keep my cricket coffin in the hallway outside. I was in my room filling a bag with clothes and I went outside and the coffin had gone. He was carrying it to the car: 'I told you I would.'

My dad would come to watch me at Test matches, but he missed the two hundreds I got in England because he and my mum were on holiday. He always complained to my mum about that. I knew he was proud of me, even if there was never going to be gushing emotion. He'd say stuff like: 'You've not done badly, have you?'

He was a farmer's son, but the family had a meeting and

decided there was no future in farming for him. His auntie suggested he worked in cars, so he had to become a motor mechanic. He didn't really have a say in the matter, and he also used to drive taxis on Saturdays and Sundays, so he never had time to play cricket himself.

Because of that experience, one of the things he used to say to me was: 'No son of mine is ever getting his hands dirty for a living.' So he was pleased that it worked out for me, though I do remember one day when I was fielding out on a muddy boundary and I was covered from head to foot in dirt. I couldn't even dry my hands, as my shirt and trousers were so wet. As I came off the field and walked past my dad, I said: 'Look at this. You said no son of yours was ever going to get his hands dirty for a living.'

He just looked at me and laughed: 'It's a different kind of muck, though, isn't it?' It was certainly that. I was lucky to do something I loved for a living. The game gave me everything – and that includes some extraordinary friendships.

CHAPTER 4

BUMBLE

'Here, you'll be able to solve this.' I hadn't seen David Lloyd for a couple of years, but I'd just got out of my car at Gloucester and there he was, now the England coach. There was no greeting or anything.

'We're playing against India and they want to use Readers cricket balls, while we want to use Dukes. But if it's one apiece, the umpires make the final decision and they always go with the away team. So how can we get to use Dukes?'

'You can't.'

'There has to be a way. What happens if I say Dukes?'

'They'll say Readers, the umpires will say Readers.'

'What happens if I say Readers? The Indians might think I want to use Readers.'

'No, they'll just say Readers, because that's what they want to use.'

'There has to be a way,' he chuntered. 'There has to be a way.'

'Bumble, there isn't.'

'Waste of money sending you to university,' he said, and walked off.

I didn't really know Bumble until I started playing in the first team at Lancashire. I'd played a few games the year before, but in 1980, when I got that maiden hundred, he was the first person to meet me at the bottom of the steps. He was thrilled to bits.

A year later, before the season started, Jack Bond saw me in the car park at Old Trafford and asked me how my hands were, which I thought was bit of a weird question. He explained it by saying he wanted me to move up to the top of the order to open the batting and to keep wicket for the first team. I asked what would happen if I didn't want to do it, and was told I would not be playing. So, all of a sudden, there I was opening the batting with Bumble.

He had a lime green Ford Fiesta – naturally – at the time, and because we were both from Accrington we used to travel together. And it was at this point I really began to understand – well, understand might be going a bit far – how the man operates. As we were driving along, bits of wisdom would pop up from nowhere – Bang! – out of his head. There was never any structure to it. It didn't have to be about cricket. It could be about caravanning, somebody we knew in Accrington, his brain used to flit all over.

One day we were going to Hove to play Sussex, and Bumble started up by asking me what my job was as an opening batsman. I suggested it was to see off the opening bowlers or to stay in and build a platform, but that wasn't what he wanted, so eventually I gave in and asked what it was. 'Soften the ball.'

Here we go. 'Boycott softens the ball. He just knocks it

into the ground. It's boring, but it does a good job. You might have scored sixty, but if you get out early, the ball's still hard and it's still going to swing around and all the glamour boys, three, four and five, they won't like it, so they'll get out. You've started a collapse. You've got to soften the ball so it doesn't swing, it doesn't bounce, and the glamour boys come in and make good.' I didn't know what to say.

'What you need to do is pick out a fielder and hit it at him, especially when the third seamer comes on. Don't twat him all over – they'll put their opening bowlers back on and you're back to square one – milk him. If there's a good fielder, aim at him. Every now and again you'll miss and you'll have to run, but don't worry about that.'

There was no stopping him now. 'Every now and again,' he espoused, 'find a bit of concrete on the ground and hit it against it, because opening bowlers don't like bowling when there's grit in the ball. So hit it against that concrete.' At last there was a pause. 'So, anyway, that's ball softening for you.' Cheers, Bumble, thanks for that.

Next day, we were playing against Sussex. We'd both got out early and hadn't got many, so we were just sitting, watching. Clive Lloyd was batting, and Imran Khan was bowling – quick. He bowled one at Clive and he square cut it. At Hove the scorebox was square of the wicket and used to have two great big loudspeaker horns on the top. Clive hit it between the two speakers, right over the scoreboard and out of the ground. It was an unbelievable shot. Everyone was dumbfounded, all our lads were shouting, and after it all calmed down Bumble turned to me. 'That,' he said, 'is the best bit of concrete finding I've ever seen.'

When Bumble's playing career hit a full stop, his eccentricities carried on unabated. When he was an umpire, for instance, I bumped into him and he told me he was buying a caravan. You either go with it or you don't – there's not really an option. 'I'm getting a caravan, because all these places that I stop in, all these strange beds, all these rooms, I wake up and I don't know where I am – there's nothing familiar about it – I never feel at home.'

'That's because you're not.'

'Exactly! So I'm going to get a caravan and fill it full of my stuff. I'll be able to tow it. I can take my home wherever I go, so when I wake up in a morning all my things will be there. I'll have a little telly and a radio. I can do what I want. I can cook my own breakfast. And most clubs let you park at the ground, so I don't need to get up too early – I'm already there. Perfect!'

So he got a caravan, and I didn't see him for a while. The next time I did there was an obvious question about his caravan.

'Caravan? Caravan? I got rid of that bloody thing.'

'I thought you were looking forward to it.'

'I'm driving at fifty miles an hour on the motorway, great queues of traffic behind me on A-roads, people flashing at me, sticking two fingers up at me, calling me a wanker. It takes me ages to get anywhere. Then, when I do get there, I've got to park up, wind the legs down in the pissing rain, and I open the door and there are plates all over the floor because the cupboards are open. There's crap everywhere. I think I'll just go for a wander, have a pint, and I'm locked in! They've locked the bloody gates. I'm stuck there all night. Caravan? I got shut of that.'

Another time, I was commentating on the same game as him and he had a beautiful Mercedes soft-top, cream coloured, lovely thing. So I wandered over to talk to him about it. 'It's a classic, an absolute classic,' he told me. 'It's going up in value. I bet yours isn't. I bet yours is going down in value. This is going up. When I drive this, I feel like a king.'

A few weeks later, we were commentating together again and I noticed him at the back of the box with a copy of *Exchange & Mart*, so I asked why. 'I'm looking for another car,' he said.

'Oh, are you just going to push your Merc in the garage?'

'No, it's got to go. It's twenty-odd years old that thing, you know. It only does sixty-odd miles an hour. I can't get anything in it. And it's a soft-top, so I'm always frightened someone's going to cut the roof. It only does twenty-five miles to the gallon and I can't get the dogs in. It's got to go. I'm going to get one of those big four-be-fours. High up. King of the Road.'

So he found a Jeep Grand Cherokee, and told me: 'I feel like a king. Leather seats, I can get the dogs in the back, I can see everything – just cruise along.'

A month or so later, we were back in the commentary box, and he was looking at *Exchange & Mart* again, trying to find another car. 'You've just got one, that Grand Cherokee, you said you bloody loved driving it,' I told him.

'I did – between petrol stations. It's thirsty as anything. I go round a corner, I'm sliding all over those leather seats. The dogs are in the back, as soon as we set off they shit all over. I'm driving everywhere smelling dog shit. It's got to go, I've got to get something else.'

'What are you going to get?'

'I'm going to get a little Alfa Romeo saloon.'

'What about the dogs?'

'Sod 'em.'

Despite all that, Bumble's got a brilliantly analytical mind. In 1981 especially, my initial full year in the first team, he taught me such a lot. It was like he saw something in me and wanted to help. It was exhausting because I was opening the batting and keeping in every form of cricket, but it was brilliant in that it focused my mind. I was always in the game, I was always playing, there was always something happening. I was the top scorer with more than 1,500 runs, basically out of nowhere, and a lot of it really was due to Bumble, because if I got out or thought I wasn't playing well, he'd reassure me. 'If it doesn't work this week,' he'd say, 'it'll work next week. Just keep going.'

Batting with Bumble, I picked up a lot out in the middle. You can practise all you want, but you don't learn unless you're doing it in a game, so he was almost coaching me while I was batting, and I enjoyed that. I'd try something and he'd say: 'Heh! No! What are you doing that for?' So instantly I'd had perfect feedback.

He taught me how to play in different areas, to my strengths, but he never wanted me to be a clone of him. He must have looked at me and thought: 'Right, this is how you're going to play.' That's something I took from him when I started coaching – don't coach someone to be like you, help them be themselves. And that's what he always did – he helped me be myself.

There was something special in that relationship. He was

getting towards the end of his career at that time – you get a bit jaded, your body aches – but he wanted to stay in to bat with me, to help me. I could sense that in him. He wasn't bothered about how well he was doing or how many runs he was scoring, he wanted to stay with me. The nice thing is, at the back end of my career, I opened the batting with his son Graham, and so I could do the same with him. It's lovely how cricket goes round in circles like that.

When it came to coaching England, there was never any way Bumble was going to fit in. He was going to stamp his way of doing things on the game, and his way was always going to have a lot of weird and wonderful components. As a player, you've got to like that environment, because previously there hadn't really been an England coach, so when he came in he was an innovator. He had slogans put up on the wall – 'Concentration. Dedication. Application.' He played speeches of Winston Churchill in the dressing room. It would have been massively different from anything anybody had been used to, but it's become a standard part of the game now. He was one of the first ones to put on 'Land Of Hope And Glory' and 'Jerusalem' in the dressing room, and they do that every day now at a Test match.

On Sky, Bumble trades on his humour, he's their stand-up. He likes that role, and it suits him, but it's easy to forget when you hear him making daft comments that he used to be England coach. There's more to him than making people laugh. At the back of it, he's got knowledge. Yes, he's had some of the weirdest ideas ever, but out of that something develops. He was the first step towards the England team having the structure it's got now. He broke a lot of new ground. In some ways, he was ahead of his time, and I can't help thinking he'd have benefited from having a good number two underneath him, who was the opposite, to be a balance.

In the end, the powers that be took the best bits of Bumble and changed direction. Because you know what the establishment is like – they want someone who is the establishment. Bumble wore his heart on his sleeve, as with his famous 'We bloody murdered 'em!' comment after a draw with Zimbabwe. He was just being himself, but that doesn't sit right with some people. He never thinks inside his head, he always thinks out loud. Once you get to know that, it puts a different slant on it. He's the sort of bloke that whatever he's doing at the time he believes to be the best – until he changes his mind to something else. I quite like that because it means he's adaptable, but it also means he's unpredictable.

Some of his notions are crackpot, but others make you wonder: 'Wow! Why didn't I think of that?' On one occasion, he suddenly piped up: 'When you're playing back, and it's short, and it's coming at your head, get square on. Go on, get square on. Now get your front shoulder out of the way and get your hands up – you can get your bat in front of your face.' Thinking about it, it made sense, and it still does. You sometimes hear commentators say: 'He's squared the batsman up,' but that's what you do, to get your bat up in front of your face.

After Bumble had finished playing, I asked him to come and look at me in the indoor nets, just to see if I was doing anything different, because I wanted to carry on playing the same way. I'd done my warm-up, put my kit on and gone in the nets, where he was waiting with a bowling machine. I said

I was ready, and the first ball went past my nose at 100mph. For the next 40 minutes, he absolutely bombarded me. This was not a gentle little session, it was a 'get out of your comfort zone and do it' session. After a while he told me I was getting too square on.

'Hang on, it was you who taught that to me.'

'Yes, well, it's wrong.'

'How can it be wrong? You taught me to be square on.'

'Aye,' he said, 'never mind.' And that was it! That was what he was like.

He is, without doubt, the funniest person I've ever met. Half intentionally, half not. Driving around together was amazing. We came up with a rule that wherever we were travelling, the first hour we'd talk about the game or what was coming up the next day, after that we'd talk about anything else. Sometimes we'd have to pull off the road because we were both laughing that much. We used to do it to each other: he'd make me laugh and I'd make him laugh, and it just seemed to escalate.

That's not to say he doesn't have a harder side. I love Bumble, but he did once reduce me to tears. We were at Worcestershire and hadn't played all day, so we found ourselves in a pub. I was standing with him and Frank Hayes and all of a sudden he started having a go at me, challenging me about my batting and what I was doing to make myself better. I remember that it was not long after I'd made my first century, so I thought I deserved some credit for that, but he said: 'That was three weeks ago. You can't get a hundred every three weeks. What are you doing? Come on!'

I'd thought he was backing me, so his criticism hit home

and I went outside, and to this day I remember standing in the car park, underneath a little overhang in the rain, crying my eyes out. Eventually I composed myself, and realised he'd made a good point that I couldn't just rest on what I'd done so far – I had to keep working, trying to be better. I went back in and told him that he was right. 'Good,' he said. 'Let's get on with it.' He'd sussed something out about me and done that deliberately. I'm not so sure he knew it was going to work, but I think he knew it was going to make me cry.

The only time I've ever seen Bumble despondent was because of cricket. When Lancashire had a poor team at the start of the 1980s, he used to get frustrated at our inability to play good cricket. When I started opening with him he was towards the back end of his career. He'd had his box smashed by Jeff Thomson on that horrendous Australia tour in 1974-75 where nearly every batsman came back damaged and no one was ever quite the same again. Lillee and Thomson on green wickets, no helmets, he'd been through all that. He knew what fast bowlers could do – and there were plenty of them in county cricket.

When Bumble and I were driving down to Hove, we weren't going to play against Sussex, we were going to play against Imran Khan and Garth Le Roux. When we went to Notts, we were going to play against Richard Hadlee and Clive Rice; Hampshire – Malcolm Marshall; Surrey – Sylvester Clarke; Somerset – Joel Garner and Ian Botham; Middlesex – Wayne Daniel. There was serious high-quality fast bowling everywhere you went. But Lancashire rarely had anybody, and it was a source of continuous frustration for Bumble. You could hear him say it sometimes when we were fielding: 'Peashooters against cannons.' We didn't have enough penetration in the bowling attack, so everywhere we went we got absolutely tortured. It was a situation where we were always hamstrung before we'd even started.

We didn't have a squad that could win first-class cricket matches. We had a brilliant one-day bowler in Jack Simmons, who should have played for England, but he didn't spin it. So in August, when it started to turn, we didn't have that weapon either. No bullets at the beginning, no spinner at the back end. Bumble, because he had such a good cricket brain and was such a great tactician, could see his own career passing by and we weren't getting anywhere. I asked him once how he looked back on his seasons. 'Well, I knew we hadn't got a team to win the Championship, so I just started batting in April and I'd see how many runs I'd got by September. That was it. There was nothing else.' It was an astonishing way to look at it, but it was because he knew we weren't going to win anything.

Our committee always paid lip service to the idea that they wanted to challenge to win the Championship, and that they would do things to help make it happen. But we recognised it was obvious they didn't give a shit about the Championship, because if they had we'd have had a different squad. We needed strike bowlers; batsmen set games up, bowlers win them. We had a fair amount of talent on the batting front – Barry Wood, David Lloyd, Frank Hayes, Clive Lloyd – but then we didn't have a bowling attack that was going to bowl anyone out twice.

I was lucky in the fact that I played half a season in 1980 batting middle order, so all I wanted to do was focus on my own performance. Then in 1981 I opened the batting and didn't want to know about the politics of the club. By 1982, I was playing for England. My focus when I went back to Lancashire was to play well enough to stay in or get back in the England team. Again, it was more of a personal drive rather than a club-based drive. I was fulfilling my ambitions at a higher level so what was happening at the county didn't worry me as much. I didn't have the same frustrations, my focus was slightly different.

That's not to say I was selfish. It shouldn't be misinterpreted as me not bothering about Lancashire because I was playing for England. I always thought it weird there should be this feeling which pervaded throughout county cricket that once you'd played for England you didn't try for your county. Playing well for your county is how you get to the England side, so why wouldn't you want to keep playing well? Also, after you've played for England, playing for your county seems a little bit easier – because it is easier – so you actually enjoy playing and hopefully get more runs.

I understood where the criticism of England players not trying for their counties came from. Then, we would finish a Test match on Tuesday night and be playing for our counties on Wednesday morning – we'd be mentally and physical knackered. We'd wake up on that Wednesday and the tanks were empty. It's got nothing to do with desire. People said: 'Botham, when he gets back to Somerset, he doesn't try.'

Well, hang on, he's just bowled 40-odd overs in a Test match and now you want him to open the bowling against Leicestershire? Do you think he can maintain that level? He can't. It's impossible. Same with Bob Willis. He got to a stage where he could only tick over in county cricket, because it was so incredibly difficult being an opening bowler in the England team. You don't have two tanks; you only have one. But obviously you can't turn round to team-mates or spectators and even try to discuss it. They're going to think you're full of bullshit, and they're not going to understand either.

The other crucial thing to remember is that, after a week away with England you haven't a clue what's going on in your county dressing room. It doesn't take long to not be part of a dressing room. Sometimes coming back quiet and getting used to what's going on can be misinterpreted as not being interested, but it can take a few days to get back into the rhythm of things – and then there's another Test to play. And let's not forget possibly the most pertinent point of all: just because you got runs yesterday in an international doesn't mean you're going to get them next day in a county game. You can get a good ball, you can make a mistake. That's cricket.

After 1981, the first full first season I had with Lancashire, without any England commitments or injury, was 1986 and by then we were getting new players in. By 1987, we had Patrick Patterson and Gehan Mendis and ended up being runners-up in the Championship, Wasim Akram joined the following year. I was lucky that, as I matured as a cricketer, I was playing in a side that was strong, whereas Bumble was in one that was tailing off. I'm sure he felt his last few seasons were wasted. You know your career is coming to a close, and I'm sure he wanted to go out on a high, but the way the committee was at Lancashire that just wasn't going to happen.

I don't think Bumble found fulfilment from his international career either. He got 214 not out at Edgbaston against India. In fact, when I got 201 against India, in Madras, I got a telegram from him. When I opened it, it just had one word on it: 'Nearly.' If you get a double hundred in a Test match, which he did, you can obviously play. So should he have played more Test matches? You could argue that, but there were some good players around. I think if he could be transferred to modern day, he'd be used as a middle-order batsman because he was far better against spinners than he was opening bowlers. He survived opening bowlers to get through to the spinners. Once they came on it was party time. He was brilliant against them.

The final thing to add about Bumble is that whatever he's focused on at the time is the most important thing. If it was fly-fishing, everything in life would revolve around fly-fishing. If it was golf, everything would revolve around golf. When he left Lancashire, and he'd had his benefit year and made some useful contacts, he started working for a double-glazing firm. When I saw him, he was full of enthusiasm for his new job: 'It's brilliant. Windows? Everybody needs windows. Look around you, there's windows everywhere.'

When I next saw him a couple of months later and asked after his new job he told me he'd jacked it in. 'What? You said everybody needs windows.'

'They've all got 'em. Have a look round. Have you seen a space where there isn't a window?'

And that was him. It was like he flitted from one odd scenario to another. You could never be sure what might happen next, and maybe that was another reason we got on. Predictability was something that was never a natural bedfellow for either of us.

CHAPTER 5

CALL-UP

Things weren't looking good. I was at the entrance to Headingley facing a gateman sat in a chair, and he wasn't about to let me in. 'I've come to practise,' I told him.

'You can't come in. Net bowlers have to go and park on the rugby ground.' This wasn't quite how I'd planned my England debut.

'I'm playing for England.'

'Have you got proof?'

'No, I haven't.'

'Well, who are you?'

'Graeme Fowler.'

'Never heard of you.' He considered the matter. 'I tell you what, son, you can come in today, but you're not coming in tomorrow.' Good to know – tomorrow was the day of the game.

To be fair to the bloke, things had moved pretty quickly.

I'd gone from being an uncapped first XI player in 1980, to having a good season in 1981, when I was capped in September, to playing for England in 1982. But that kind of thing had happened to me all through my career. People like Michael Atherton and Neil Fairbrother were talked about as being prolific, at school or whatever. I was never prolific at any level, because as soon as I got comfortable I was forever being pushed up. I'd gone from Accrington third XI, getting rid of cows off grounds so we could play, barely playing any Accrington second XI cricket, and then by the time I was 15 I was opening the batting in the Lancashire League. It was really hard, then the following summer when I was still trying to establish myself, I was picked for Lancashire seconds, another big step up.

And so it went on until I was shoved up to play for England, but I wasn't ready for that. I didn't know half the players' names. I kept looking and thinking, 'Who's that? Who does he play for?' I just didn't know. I recognised the likes of Ian Botham and Bob Willis, of course, but I hadn't been playing county cricket that long, so it wasn't as though I knew everyone from the circuit. Basically I'd been living in a bubble.

I had no inkling the England call was going to happen. To this day I have no real idea what had happened in the England team that meant there was an opening for me. It's not that I have no memory of it, it's just that I wasn't interested. It wasn't my concern. I was opening the batting for Lancashire. That was it. Test matches were something that happened on telly. My team-mates had realised the press had been writing about me, but I hadn't. I never read newspapers and still don't. If a report on a game was accurate, I knew because I'd played. And if it was inaccurate, you just got fed up. The upshot was I had no idea I was being talked about as a candidate to be picked for England.

I wasn't even really aware of my own progression. I knew that I'd played well in 1981, but in 1982 I was reacting to people telling me my second season would be harder than my first. I knew that would be the case because, when I was opening with David Lloyd the year before, they were focusing on getting him out. Some little kid at the other end didn't matter so much, as the bowlers would have thought they'd get me out anyway at some stage. And so, kind of unnoticed, I'd be on 40. I was aware of trying to disprove that – it wasn't because they were concentrating on Bumble, it was because I could play – but I wasn't aware of anything else at all.

In fact, I was so new to everything that a lot of my mates were still in the second-team dressing room, always more raucous than the first, and so that's where I was when I heard the news. It was raining and the lads were playing cards when dressing-room attendant Ron Spriggs, great fun and a former Desert Rat, came in to tell me that Bob Willis was on the line upstairs. It was pretty clear to me that someone had rung up to have a joke. Hardly bothering, I went to the phone and said hello. 'Hello,' came this voice. Oh, it was Bob Willis. 'We'd like you to play next week at Headingley.'

'Why?' Why! My first word to the England captain. It obviously flummoxed him.

'Er, well, we want you to open the batting.'

'Oh, right. OK.'

I went back downstairs where the lads were waiting. 'And?' they chorused.

'I've been picked for England.' The place erupted, and I was just standing there. 'I've been picked for England!'

I think everybody needs luck in these situations, and for me that luck came in the fact that Willis's county was Warwickshire. I'd had seven consecutive first-class innings against them where my lowest score was 55, and I'd made four centuries in that time, and it obviously hadn't gone unnoticed. I found out later that Willis had rung Bumble and asked what I was like. His answer was: 'He always gets runs against you.' I'm sure that was a contributing factor.

That run against Warwickshire included two hundreds in a particularly bizarre game at Southport. First morning I was fielding at cover and the ball fizzed past me. I was haring towards the boundary, about to scoop it up, when I realised there was no fence to stop me, just three steps down and all these old codgers in deckchairs. It was like athletic Dignitas, I was going to clear them out. I had to put the brakes on. My left leg slipped and then gripped and for the only time in my career I pulled a muscle in my leg and had to go off. I sat there all day as they racked up 523 for four. Alvin Kallicharran got 230 not out and Geoff Humpage made 254. It was carnage.

Eventually, they declared, and I was allowed to open the batting. I'd been sitting there for five-and-a-half hours with my leg up, so I was fine about going out. At the end of play I was 26 not out. Bumble was out in the last over and was furious. The following day my leg had gone really stiff so I needed a runner. As the only man out, Bumble, ten years older, had to do the job. I started at 11 o'clock on 26 and I was out at five past one for 126. I walked off sprightly – Bumble was carried off on a stretcher. That's not quite true, but he wasn't happy. He was knackered. I'd got a hundred in the morning session, without a lot of boundaries, so he'd done some running.

We declared on 414 for six, so then I sat and watched again. In the second innings Les McFarlane got it swinging and we bowled them out for 111. I enjoyed watching from the pavilion with a cup of tea and a bacon sandwich. We needed 228 to win. Obviously, I wanted a runner. It couldn't be Bumble again, because he was opening the batting, not that it would have made any difference. 'You can eff off, I'm not doing it,' he told me.

As with any team, the junior gets the shitty end of the stick so we picked Ian Folley. I was on 48 when Gladstone Small came on. I had a couple of heaves outside off stump, and it was then that Folley piped up: 'Hey, Fow! Get your head down. I've never had a fifty before.' When I got my hundred, I turned round, and there was Folley with his arms in the air. He took his cap off, waved his bat to the crowd, and went and shook hands with all the fielders – it was hilarious. We beat them by ten wickets.

A month later and I was driving to Headingley as an England player. I didn't have a sponsored car, just a 15-year-old maroon Triumph 2000 on which the paint had long lost its shine. I was putting on my Lancashire tracksuit (England didn't have one then) when Bob Willis suddenly went 'Foxy!' The only other person in the changing room was Ian Botham, and he didn't respond. I looked at Willis. 'Foxy!' he repeated.

'Why have you called me Foxy?'

'That's your name now.' I thought then, and still do, that's a weird way to start an international career.

Vic Marks was also making his England debut. I was number 498 in the list of England players, he's 499, and Norman Cowans would be 500. Outside at a pre-net chat, Willis introduced us to the rest of the team: 'Skid and Foxy – make them welcome.' So I spent that Wednesday afternoon running about with people shouting 'Foxy!' and I'd no idea who they were talking to, until I realised it was me. And that happened all through my first Test match. It was bizarre. I've learned since that Foxy Fowler was a prolific prison escapee from the 1950s. Everybody calls me it now, except for one person, of course – Bob Willis. He's the only person to call me Graeme.

In those days, you met for a net on Wednesday afternoon, checked into the hotel, had a meal with the selectors, a team meeting, and played the following day. It was on that Wednesday I met my opening partner, Chris Tavaré, for the first time. He was looking at the wicket, so Willis took me across and we shook hands. Although he was the most conservative man (with a small 'c') ever, Tav and I became good friends as I loved his great, dry sense of humour. If he went blind he'd know where everything was, all his socks were in line in his drawer.

'How do you like to play the game?' he asked me. I looked a bit confused, so he tried again: 'How do you like to build your innings?' But I still wasn't sure what to say.

'Do you like to set off aggressively and calm down? Do you look to leave the ball as much as possible? Try to get ones to get up the other end? What do you look to do?'

I'd never thought about this, but it occurred to me that he was going to want an answer. 'Merit,' I said. 'Merit. If it's a good ball I block it; if it's a bad ball I hit it.' It was all I could think of.

We turned up the next day and it dawned on me I hadn't got any England shirts or jumpers. Alec Bedser, the England selector, appeared. He had a brown paper parcel with string tied round it (honestly) and threw it at me. It contained my shirts and jumpers. He threw my cap at me, too, but when it came to the tie he walked over and shook my hand. He thought that was more important than anything else. 'You're entitled to wear that every day of your life now.' Then he added, 'Enjoy today, because this will be the best day of your life.'

Initially, I thought that was nice, but then it struck me: 'Hang on, if this is the best day of my life, does that mean it can only be downhill from here?' But I knew what he meant.

I remember running around in the field looking at these three lions on my chest, unable to believe that I'd achieved this, but there were still moments that threw me. At one point I ended up fielding at leg gulley: 'What am I doing here? I'm at leg gulley for England. I've never been here in my life. This is weird. Put me somewhere I've been, please. Please!'

This being the era where they picked you, dropped you, picked you, dropped you, and with the way I batted not being how an England opener should play, it's my view I was almost picked to fail. After the departure of Graham Gooch and Geoff Boycott on the rebel tour of South Africa, England didn't have a settled opening pair and I felt I was selected because they had to, not because they wanted to. In fact, before the game Peter May actually told us, 'Currently, you are the best team available' – obviously referring to the rebels.

A great morale booster. I wasn't a player they'd picked looking to the future, I felt like a stopgap. It was the last Test match of the summer, so I imagine the logic went something like: 'If he doesn't get any runs we can move on, get somebody else in. He'll just have to go back into the county ranks and work hard to get back.'

But I confused matters slightly by getting the top score in the game, 86, in the second innings. I came off, went for a shower, and it was then that Bedser appeared in his three-piece suit. He stood in front of me, stuck his hand out – and didn't let go. I was thinking: 'This is bizarre. Here am I, stark bollock naked, with shampoo in my hair, he's got hold of my hand, and he won't let go.' The shower water was going everywhere.

He started to talk to me. 'Well played, Fowler. I thought you were going to get a hundred. You actually played too straight really. If you'd not done that, you might not have nicked it. You're going to get a lot of advice now you play for England.' All the time he'd got hold of my hand. There was water coming over my shoulder, soaking him from the knees down and drenching his arm. He'd got a pale grey suit on which now appeared almost black – and he was still carrying on. 'My advice is don't listen to any of it. Anyway, well played.'

Off he went, but as he grabbed the door handle, all this water ran out of his sleeve. Some of the lads looked round, their faces were a picture.

That was my first Test match. It was also my first time playing with someone who was going to loom large in my life from then on.

CHAPTER 6

BEEFY

'Where is he?' Beefy had stuck his head into our dressing room. Everyone turned and looked at me. 'You're out with me tonight.'

My team-mates were sympathetic: 'Good luck, Fow! Been nice knowing you!' It was followed by lots of laughing, while I had one overriding thought: 'I'd better get my drinking boots on.'

Lancashire's last away trip that season was at Somerset. I'd always loved playing at Taunton – cider, flat wicket, what's not to like? Apart from lining up against Ian Botham, Joel Garner and Viv Richards. Our three-day game was one of those Saturday, Monday, Tuesday affairs, with a Sunday League match in the middle. During the lunch break on the Sunday, the PA announcer gave out the England touring party for the Ashes tour that winter. This was, believe it or not, how players found out if they'd been selected: no phone calls, no personal meetings, just some random bloke on a PA system.

At the time I was at the back of the changing room and didn't happen to hear either the announcer or his message. It was only when one of my team-mates came in from the balcony to congratulate me that I found out I'd been selected. I was stunned; pleased, but stunned. And then Beefy appeared. Apart from standing in the same bar as him once or twice, Headingley was the first time I'd really met him. Now, with an Ashes tour ahead, he wanted to get to know me properly.

The night was going well; we were standing side by side, leaning on the bar. I needed it for support, he was just leaning on it. The bar had a brass hand rail running round the top, and my arms were folded on it. All of a sudden a glass of whisky was put in front of my face. 'I don't drink whisky,' I told him.

'You do now!'

'No, I don't.'

He instantly put me in a headlock. I had a choice: try to fight one of the strongest men I have ever met, drink the whisky, or stay in the headlock until he let me go. I chose the latter. Every couple of minutes he'd ask if I was going to drink it; each time I replied 'no'. Meanwhile, every time he wanted to order a drink, he gently tapped my head on the brass rail. After about 20 minutes he came up with another plan: 'If you're not going to drink it, you're still going to have it.' At which point he poured it on my head.

With that he released me from the headlock. I looked up at him: 'Right, can we get on now?'

'Yes.'

'Good.'

It was an unusual 20 minutes, but something happened. He proved he was dominant, strong. I proved I wouldn't give in. It was in that exchange that a mutual respect was formed – as well as establishing who was the alpha male. Ever since, we have been good friends, through thick and thin – and that includes my illness.

In 2004, when I suffered my first major bout of clinical depression, Beefy found out I wasn't well, although he had no idea as to the actual nature of what was wrong. He phoned Sarah and said: 'Tell Fox there's a board meeting on Monday.'

I should explain. Beefy retired from cricket in 1993, while I finished in 1994. The next year, Beefy called me and suggested we get a few guys together for lunch. I can't remember who was there, and I certainly can't remember leaving. What I do remember is Beefy paid for us all.

A few months later, he called me again: 'Fox, organise another lunch.' It was the same format – meet at noon, leave when you can't see straight. There was only one rule – no one was allowed to drive. As Beefy had paid for the first lunch, I decided to pay the bill this time. The food was £76, the total was £490. Beefy was in fine form, being both funny and bossy. I remarked this was more like a board meeting than a lunch, at which point Beefy said: 'It is. I'm chairman, and you're secretary.' Our lunches have been called board meetings ever since.

Anyway, on this occasion, the way I was feeling, I didn't want to go. He thought differently: 'I'll look after you.' He sent a car for me and I was taken to the restaurant. Beefy was sitting at the table on his own. It was noon, our normal time, and I wondered where everyone else was. 'They're coming at twelve thirty. I thought we could have a chat first, before the idiots arrive.'

The car I'd come in was parked outside. 'That car is there for you,' Beefy told me. 'Whenever you want to leave, just go. I'll pay for you today. If you want to drink, fine. If you don't want to drink, fine. You don't have to join in the conversation. Just relax and enjoy being here. You are among friends.'

My mental health was low, but I managed to eat, drink and talk a little. It was a gentle meeting compared to the usual. No one asked me how I was or directed conversation at me. Looking back, the guys were brilliant. Halfway through lunch, Beefy asked: 'What are you doing on Saturday?' I didn't know.

'Well, I do. I've spoken to Sarah and you're coming with me. We're going to Spain for a few days. It's all sorted, just be at my house late Saturday morning.' I didn't argue. He thought a few days away in the sunshine would do me good. Among the party was Jez, a former landlord, a quiet man and good listener, and Joe Neenan, the former Scunthorpe goalkeeper. Beefy paid for all of us. It was remarkable in its simplicity, incredible in its generosity.

Usually when Beefy organises an event, we all have to fall in line with how he wants it to be. I wouldn't say he bosses people, but we all know what we're expected to do. As soon as we put our bags down in the villa, he looked at me and said: 'Fox, you do whatever you want, whenever you want. We'll fit in around you.' He gave me the car keys and told me it was mine to use. During the day, while Beefy played golf with Joe, Jez and I set off in the car to explore. We spoke very little, Jez only talking when I started a conversation. He was easy company and we managed very well. In the late afternoon we'd go to the clubhouse for a glass of wine and some food.

There's a lot of that trip I can't remember – and it isn't due to the consumption of alcohol. It's simply because my head wasn't working as it should. What I do remember is the feel of it: gentle, I felt safe. And the black dog of depression faded a little. I found out months after we returned home that every morning at 8.30 Beefy rang Sarah to tell her how I had been the previous day.

Beefy might not understand depression, but what he did have was a clear understanding in his own mind of how to help. And he was right. That trip didn't cure my depression, but it did lift me from the bottom of the well towards the light.

The same thing happened when I had my first anxiety attack, also when I was out in Spain. I was driving a golf buggy, following Beefy and his pals round on the course, having a right laugh, and then all of a sudden I became absolutely petrified. I didn't know what the hell was happening, so I drove the golf buggy straight back to the house, quickly went inside, and sat myself down. It was horrific; I couldn't handle it and didn't know what to do. I'd never had anything like it before. It came completely out of nowhere. At one point, I honestly thought I was going to run at the wall and head-butt it. It seemed the only way to make it stop.

In the end, all I could do was talk to myself: 'Look, you're in a safe place, you're with good friends, there's no danger, you're OK. Just sit down, breathe, keep calm, and you'll be all right.' Thinking about it logically had saved me. 'It's just your head playing tricks with you.' But it left a shadow of being frightened. That night I stayed in Beefy's house as I couldn't face going out. I told Beefy, and he was great. He knew to just leave me alone. His instinct was absolutely right.

Those occasions weren't the first time I'd seen his sensitive side. One night in January 1983, Beefy asked me what I was doing that evening. I didn't have any plans, so he said: 'Be at my room for seven pm.'

I knocked on his door at the agreed time and he opened it wearing shorts, T-shirt and in bare feet, so we obviously weren't going out. He picked up an expensive bottle of wine and poured me a glass. 'I'll just have a beer, Beefy. That's too good for me.' He insisted I take it. We were the only people in his room.

'We're celebrating,' he said.

'Celebrating what?'

'It's my wedding anniversary.'

'How many years?'

'Seven.'

'And how much time have you spent together?'

'About twelve months.'

We sat and talked, had a bottle of wine, and ordered a room-service supper. I've never asked him why he asked me to share his anniversary, but I was touched that he did, and I guess I still am all these years later.

The thing with Beefy is he just doesn't like being on his own. Another time we were in Christchurch and had an afternoon off. I was lying on my bed watching *Victor Victoria*, the Julie Andrews film. In Beefy walked, didn't say anything, and picked me up like a baby. He carried me out of my room and started walking down the corridor. I was worried that I didn't have any shoes or socks on, but he told me I didn't need them. I put my arms round his neck, because there's nothing else you can do; you can't fight him or argue, you just go with the flow. He went into his bedroom – he had two double beds – and he threw me on to the spare. He was watching *Victor Victoria* as well. 'Kettle's there, fridge is there, get what you want.' He just didn't want to be on his own, and he hates not having anything to do.

I think I was a curiosity to Beefy at first, a little skinny bloke who'd turned up out of nowhere. But I think he respected how much I got stuck in when I played, and I think he liked the way I was off the pitch, too. Whenever he was doing anything he used to invite me. Once in Auckland he asked: 'Do you want to come with me?'

'Why, where are you . . . ?' I got halfway through the question.

'Downstairs, seven o'clock,' he said, 'and bring a towel.'

So I was downstairs at seven o'clock, and there was Vic Marks, half asleep, and he had a towel as well. Then Beefy marches down, and we got into a taxi that took us down to the docks area, where there were shipping containers all around. We stood there, Beefy wasn't saying anything and neither were we. Then, all of a sudden, it struck me – there were no boats anywhere. What were we doing? Then a seaplane appeared, landed and rolled up a ramp. Beefy told us both to get in. 'Don't touch anything,' the pilot said to me as I clambered in the front. 'Er, yes, all right.'

Off we took, flying above these beautiful islands, the bloke even let me have the controls at one point, and then we dropped down, landed, and pulled up by a beach, so I got out and lay my towel on the sand, but this wasn't the plan.

'Forget sunbathing, get on that!' Beefy said. A 60ft yacht had appeared. 'We've been out and caught fresh fish,' said the captain. 'There's beers in the fridge.'

We sailed around on a glorious sunny day, having a quiet beer and just loving where we were, before, at lunchtime, the captain pulled up at a jetty on an island. There was a single building, halfway up a mountain – a restaurant. In we went. Beefy had already sorted out the bill. We went back to the yacht, sailed back to the beach, got on the seaplane, and finally back to the hotel. It must have been eight o'clock when we got back. Recognising how much it must have cost him, I offered to chip in, but Beefy was having none of it: 'I asked you if you wanted to come with me, so I've sorted it.' I'd had one of the best days of my life.

I think the fact we get on is born out of my ability to understand people and work out how to relate to them. I've spent a lot of time with Beefy when there's just been me and him, not really doing anything, sometimes not even speaking much. Some people get carried away and anticipate what is going to happen, but I've never expected anything of him. He knows he can rely on me because I've never been any different. When he's in a bad mood I know how not to inflame it, and if he's in a humorous mood – and he can be really funny – I can get him going. But I've never been out of order with him. Out of order, yes. With him, no. We just get on.

It helped that I didn't have any preconceptions of him. I had no trepidation about meeting him, because he was a cricketer and cricket was what I did. It was the same with Derek Randall, Bob Willis, David Gower – they were cricketers like me. But the first time I met Eric Clapton, Elton John or

Bill Wyman, that was special. But then I remember how Bill Wyman once moved Bob Hoskins and Stephanie Powers from opposite him so he could talk to me. To him, they were just in showbusiness, whereas I was an international sportsman. I was interesting to Bill Wyman; they weren't. When it came to Beefy, I considered him a cricketer, albeit an exceptionally talented one, and so he didn't faze me. I always viewed it as a privilege to be in his company, because in a hundred years people are going to look back and say: 'I'd love to have met him. I'd love to have watched him play, to have had a beer with him.' And I'm in that situation.

A lot of his time, of course, has been spent fundraising – his foundation now raises money for five different charities. It began with his charity walks, inspired when he visited a children's leukaemia ward, shattered to hear that many of them wouldn't make it to Christmas. 'I want to do something for kids with leukaemia,' he told Kath afterwards. She thought he simply meant a golf day or something; she had no idea.

When Beefy started his walks, 80 per cent of children with leukaemia died and 20 per cent lived. Now, helped by all the money he's raised, it's the other way round. He found it unacceptable, so he said: 'I'm going to change it. I'm going to walk from John O'Groats to Land's End.'

And once he decides, that's it. Nobody has got a constitution like him, or a will. I've done legs of those walks with him, and they kill me, especially bearing in mind I've had four operations on my feet. The pace he walks, between 4.5 and 4.7 miles an hour, is at my very limits. We had three days on the south coast and I ended up jogging between 17 and 20 miles every day because I couldn't keep up.

The first time I joined him was on the east coast, in Yorkshire. At dinner, if you were new to the walk, you were on his table, so I sat next to him. Everyone had a set menu, except Beefy who had what he wanted. Now Beefy's a lover of seafood, and that night he had mussels. The following morning I discovered he'd been up all night throwing up. All the lads who walked with him were worried what it meant for that day. When he came down, he'd put on long johns, tracksuit, bin liner, big thick coat and waterproofs. Added to that was a woolly hat, gloves, dark glasses and hood pulled up; he might even have had a scarf on. And he just set off, walking even faster than normal. And that's why the lads were worried when they knew he had a problem, because most people when they're ill, they walk slower – not him, his mindset was: 'Right, let's get this over with.' When we got to the end of the walk, everybody was knackered. He walked at touching five miles an hour that day. It was torture.

At the end of every day he'd get to the hotel and be packed in ice, and he'd have the end of his bed raised so all the fluid would drain out of his legs. After about half an hour, I thought I'd go and see him. He was lying in bed with ice packs all over his legs, and he'd just done a TV and radio interview. 'Give me ten minutes,' he said, 'I'll have a shower and I'll see you in the bar for a pint.' I've never met anyone like him; he's 60 and he still does it.

But this is what he's always been like. When I moved to Durham, the first match I played was back at Lancashire. During the game we were asked to go as guests to a dinner at a club in Stockport. There was me, Beefy and a couple of other blokes on the top table. The owner gave Beefy the run of the wine menu. By the end of the evening I'm fairly sure he wished he hadn't. There were 12 bottles of good red wine brought to our table. I had a few glasses, the bloke next to Beefy maybe had one, and the bloke on my side had nothing at all. When we got up to leave at the end of the evening, the manager already had the cork out of the 13th. 'You might as well take this with you,' he told Beefy. And he did. He had it in the taxi on the way back to the hotel.

We walked into the foyer and I headed for the lift. We were halfway through a game, so I was planning on going to bed, but he wanted to go for a drink in the bar. He's like no human being I have ever met; he has an iron constitution.

However, he has changed down the years. He used to be on fire all day every day, all night every night. Life was huge. He was full-on at absolutely everything; now he's more reflective, a little bit more mellow. He's like a good fire – he's got those good embers, but he's still bloody hot, so don't take him for granted. If something winds him up, or he thinks something is unfair, he goes nuts. But that's what he is. You can't walk however many thousands of miles for charity, raise millions, be the best cricketer in the world, without passion.

There have been times where I've physically had to get between him and other people, not because they were going to come to blows, but because I would spot what was going to happen and stop it before it started. I didn't do it to stop them hitting him, but to stop them being absolutely pulverised. I did it for their protection, but also he'd have been in the papers and all sorts. He's had to live with that for decades, and I'd always intervene and get in the way. And he's done the same with me, like that time he took me to hospital in Auckland.

As a sportsman you get used to being judged. It's not nice, and the outcomes are not always good. I've seen at close quarters what it can be like to be in Beefy's shoes. I was with him once, way after we'd both finished playing cricket, and he just wanted to watch his son Liam, who was about 15 at the time, play rugby. He was playing in North Yorkshire somewhere, so we both went along, found out what pitch he was on, and walked out to watch. After about 20 minutes, someone must have realised Ian Botham was on the ground, and within another ten minutes there was a queue of people wanting his autograph. I was trying to explain he just wanted to watch the rugby, but at one point this woman pushed past me to get her autograph. Beefy refused: 'I want to watch my son play rugby.'

'It'll only take a minute.'

'There's only eighty minutes in a rugby match. I'll be here at the end and I'll sign as many as you want when the game's finished.'

She wasn't satisfied: 'But I have to go straight away afterwards.'

He looked at her: 'But that's not my fault.'

'You are an arsehole,' she told him, and walked off.

I've always said one thing about Beefy: 'If anybody doesn't like him, they don't know him.' Everybody has an opinion, but they haven't met him. Because if they had met him, and been polite, they'd know.

Beefy knows he's blessed with an amazing constitution, but I don't think he knows how great his capacity for life is. I don't think he knows how generous he is, though perhaps it is starting to dawn on him – I suppose a knighthood is a pretty good indication you're fairly special.

All I can say is that my life would be incredibly poorer if I didn't know him. I know that if I got run over today and died, and Sarah was made unemployed, he would look after our family. I know he would, because that's just him. He would just do it. And it's hard to thank a man like Beefy for something like that. Ever since I met him in 1982, I seem to have been in his debt. No matter how many times I say 'thank you' or do something for him, it will never be enough. It's always been a privilege to know him.

CHAPTER 7

AN OPENING OF EYES

It's a bit deflating to reach the pinnacle of cricket and then find out the set-up is shit. I was so proud to play for my country, to pull on that shirt, and then I realised they don't give you anything else. Quite literally – not a tracksuit, nothing. I was playing for my country and thinking: 'Fucking hell, it's like Accrington first team, only with better players.'

To give you an idea of how bad it was, at the World Cup in 1983, every cricket nation in that tournament had a tour uniform. We, the hosts, were told to buy a suit, not the same suit – any suit would do. There's a picture taken by Patrick Eagar from the balcony at Lord's looking down on to the pitch. All the other teams are in lines, in uniform, apart from us. We look a shambles.

That was the only time I met the Queen, and she actually said – and how embarrassing is this? – 'Why don't you have a team uniform?'

We couldn't really answer: 'It's because the TCCB don't give a shit about one-day cricket, or us. They're asking that we perform well, but they don't give a toss. It's just lip service.'

At the time, the rest of the cricket world played one-day internationals across 50 overs. We played them over 55. We couldn't even be arsed to play by the same rules, or buy the team a blazer. If that was the background, it's no surprise there was no analysis in the dressing room. We didn't have a coach or anybody to help out. Once the selectors picked the team, they buggered off, so it was just the captain and us. We were on our own; we had no one to go to, only our team-mates.

Thinking back to what Chris Tavaré had done when I joined the side, I decided to find out for myself. I remember asking David Gower how he set himself up to play at international level, and he said: 'I always target the first Test match of the summer to get a big hundred.' Great, but that didn't really help me, as he was somebody who played in every Test match, not someone like me who was just finding his way. I tried getting some help from Allan Lamb: 'How do you set yourself up to play against the West Indies? Do you look to leave it, then to dominate, then calm down? Do you look to play shots? Leave some shots out? Look to get forward? Play off the back foot? What do you do?'

He just looked at me: 'I rely on instinct.' So that didn't help either. Sometimes, if you've only got senior players to talk to, you don't get a lot back. It's not because they're being unhelpful, but they simply do stuff their own way, rather than being able to give advice that was applicable to me, so I had to find my own way to do things, too.

It wasn't that no one gave me any advice. Before I went to Australia, Jack Bond said to me: 'You'll be able to cope with the cricket, it's the off-field stuff you won't be able to cope with.' I felt he actually got it the wrong way round: I could deal with the off-field stuff – the travelling, the functions, the expectations – because I didn't need to think about them. I just lived inside a little bubble. It was the on-field stuff I couldn't cope with, because I'd never really thought about it. I'd never sat down to think about what was needed to be a successful international player. Only after my first England tour, to Australia, did I start to analyse what I had to do.

With no one around to guide me or help, it was all unknown territory, so a few simple pointers wouldn't have gone amiss. For example, during the 1983 World Cup I averaged 72, but looking back I should have done even better. I got four consecutive fifties, but they were fifties, not hundreds. I was not out in two of them, guiding England to victory, but it wasn't down to any kind of plan. If somebody had said: 'Look, once you get to fifty, just occupy the crease, bat through the overs, and everyone else will bat round you,' that would have been great advice, but there was nothing.

I'd get out for 60-odd and someone would say 'Well played', and that was it. There was no one to point out that if I'd stuck around, we might have ended up scoring 270 rather than 230. We had no analysis of that type, because the England establishment didn't care about one-day cricket. I was awarded Man of the Match for my 69 against Pakistan at Old Trafford, not that I actually received anything – no cheque or medal, not even a tie. Once again, thanks TCCB. I thought I might have won it again for my 81 not out off 77 balls in our win against

Sri Lanka at Headingley, but Richard Hutton gave the award to Bob Willis – for winning the toss.

We used to get angry and voiced our opinions. We believed that being an England cricketer should have meant that we were more professional, but we felt they were making us play with one hand tied behind our backs. If you were lost, you were lost. If you were out of form, there was no one to go to – you just didn't get picked.

Over the years, it's changed – a lot. England played a one-day series recently and there were 16 backroom staff, so it's gone from one extreme to the other. Sixteen backroom staff? You wouldn't know all their names, and I think it has gone too far.

We always said our dressing room was sanctuary, a private place where we could go and express our emotions, get all our frustrations out, and have huge arguments if necessary. It was completely our space. I got out one day and walked into the Lancashire dressing room and the chairman Bob Bennett was there with this bloke. I was furious at being out and I went up to David Hughes, the captain: 'Get them out of here!' To his credit, he went to Bob Bennett and kicked them out. It turned out the guest was Alex Ferguson. A couple of years later, I was at a luncheon, speaking at a Manchester United Supporters' Club event, sitting in between Alex and the United chairman Martin Edwards. I turned to Alex and apologised for sending him out. 'No, no,' he said, 'you were absolutely right. I should never have been in there. I didn't want to go in there anyway.'

He knew how it should be, but how can a dressing room be a sanctuary now with 16 backroom staff? These people don't have the same value on privacy as the players. What's to stop them from gossiping down the pub about what they've seen and heard in the England dressing room?

In any team there are some you get on with, some you don't, and some, if truth be told, you don't even really like, but you have to have a professional relationship with them all. However, that's not a problem, because that's part of being a cricketer. But why should you have to deal with 16 backroom staff on top of all that? Why should you have to get on with them? You probably can't even remember what some of them do. You don't know them and you don't socialise with them.

Just imagine this scenario. You and I are fairly regular openers for England. We're not playing badly, we've had scores in the last couple of games, but today we're out in the first and third overs. It's a 50-over game, so we go off and sit in the dressing room. I simply want to sit there and watch the game – I know I'm not in bad nick. The analyst comes up to me and asks if I want to see my dismissal, but I don't need to because I know what I did. The statistician then wants to show me what I've done in the last three weeks, but I'm not interested. You, on the other hand, go and watch your dismissal, and talk to the statistician. Then the strength and conditioning coach asks me if I want to do a core session, but I'm fine. However, you agree to do one. Then the assistant coach or batting coach asks if I want some throwdowns, but I'm happy watching the game, while you agree to do it after lunch.

So, by the end of the day, all I've wanted to do, because I'm my own man and I like my own space, is watch the game, but almost inevitably some of those backroom staff will go to the manager and say I did nothing and that I was really difficult to deal with. Whereas you, the other opener, are a great bloke and easy to get on with, because you gave them something to do. At the end of it, I'm going to be seen as an awkward character, and you're going to be perfect to work with, a true professional.

And that's just bollocks, isn't it?

If I was in a Test match dressing room now as a player, the only people I would like in there would be the players, obviously, the dressing-room attendant, the coach, bowling coach, batting coach and a strength and conditioning coach. If you want to have a fielding coach as well, fine. But that's it; the analysts, statisticians, sports psychologists can be available to the players if they want to see them, but they're not in the dressing room. The last thing you want is to clutter up that room with people. It dilutes the energy the players generate. There has to be a closeness in a team for it to be successful (though closeness doesn't always mean friendship) and it's impossible to have that if there are too many in the room, which can weaken the whole unit.

That's not to say the increase in staff numbers is bad in itself. It shows the ECB have tried to identify areas that need support, which is good. However, they've not known when to stop, so if the physio doesn't give massages, they will get a masseur. So what's next? An optician to check the players' eyes? They've grown it so far and then all of a sudden they've realised that people who should be used on a consultancy basis have become full time. Those extra people must then feel they have to justify their own job. To make matters even worse, you're taking all the key decision-making away from the player, who then gets in the habit of doing what he's been told. Well, I don't like being told how to play. I don't like being told I need this or that. Let me find out what I need and then you help me.

David Hughes, when he captained Lancashire, would occasionally say to me and my opening partner, Gehan Mendis: 'Go on, fellas, forty for none off the first ten.' And we'd just look at him and nod, and then he'd add: 'If we get to eighty off twenty, then we'll start going a run a ball.'

We'd walk out, look at each other, and wonder what he was on about. The way we played we might be 60 off ten, or even 80 off eight. We knew how to bat, how to play and what to do. You can't make it a formula; you can have things in mind, but it didn't make any sense to set those sorts of targets. The way we looked at it was: 'We're capable of doing this. You have to give the responsibility to us. You have to let us read the wicket, the bowlers, the circumstances.'

I want the freedom to think. I've always challenged things, asked questions, and if I don't agree with something I'll say so. Again, a lot of it goes back to my mum. Because she was always shouting at me and ordering me around, I rebelled against it as I wanted make up my own mind and didn't want to be told what to do. I would not have liked to have been told what to do 24/7 as a lot of players these days are. When they get out in the middle, if the script doesn't go to plan, they don't know what to do.

It goes back to a core belief I have about cricket. Yes, there's a lot of science in the game, but the performance is artistic. That split second when the ball is coming towards you, that's your performance. You decide what to do and how to do it. You can pre-load things, like 'if he bowls me a bouncer I'm not going to hook because there's two men out', or 'I can't trust the bounce, so I'm not square cutting', but that particular instant is a performance, artistic not scientific.

That's the way England played when Trevor Bayliss came in. They were given a licence to express themselves, and they were allowed to perform. I disagreed with the ECB when they said the coach is the most important person in the set-up. I don't think he is, because he never gets any runs or any wickets. He isn't out there making decisions. They made all this fuss about Peter Moores being the best coach of his generation, but he's been England manager twice and sacked twice. He was coach of Lancashire, and, yes, they won the Championship, but the following year they got relegated. So was he that good, and then became that bad?

To say Peter Moores is the best coach of his generation is insulting to a lot of other people. And how accurate can that be? There can't be a 'best coach'. Being a coach is a bit like playing, you have times when you know you're getting through to players and it's helping them, and there are other times when you're out of nick and you're not making sense to anybody. It's just as flighty as actually playing. Coaches have form as well. There's nothing in life that remains constant; it goes up and down. Human nature rules out constant. So I don't believe there is a best coach of a generation.

What I do believe is that Peter Moores wasn't the right selection for England. I know a lot of people at Lancashire who think he's brilliant and he probably is – at that level. For England, I didn't think he had a deep enough understanding of the emotions involved. I wouldn't necessarily say that's because he hasn't played at that level. I'm not of the school that says you have to have played at a certain level to coach that level. There are some who haven't played Test cricket who do understand it, but I didn't sense that he was one of them. It felt like he got everything from a book. I respect him, and I'm damned sure he's a great county coach, but when it came to England it was like putting Allan Lamb in charge. Love him as much as I do, he wouldn't be the right bloke. He just did it. As a player he didn't really analyse what he did, or how things were done. He couldn't deconstruct the game, work it out, and then construct it again. I wouldn't be the right bloke either. I don't have the overall vision and direction. I'm better at going into small areas and then expanding them. I've always felt that about team coaching – I'm better working with individuals than I am with a big unit.

For England, I thought the Andy Strauss and Andy Flower combination was fantastic – you could see it working. And since Trevor Bayliss came in there's been a different look on everybody's face. There's a joy, and you can hear it in players' voices when they're interviewed. They want to speak, not simply give pat answers. (There's another classic who shouldn't be allowed in the dressing room, the media relations officer. If that had been me, I'd have said: 'I'm an intelligent bloke and an international cricketer, I can speak. If I get it wrong, fine me.')

What's needed with support staff is a happy medium, but now the pendulum has gone way too far the other way. Progress does not always mean better. I'm sure there are some players in the England set-up who absolutely love everything that is going on, but that's because they've been brought up in that system and they don't know any different. And they probably, as we have seen, don't have the ability to think for themselves or to do things the way they want to.

To give an example, when I got to a cricket ground at 9.15, I was out there by half past for an 11 o'clock start. At Lancashire we did a routine where we ran and warmed up and stretched, then we did group fielding, and then we went off and did our individual stuff. I could have told you, purely by what we were doing in my match preparation, exactly what time it was. That hour between half-past nine and half-past ten turned me from a civilian to a professional cricketer. That was repeated every day, and every game I played in I treated it the same way. When I was coaching, I used to stress that if you get to a Test match or a one-day final and you need to do something extra, it means you've not been doing enough on all those other days.

I could not imagine turning up to a ground now and seeing all those cones and discs everywhere on the field. I don't want to be your monkey while you grind the organ. This is my time to turn me into a cricketer, not your time to demonstrate how many stupid exercises you can come up with. OK, it might loosen me up, but it's stopping me preparing myself to be a cricketer. My mental process has been stopped. Transforming myself into a cricketer has been altered to participate in silly little games, and that is not what I wanted. You can do all that stuff on preparation days. Then, I'll be your monkey and do what you want, but on the morning of a match, can we have a simple routine, so we're all doing exactly what we want and it's repeated day after day?

I absolutely understand that not everybody is the same as me. If some players like doing these different things, because it takes away them having to think about the game, fine. But there should be limits. As a coach I never allowed any of my players, before training sessions or games, to play football, because to me that's unprofessional. You only have to see the statistics about football-related injuries. When Lancashire used to come down and play at Durham University, they played football every morning. They appeared more interested in the football than they were in the cricket.

That's not to denigrate everything about the modern set-up. There are elements of it I'd have really enjoyed. They're fitter and stronger these days, for example. That was something I aspired to, having qualified as a PE teacher, but I didn't really know how to go about it then. As it was, at the start of a season I could easily run five miles in 27 minutes, but after the first day's fielding I was tired. By the end of the season, I could field all day every day, but I couldn't run five miles in 27 minutes. Physical training or strength and conditioning to prepare players for what they needed in the season weren't even invented back then.

Nowadays I'd also have the option of talking to a sports psychologist, something I would have loved, even if it was just to understand that other players have the same difficulties, playing-wise, as me and to realise that other people lack real inner strength and have doubts sometimes as well. I recognised I wasn't the same as everyone else that I played with; I thought my head was completely different as well. It's only donkey's years later you find out that other people suffered with the same issues, too.

To have had someone like Mark Ramprakash as batting coach, like the current England set-up, would have been brilliant. I'd argue he is probably a better batting coach than Graham Gooch, because Gooch was an unbelievable player and if he explained how he did it, and suggested someone followed suit, the problem is they might not have his talent. I love him, but I remember he'd say things like: 'If I was struggling in a one-day game, I'd just go back to my go-to shot. I'd go inside out and hit it over extra-cover for six.' He was being genuine, because he could do it, but the rest of us couldn't play like that.

When Peter Moores and Paul Farbrace were head and assistant coach, I would have had my doubts about talking to either of them. Moores wasn't even a good county batsman, let alone Paul Farbrace. I wouldn't have been able to talk to them technically about batting, because they would have to go on theory; nor could I discuss the mental side of batting either. However, Ramprakash's international career for a large part was a struggle, so he'd be more sympathetic, more analytical, and understand what it's like to battle in those circumstances. Not only that, but he got 150 in a Test match, so he knows what it's like to succeed as well. I actually think he'd be good to talk to, even if it's just to pat you on the back and reassure you that you'd got out to a great ball.

That would definitely have been an improvement on what I had. In these days where even club players can have video analysis of their game, it might surprise you to learn that the first time I saw myself bat was on the BBC highlights after my first Test match. I was horrified, because the images didn't match up with what I thought I was doing. I saw myself and it was a real wake-up call. But when it came to progressing, to practising the detail, we didn't even have a bowling machine at Lancashire. I asked Jack Bond if we could have one: 'What, so you lot can back away from that as well?'

I was incredulous: 'One, have you just said that? And two, I don't care what anybody else does, I'd like to practise properly.' We didn't get one.

Everything in that era was so random. Back then, the players said goodbye at the end of a Test match and that might be it. There was no settling-in period, you could get dropped if you hadn't performed on that occasion. Derek Randall felt he had to score runs every game or he'd not get picked. On the New Zealand and Pakistan tour of 1983-84, he averaged 40-odd and was by far and away our best batsman. We got back to England, he played the first Test match against the West Indies, made 0 and 1, and never got picked again. The message from the selectors was that he didn't like playing against the real quick bowlers. Well, he did all right against Lillee and Thomson, didn't he? In that first West Indies Test, after usually batting between five and seven all winter, and being a success, they made him bat at three. Why do that? Give him one game, and then never pick him again? Essentially, they were picking him to fail, but why would you want to get rid of your best batsman?

To treat Derek Randall that way was dreadful, but at that time you got the feeling the selectors wanted you to be like the archetypal English public schoolboy, in how you both behaved and dressed. But Derek wasn't like that – there aren't many players who are – and he suffered for being unorthodox. He had to perform every time he went to the crease, while other people didn't. Some were given a much longer run. For example, Mike Gatting made his first hundred in his 30th

Test match. After that he was a good player, but before that he wasn't. Everybody would have enjoyed being given that many opportunities, but they just didn't do it. How many players had one Test? People like Alan Wells at Sussex. One Test! If you have four or five bad games, then you can expect to be dropped, but not if you have one. I would have loved to have played in this era where you're given the opportunity to play a few games so that you become part of a team and you know that, if you don't play well in one game, you're still going to be there for the next one. It allows players the freedom to play.

It must have taken me a good 10 to 15 matches to feel comfortable at Test level. Not many people make that step up and find it easy, go out there and smash it to pieces. I got 80-odd in my first Test match in the second innings, so I had a little bit of leeway, but that's still some way removed from actually feeling settled and comfortable in that environment. Players were given no consistency and it made a mockery of the selection procedure.

Even if you were playing well, there were no guarantees. In New Zealand, I was the leading runscorer before the opening Test match. Two games previously, all three openers had played – Chris Smith, Chris Tavaré and me – because the selectors couldn't decide who to pick. The other two both wanted to open and so, me being me, I agreed to bat at three. I made a century and 80 and was rested for the next game, which was a good sign, as it generally meant you were in for the Test. Bob Willis was interviewed before that match and asked if it was the team he'd be going with in the Test and replied: 'No, no, because if it was Graeme Fowler would be playing.'

Then Chris Smith got a really good, but slow, 138 not out in that game. When Bob announced the team, I wasn't in it. Graham Dilley, the leading wicket-taker on tour, wasn't in it either. Bob explained the decision to me: 'I've gone for someone else, because you score too freely.' What a thing to say. Can you imagine someone being told that now? 'What am I supposed to do?' I asked. 'If you don't pick me now, when am I ever going to play?'

Bob didn't really understand batting, but what he did understand was taking time out of the game. He'd rather have Tav getting out at teatime for 60, than me be out at lunch for 80. I half understand that, but can you imagine someone being told that now? If someone bowled a bad ball, what was I supposed to do? Block it? In the continuum of batting, there's two extremes: every ball is there to be hit, but if it's a good ball block it; or every ball is there to be defended, and occasionally you'll get some runs. I was the first one, Boycott was the other. I'm not saying I was a better player than Boycott, because obviously I wasn't. It's just two different approaches. I was one, Tav was the other, and Bob preferred the other. But if that was what he thought, why had he brought me on tour? Why not bring another blocker? Why bring me?

So I had hardly played any cricket, and then all of a sudden I got picked for the second Test at Christchurch. It was the worst wicket I have ever played on, including club wickets. You could pick pieces of grass and lift lumps out. Tony Pigott turned out for us, drafted in because he was playing in New Zealand. At the team meeting the idea was they couldn't play bouncers, and that none of them liked the short ball. Poor sod, he didn't know what was happening, so he bowled bouncers, as did everyone else, and they got 307. We thought we'd done well. Then Richard Hadlee came in, pitched it up, and we were 82 and 93 all out. I batted for an hour and a half in the game and got 14 runs. We then went to Auckland where they chose to bat and made 496. I fielded for two days, went out to bat, Richard Hadlee ran in, and I nicked it first ball. On that tour, having been the leading runscorer before the first Test match, I averaged 4.6 for the series.

But it was nothing I wasn't used to. In 1983, after my successful World Cup, I went on to make my first Test century, then I didn't do anything in the next Test, and then I was dropped. Can you imagine that now? Unless you were Lamb, Gower, Botham or Willis, you played for your place every match. We never felt like a team. It was just 11 individuals playing in that particular game who then went off not knowing if they were going to see each other again. No one ever communicated with you concerning your selection or non-selection. I found out I'd been dropped because a journalist rang me up. If the selectors thought you were doing well, you didn't know. If they didn't think you were up to standard, a local journo informed you.

At the time, Peter May was the chairman of selectors alongside Phil Sharpe and Alec Bedser. After being left out I bumped into Phil Sharpe, who told me he had voted for me. Later in the season I saw Alec Bedser, who said the same thing. When Peter May repeated the statement, I was angry. None of them would tell me why I'd been dropped and what I needed to do to improve and get back in the team.

I remember thinking I was only a member of England team for the duration of the match. As soon as the Test was over, I would trundle back to Lancashire and become a county cricketer again, and await my fate. I never felt I was an England player between matches. And that's why it was my generation of cricketers who in the end said: 'This is not good enough. We're trying our best here. We want a bit of help. We get all this stick and criticism, but you're not doing anything to help us represent our country the way we want to.'

In the meantime, despite the lack of preparation or consistency of selection, we had to hope we all came together and played well for those five days. Sometimes it worked, sometimes it didn't. Foresight and planning were non-existent. When we went to Australia in 1982-83, we were travelling economy class in the blazers, shirts, trousers and ties we'd been given the day before when we met up at Lord's. Of course, they didn't fit. Can you imagine big blokes like Derek Pringle, Beefy and Bob Willis in economy class having got on the plane in blazer and tie for a 20-hour flight to Australia? Thanks TCCB, that really makes sense.

Earlier we'd had a medical. It wasn't exactly rigorous. Basically, if you pissed on a stick and it didn't melt you were in. We had our blood pressure taken, stuck out our tongues, and had a couple of injections. Weirdly, we did all that in pairs. For the Australia tour, I was with Norman Cowans, but he was so afraid of injections, his muscles became so tight they broke three needles in his arse. I was killing myself laughing.

The laughter didn't last long – my top score during the first six weeks of that tour was 14. It was no surprise I wasn't picked for the first Test match in Perth. Instead, Geoff Cook and Chris Tavaré opened. We drew. During net practice before the second Test at Brisbane, Geoff asked Beefy to stay behind and give him some practice against the short ball. Beefy was happy to do so as he preferred to practise in small numbers – he sometimes would ask if I'd stay behind so he could have a proper bowl. On this occasion, however, he hit Geoff in the ribs and cracked a couple. On the morning of the game there was a knock on my hotel room door and Bob Willis told me I was in the side.

In the first innings, I scored 7 and lasted all of 28 minutes. The second innings defined how I would approach batting for the rest of my career. Our backroom staff was Doug Insole (manager), Norman Gifford (assistant manager and catch hitter), Bernard Thomas (physio), and Geoffrey Saulez (unkempt scorer). That was it: four. Doug Insole, as manager, would stick his nose in and tell us how to play, or, to be more precise, how not to play: 'Don't hook, don't drive outside the off stump, the cut is a dangerous shot in Australia.' For the first part of the tour, I listened. After all, he was the manager – I felt he must know best. But what that meant was I was now trying to play like an England opening batsman, rather than in my own way. I was listening to someone who didn't know my game tell me how to play, and I was failing abysmally.

For the second innings in Brisbane, I thought: 'Fuck it, if I'm going to fail at Test level, I'm going to fail being me and not trying to bat like someone else.' Taking that decision was quite liberating and I decided there and then no one would ever tell me how to bat again. Take advice and learn, yes. Tell me how to play, no.

At tea on the third day, I was 30 not out. I hadn't played well but I was still in. Chris Tavaré batted 111 minutes for his 13, so the scoreboard wasn't exactly rattling round. After tea we went off for bad light and when we came on again it was murky to say the least. Not exactly ideal – I was on strike to Jeff Thomson for the first time in my career. I had a thigh pad, pads, gloves and a helmet which had very small cut-down Perspex ear pieces. I had no visor, chest guard or arm guard.

When it came to the first ball from Thommo, I saw the bottom of his foot in his delivery stride, then the ball whistled past my face. I hadn't moved. I had never faced anything that fast. The second ball, like the first, whistled past my face. Again I hadn't moved. I had seen both balls, but they were too fast for me to react. It was then I started a conversation with myself. Sportsmen and women often have internal dialogues with themselves, referring to the other voice as being a little man on their shoulder. This little man is often annoying as he's usually negative and tells you to do stupid things. Occasionally he can be the voice of reason, but in my experience he's usually a little prick. Anyway, up he popped. This was the conversation.

Him: 'Kin 'ell. How are you going to play this? It's too fast.

Me: I've no idea. I've never ever played anyone this fast.

Him: Well, you'd better think of something – he's reached the end of his run-up.

Me: Just stand still, use your eyes and hands, something will happen.

And so that's what I did. I stood perfectly still and let my instincts and reactions take over. I don't know how it looked, but it worked, and gradually I got used to his pace. Thommo did get me out, a thin glove down the leg side caught by Rod Marsh, but I had batted for four minutes under six hours for 83, which was the top score of our innings. And, in the absence of anyone else to advise me, I'd worked out how to do that myself.

When I was out, though, all the manager said was: 'What were you doing? Even if you'd middled it you were only going to get a single.' Clipping the ball to fine leg is bread and butter for a left-hander. Do it a hundred times and you have a century. 'Too high risk,' he said, 'for too little reward.'

I walked away saying nothing, but thinking plenty. I smiled to myself. Before that innings I had decided to be my own person and not be told how to play. Six hours later and I was vindicated. I had the feeling Doug Insole never liked me, while I didn't trust him. To him I was immature, to me he was headmasterish. At the end of the tour he gave me a poor report, or so I am led to believe. In that era there were players and officials, 'us and them', he was definitely 'them'.

Having lost in Brisbane, the next Test was in Adelaide. Bob Willis won the toss and stuck Australia in and they scored 438. We were bowled out for 216 by tea on the third day and forced to follow on. I was alone in the changing room with Beefy and padding up: 'Come on, Fox. If you bat all day today and tomorrow, we can save this.'

'Bat all day?' I replied. 'I'm not a superstar. I'm just a little lad from Accrington.'

Beefy walked over, grabbed me by the shirt and vest, lifted me completely off the floor, and pushed me against the wall. He leaned in quietly. 'How do you think I started?' He put me down and walked out. It was a seminal moment for me. I was being an idiot and he was right. We all start from the same place. Where we end up is largely up to us (and good genes). I may have scored only 37, but I batted with new ambition and was out early the next morning after batting for 139 minutes. I had played in three Test matches and twice I had been the top scorer in the innings. Twice I had scored over 80. I was good enough to play at Test level. What I had yet to find out was whether I was good enough to do a good job at Test level.

We moved on to Melbourne for the Boxing Day Test match. The little matter of 83,500 people turned up for the first day's play. Not that they watched me for long – 24 minutes to be precise. We were bowled out for 284, then Australia replied with 287. In the second innings, I had just passed 50 in 77 balls when Thommo bowled me a yorker. The ball hit the very bottom of my bat, which itself happened to be immediately above the big toe on my right foot. The end result, as X-rays proved, was he'd broken the end bone into three pieces. It hurt. I did all my batting using my right leg. I went forward and all my weight was on it, and I used it to push me backwards on to the back foot. Still sitting on the wicket, I tried to explain this to Bernard Thomas. 'Well, stand on the other leg for a while,' he advised. I could hardly stand up. A runner came out for me, David Gower. There was never any discussion about me going off.

I knew that Thommo would bowl a bouncer at me, but I couldn't duck because of my foot. In essence I was a target. As I very rarely hooked, I decided to let my instinct take over. He bounced me, and somehow I hooked it straight down fine leg's throat. Just as I was thinking of walking off, I heard the umpire's call of no ball. 'Shit, I'm going to get another bouncer!' I did. I missed it. It missed me.

I was out shortly afterwards for 65, bowled by Rodney

Hogg. I limped off the pitch and out of the tour. Famously, we won that Test match by 3 runs. Last pair Thommo and Allan Border put on an agonising 70 before Thommo edged one off Beefy to Chris Tavaré at slip. He fumbled the catch only for Geoff Miller to pick up the rebound. It was an incredible moment, but I wasn't even at the ground. Bernard Thomas said it would be too difficult to get me there, so I watched us secure one of England's most famous victories, which I'd been part of, from my hotel bed. When it came to the England set-up, it kind of said it all.

CHAPTER 8

QUICK

Jeff Thomson was one thing; the relentless quicks of the West Indies entirely another. In 1984, England faced a full summer against the men from the Caribbean. My place in the England side was tenuous to say the least, and here I was about to play against the best team ever. Physically, mentally and emotionally, it proved to be the hardest cricket I ever played.

There was an early sign of things to come. The first one-day match, at Old Trafford, produced the most remarkable innings I have ever seen – I.V.A.Richards' 189 not out. They were 166 for nine and we were in control of the match when last man Michael Holding strode to the crease. He batted for an hour, scored 12 not out, and yet the West Indies finished up on 272 for nine. Viv not only farmed the strike, but he added another 93 runs to his tally. It was brutal beauty in the extreme.

We walked off stunned. As we sat down in the dressing room, no one spoke. Then Beefy said simply: 'Smokey, you bastard.' Viv was known as Smokey because of his admiration for the boxer Smokin' Joe Frazier. We lost heavily that day, and the series 2-1.

The first Test was at Edgbaston. We won the toss and elected to bat. I took first ball. The second was a bouncer. It set the tone for the series – fast and hostile – and I was out for a duck. Sitting dejected in the dressing room, I was staring at the TV watching the game. Between me and the pitch were two doors, both of which were closed. Malcolm Marshall was bowling to Andy Lloyd and hit him on the helmet. I heard the loud crack of the impact through the doors long before I saw he'd been struck on the TV. I shouted for Bernard Thomas: 'That's hospital.'

As Lloyd was ushered in, I asked him how he was. His reply was sickening: 'I'm all right apart from this blind spot.' I knew he'd detached his retina, and he never played for England again. In that match I scored 0 and 7 as we lost by an innings and 180 runs. The technical term for that is a good stuffing.

The next Test was at Lord's. It was being written in the press that I wasn't good enough to play at this level. To be honest, I thought if I have to play against this lot every week, I'm not so sure if I am good enough. We were staying in a hotel opposite, and my room overlooked the ground. The night before the Test, as usual, I ate and had a couple of pints before retiring to bed. I was nervous, and I didn't usually get nervous. I think it was for a couple of reasons. One, this could be my last Test match, and I didn't want that to be the case. And two, I knew how bloody difficult it was to bat against them. Not only were they extremely skilled but physically threatening. Playing against one world-class fast bowler is one thing; playing against four is a different thing altogether.

Each brought their own problems. During that summer,

Joel Garner and Malcolm Marshall usually opened the bowling. Marshall was about 5ft 10in and skiddy, so he might bowl a ball that you had to play forward to. If Garner pitched the ball in the same spot, you had to play back because he was 6ft 9in and had a shedload of bounce. See off the opening bowlers and then you'd have Michael Holding and Eldine Baptiste. I found playing Baptiste difficult. He wasn't as quick, but he leaned back and angled the ball across me at an acute angle. He was awkward. Holding? What can I say? Often in my stance I would watch him run in with that beautifully silken, athletic, poetic stride, enjoy its elegance, then realise he was about to bowl and I'd better do something.

So there I was in my room, nervous, unable to sleep, literally pacing the floor, looking out the window at Lord's bathed in darkness. Then I thought: 'Bollocks, this is ridiculous, I need some sleep.'

The practical side of my brain kicked in. How do I get to sleep? One answer sprang to mind – drink alcohol. Better off with a bit of a hangover having slept than being awake all night. I rang down and ordered three pints of Guinness. When they arrived I drank them as fast as I could and went to bed. It worked, I slept.

At the end of the first day I was 70 not out. I was also nursing sore bollocks. Joel Garner had smashed my box just before lunch. When I say smashed, I mean into little pieces. That wasn't funny – although everybody else seemed to think so. Clive Lloyd was taking the mickey out of me. I said something along the lines of: 'Can you take away the pain and leave the swelling?' He just laughed.

I carried on batting, but I felt sick. I had water brash, my mouth was salivating. My nuts were on fire. The strange thing is they felt wet. I thought I was bleeding, but there was no blood, and it ached like nothing on earth. It was not like you've trapped your finger in a door and it slowly subsides – this was not going away. I stood up, didn't even check my box, carried on batting, obviously feeling terrible, but I'd been hit in the bollocks before – you just get on with it.

We went off at lunch. I deliberately waited until the entire dressing room was empty before I took my trousers off to have a look. I took my box out – it had split in two. Thank Christ I hadn't got hit again. I was one of the early players to use a baseball box, which curves round and keeps everything in place. The problem with a normal box is if it gets hit on the side it moves, and it takes everything inside with it, and that is horrific. As it was, Joel Garner hit me straight on. When it had split it had trapped me as it came back together. It looked like I'd been given a lovebite by a Rottweiler. Where the box had got compressed into me, all the skin had gone through the breathe holes. Imagine a hole-punch – I had purple circles all over my bollocks. It was horrific really, and they were just so tender. I put some ice on, which is not a pleasant feeling, and the pain had calmed down by the time I went out again after lunch, but it looked a right mess.

That night it was the same routine: evening meal, a couple of pints, and bed. At 1am I was still awake and nervous, but I knew the solution. The night porter delivered three pints of Guinness and I slept. The next day I scored 106.

I was on 95 and Roger Harper came on. I don't think Clive put him on to help me. He knew what I liked, and that I batted well against spinners, but also I did tend to hit them at that time so maybe he believed I might give a chance. I suppose he thought, 'If it works, it works.' Where you'd think most people would have tried to take singles, I slog-swept Harper over long-on to go to 99, then I cut him behind square for the hundred. At the time I don't think I understood it would be one of the moments that defined my career. I didn't even realise the significance of being put on the board of century-scorers in the pavilion. It was only when I went back years later and saw my name up there that I thought, 'Wow!' But that was just me: I was so bloody ignorant of stuff. In some ways, however, naivety was a godsend; my ignorance was bliss. If I'd understood the gravity of things, in the 90s I'd have been a hell of a lot more nervous. If you don't know anything, you don't put any pressure on yourself. What I did know is if I hadn't got a hundred in that Test match I probably wouldn't have played another game for England. And I didn't want to be dropped; I wanted to play.

I had no real plan in that innings. All I had – and this sounds ridiculous – was to try to get forward. I knew that most of the time I wasn't going to be playing forward, but the dangerous balls are the pitched-up ones. They're the ones that get you caught behind, LBW, bowled; the short ones are just uncomfy. But what the West Indies would do is push you back, push you back, push you back, then pitch one up. So you had to be looking to get forward.

As a rule, I didn't really hook, but I played two hook shots in that innings, off consecutive balls from Malcolm Marshall, and they were the best I ever played. I watched the highlights later. Ted Dexter said: 'Fowler taking advantage of the old ball, which he should do. Get a few runs before the new ball's due.' I hadn't thought of that! I just hit the damned thing!

It wasn't all like that. Malcolm Marshall bowled me a yorker which beat me through the air for pace. If somebody beats you through the air for pace, that comes as a shock. It missed off stump. I nicked another and it went between wicketkeeper Jeff Dujon and Clive Lloyd at slip, so it wasn't a flawless innings. Also, something very strange had happened. At one point, Desmond Haynes at short leg asked: 'Why are you shouting?' I didn't know what he was on about. He explained when Joel Garner was running in, I was shouting out loud 'Come on!' And I hadn't even noticed. That shows more than anything how involved you are in the moment.

It helped that we were constantly interrupted. We kept going off for drizzle and bad light. It may have meant that Joel Garner and Malcolm Marshall had a rest, but it also meant I got one too – a mental rest. I was able to switch off when I got in the dressing room. In cricket it's vital to learn to switch on, switch off. In the middle, you do it in 20-second batches. You cannot possibly concentrate for six hours. My ability to do that was partly down to my character. I could always, in the middle of a conversation, come up with something flippant, something funny, and then go straight back to being serious again. And that ability worked in cricket. I could talk to the non-striker, wicketkeeper, have a look at the crowd, see what was happening, but as soon as the bowler turned round I was in my stance. I was switched on. As soon as that ball was completed, I switched off again. Everybody's different. Chris Tavaré would be intense the whole time, whereas I was completely the opposite. Like Clive Lloyd always said: 'Batting is an extension of your personality.'

I learnt a lot of the psychology, the philosophy, of batting from Clive. He said to me one day: 'If you go in a pub and talk about religion and sex and football, and you get your head kicked in, you stop talking about it. If you go in a pub and talk about those things and everybody has a good night, keep doing it. Batting is the same, young Fow. If you can get a ball from outside off stump and hit it over deep midwicket and it gets you out, don't do it. If it works, keep playing it. It's the same for everything.'

I had the belief I could make a century against the West Indies instilled in me through experience, but that experience was started by those words from Clive, stood there at slip, about what you can do. When I reached the hundred, I was batting with Beefy. He shook my hand, I acknowledged the crowd, and Clive must have just stood and waited. The applause died down and then he walked slowly over and shook my hand. That was just incredible, but he was an incredible bloke. In Australia, when I was picked for the second Test at Brisbane on the back of a run of low scores, I was not out overnight when the phone rang in my room. It was Clive. You have to bear in mind this was the era with no mobiles, so he'd obviously made the effort of finding out which hotel I was in, working out the time difference, staying up until that time, and ringing me. All he said was: 'Fow, you've done this before, you did it at Headingley, you can do it again. Just play like you.' He was the captain of the best team in the world, and he made me feel honoured when he did that.

On the fifth day, we declared, leaving the West Indies 342 to win. They won by nine wickets. West Indies 2, England 0. Marshall 1, Andy Lloyd 0. Garner 1, my bollocks 0. Could this game get any harder?

The next match was at Headingley, a ground which, during the 1980s, produced incredible cricket matches, partially due to the fact the wicket was, shall we say, sporting. Michael Holding, as you'd expect, was playing after having missed out at Lord's, and by this time I'd known him a while. In 1981, while he was the professional at Rishton in the Lancashire League, he also played a handful of midweek games for Lancashire. Michael's first match was at Northampton in a three-day Championship match. Clive Lloyd was captain – at that time we could play two overseas players – and I was wicketkeeper. Terrible – not so much a wicketkeeper as a fielder behind the stumps with gloves on.

During Michael's first spell, he bowled a bouncer that was going down the leg side and I set off after it. As it pitched, it swung back to the off side, so I turned round and set off the other way. Diving full-length, I caught the ball one-handed exactly in the spot where I'd been standing four seconds earlier. Clive Lloyd, with his hands on his knees and head bowed, was chuckling: 'Oh boy, this is going to be a long season.' Michael looked on quizzically. In a short period of time, he realised I was rubbish but tried my best, and weirdly I caught most of the catches. We became friends.

During the Test series in 1984, Michael and I would sometimes go out for supper during matches. As soon as play ended, we stopped being cricketers and went back to being friends. When it started again, vice versa. One such occasion was Headingley. As we were parting after our meal one evening, Michael said: 'Fow, I will say goodnight. I will not be saying good morning.' A brilliant comment.

Next morning, the first ball he gave me was one of the

fastest I ever faced – a bouncer straight at my head. So taken aback was I that I tried to hook it. To say I was late on the attempt would be an understatement. By the time I'd finished the shot, Jeffrey Dujon had thrown the ball to Clive Lloyd at first slip. I knew it was comical. I bowed my head and started laughing. I didn't want Michael to see me, so I kept my head really low. However, I could see the tips of his bowling boots just poking into my field of vision under the peak of my helmet. He was stationary, not going anywhere. I knew I had to look at him. I raised my head and met his gaze.

'Fow.'

'Mikey.'

'Fow, put that shot in the cupboard.'

'Mikey.'

With that he walked away. I love that memory. It's a special one, involving an incredible bowler and a fantastic man. A true gentleman. He didn't get me out – I was caught and bowled Marshall, who had a plaster cast on his left arm. Only I could do that. We lost again, 3-0.

On we went to Old Trafford. Being two local players, *Look North* wanted to interview me and Paul Allott live on the eve of the game. We'd both done this sort of stuff before – we weren't brilliant, but we weren't bad. As we took our places in the studio, with microphones being shoved up clothing, it was all going well until the floor manager said: 'You'll be great, just don't say "fuck".' He completely stuffed us. For the entire interview, it was the only word I could think of. It didn't help Walter either. In response to one question, he said: 'It will be great to play in front of the Old Trafford crowd, because not only are they one of the noisiest crowds, they're also the loudest.'

Next morning we had a team photo on the outfield. This is how bad we were, it was my 14th Test match and I was on the front row. As the photo was about to be taken, Beefy said out loud: 'I wonder what they'll say about this team in the future.'

At the time, the wicket at Old Trafford was a slow, low shit-heap with variable bounce. It wasn't the groundsman's fault. The square had died and needed digging up; a year or so later it was. Being 3-0 down in a five-match series, the selectors must have thought they needed to do something drastic. They did: they picked Pat Pocock.

Universally known as Percy, Pat is a delightful man and one of my favourite room-mates ever. I've never met a more irrepressible, upbeat bloke. The more I got to know him, the more I loved him. He made his first-class debut in 1964, and once took seven wickets in 11 balls. In his career, he amassed 1,607 first-class wickets. However, this was now 20 years after his first-class debut. He was 37 years old.

In professional cricket, I was hit on the head only twice while batting. One of these occasions was in this Test match. Winston Davis (in for the injured Marshall) bowled me a bouncer, I ducked, but the ball didn't bounce and skidded at me. I ended up on one knee and turned my head away. The ball thudded into the back of my helmet. Such was the lack of bounce, if it hadn't pitched outside leg stump I would have been LBW. The impact was loud inside my helmet, and I ended up flat on my back. Don Oslear, the umpire, was a man who loved getting involved in the game and could turn any drama into a crisis. He ran over, bent down beside me, and basically pinned me to the ground. 'Get off me! I'm fine.'

I looked up and saw Clive. 'Clive, get him off me!' Oslear let go and I got up. I was perfectly fine, just shocked I'd been hit on the head and how loud it was.

Paul Terry, in only his second Test match, wasn't as lucky. A Garner delivery kept low and smashed into his wrist, badly breaking his ulna. He needed an operation and a steel plate was put in his arm.

Towards the end of our innings, Allan Lamb, playing brilliantly, was nearing a century and Terry was told to pad up. The idea was to help Lamb to a hundred and possibly avoid the follow-on. I was in the physio's room with Terry and a few others, one of them being an England selector. I couldn't believe what I was hearing. Terry's left arm was in a cast. Usually your top hand controls the bat, the bottom hand adding a bit of punch to the shot. This, of course, is a generalisation, but usually the case. What is true is that both hands work together. What is also true is that you stand sideways in your stance and all your cricketing life the ball has been delivered to you in that way. This meant that, for the right-handed Terry, the ball came across the field of vision from left to right. This had been the case since he first picked up a bat, all the way through to his Test career. In the 1980s, the purists said the top hand was the most important, so the selector told him that, should he go out to bat, he should do so left-handed. He had only one hand, his right, and that would become his top and therefore dominant hand. I'd never heard such crap in all my life. He's a right-handed batsman. It's hard enough to play against the West Indies batting the right way with two hands and now the selector wants him to bat the wrong way round with one hand! Utter madness.

In the end, he did bat right-handed with one hand. His injured left hand was in a sling under his jumper – it must have been petrifying. Thankfully, he didn't get hit again. He managed to hang around until Garner bowled him shortly after Lamb had reached his century. We didn't avoid the follow-on. In the second innings, I was out second ball, bowled by Holding. We lost by an innings and 64 runs. Actually, to say we lost would be wrong. We were crushed. Again.

I often wonder if Viv Richards struggled to sleep thinking about the prospect of facing Percy in that game. But his selection as a bowler was justified. He bowled 45.3 overs and took four for 121. His batting was less impressive – he made a pair.

The Oval was the venue for the fifth and final Test match. Obviously, we stayed in the hotel opposite Lord's. The commute to and from The Oval was a ball-ache to say the least. Jonathan Agnew and Richard Ellison made their Test debuts on a quick bouncy wicket. Years later, Malcolm Marshall told me it was one of the fastest wickets he ever bowled on. Beefy swung the ball and took a Michelle (Pfeiffer – five-for). They were bowled out for 190. Bowling them out cheaply was brilliant, but it left one of those awkward little periods if you're an opening batsman. You just know it's going to be hell until the close of play.

With two balls left in the day, Garner, bowling from the Vauxhall End, uprooted Chris Broad's stumps. I was staring at the pavilion to see who would come in. I couldn't believe my eyes: it was Percy. Every part of his body seemed to be covered with padding. Thigh pads, arm guards on both arms, chest pads, and all topped off with a helmet. It wasn't an

England helmet – we didn't have them – and it wasn't blue or white, it was bright yellow. The West Indian bowlers didn't need a target usually, but Percy brought one just in case. He walked past the slips saying 'Afternoon!' to them all. He then carried on for another 35 yards until he got to the stumps at his end. He proceeded to walk past them and headed for me. I walked to meet him. 'Foxy, I can do this.'

'Good.' I turned to walk away.

'Foxy, we're not running unless it's a two or a four.'

'You've got that right.' I turned again.

'Foxy.'

''Kin 'ell – what?'

'What's happening? It's hard to tell what's happening from the dressing room as everything is happening too fast.'

'That's exactly what is happening.'

Percy walked back to his crease and took guard. He ambled down the pitch and did a bit of gardening and went back. This was taking forever. He then looked round at the fielders. There was only one within shouting distance, the rest were 100ft behind the stumps waiting to catch his yellow helmet. The one fielder who was near was Desmond Haynes at short forward square leg. 'You're safe, Dessy,' Pat told him. 'I don't hook.'

Neither Haynes nor I could quite believe what he'd just said. Garner ran in and pitched the ball up just outside off stump. It climbed and Jeffrey Dujon took it above his head. At the same time Dujon caught the ball, Percy was still coming forward to play his defensive shot. To be fair, it was a perfect forward defensive shot, but it was a second too late. The next ball whistled past Percy's head. It missed him and his padding in a fraction of a second. Dujon caught the ball and turned to walk off. I walked towards the pavilion; Percy didn't. He walked towards me, and as he approached he was wearing a massive smile: 'Told you I could do it.'

On the morning of the second day, I was quietly going through my pre-match preparations when Percy made a bee-line for me. 'I don't want how I bat to affect how you bat,' he told me. 'I could hang around for a while, but I don't think that's the best way. Once I've got used to the pace and the bounce I'm going to play a few shots.'

'Good luck with that.'

'Also, if we have a mix-up running, I want you to know I'll sacrifice my wicket, even if it's your fault.' He faced 19 balls that morning. How he wasn't killed I'll never know. We had a partnership of 11. He scored his third duck in succession.

In my career, Malcolm Marshall hit me more than any other bowler. It was always the same ball, same result. It was a skiddy bouncer that, after it pitched, swung back at me. I could neither duck nor sway. My hands would go up as I was getting into a tangle and it would always strike me on the flat palm side of my wrist. I was on 12, still batting with Percy, when he nailed me. The sensation was of extreme burning. It didn't really hurt, but this burning feeling was accompanied by an inability to use my hand. Next over, Percy was on strike. Predictably, it was a maiden. All through the over I had been trying to grip my bat. It was hopeless. I called for Bernard Thomas, otherwise known as Bolt. On explaining to him what happened and how my hand wouldn't work, he said: 'Use your other hand for a bit. The sensation will come back in the end.'

'Bolt, you may not have noticed, but I'm not doing very well with two hands.' With that I retired hurt. X-rays proved there was no break, but I couldn't pick up a pint properly for a month. In the end I switched to left-handed drinking.

In their second innings, starting with a lead of 28, they scored 346. Predictably, we didn't get close: all out for 202, and I made 7. As I was walking off the field for the final time in the series, an overwhelming feeling of relief came over me. I was in one piece. I hadn't been aware of this physical pressure until it was lifted. It was a realisation after the fact, not a thought before it. If you thought like that beforehand, you couldn't play. I'd been hit on the left nipple by Garner, had my box smashed by him also. Winston Davis hit me on the head, and Malcolm Marshall made me retire hurt. All the same, I was OK. Andy Lloyd and Paul Terry sustained very serious injuries and they never played for England again. Lloyd still has a detached retina.

As an opening batsman, the sheer physicality of that attack was enormous. They had three, sometimes four, bowlers who had the ability to bowl around the 90mph mark. When you face an attack that has a very fast bowler, the tactic is to see him off. A six-over spell is 36 balls. If my partner and I split them, then that's 18 each. I have to face only three overs, then he's off. He may come back later, but I'll be seeing it better by then because I will have found my timing, got myself in against the other bowlers. Not so against the West Indies. Marshall and Garner open, Garner comes off, Holding comes on. Marshall has a rest, Winston Davis or Eldine Baptiste come on. Holding comes off, Garner comes back. Baptiste finishes, Marshall's back. Relentless.

They bowled 16 overs per hour. At the time it was considered a painfully slow over-rate – these days that's express. Modern Test match over-rates are appalling and cheat the paying public. If the West Indies could bowl 16 an hour with four fast bowlers, any team can. No excuses. My point is that hardly ever did you get a break from really fast bowling, and I haven't even mentioned how wonderfully skilful they all were. If Roger Harper ever bowled it felt like your granny was bowling. No disrespect to Roger, who was a fine spin bowler, but he bowled at only 55mph.

The series was nicknamed 'blackwash'. It was then, and still is now, a term I don't like. I don't like whitewash either. If it's wrong to use colour in an expression that is negative, it's also wrong to use it if that expression is positive. There is no need for either expression, as there are plenty of others. 'Absolutely hammered into the dirt' is one is one that springs to mind for that series.

Lamby got four hundreds, I got one, and nobody else got any. Beefy got 80-odd at Lord's, the game I made my century, and in the newspapers the next day it was all about that. In one of them I didn't even get a mention. I thought, 'Oh well, at least you know you did it.' As an opening batsman at that time, to get a hundred against the West Indies was good. We didn't know they were probably the best team ever, but we knew it was tough. Years later, Viv Richards, the best batsman I've ever seen, and I were talking. I said: 'Look, I'm just an average international player who had some good days.'

And he replied: 'Fow, you were better than that. You did something I never did. You got a hundred against the West Indies. Respect.'

When somebody like him says that, it means something.

CHAPTER 9

ANYONE FOR A DOUBLE?

When it comes to my double century in Madras or the West Indies hundred, I can't separate the two. I can't have one without the other. West Indies were the best team in the world and, as an opening batsman, I got a hundred against them at Lord's. And then to make a double hundred for my country in India, to be the first to do it, to prove you can play against spin, that you are a complete batsman, that was incredibly special too.

All around India people had been telling me that Graham Gooch had got a century at Madras and played really well. Because people thought I was in the team because Gooch had gone to South Africa, they perceived that I'd be keen to outdo his 127, but that had nothing to do with how I batted. I never thought like that at all. That would never be part of how I approached an innings. I remember Kim Hughes once scoring a double hundred and saying afterwards: 'I got a hundred for each of my twins.' No you didn't – don't make up stuff like that. I didn't get 200 because Gooch had got 100. Anybody who says that sort of stuff is talking rubbish.

The first couple of overs of that fourth Test, I was at cover as usual, Neil Foster was bowling, and Sunil Gavaskar cut it. The outfields out there were murder, so when I dived for the ball, I ripped my trousers and took a chunk of skin off my knee. By lunchtime it was going septic. The first over after lunch, I dived the other way and did my other knee. I now had bandages on both knees. When I came in to bat late that day, after we'd got them out for 272, they were still really painful.

On the second day, Tim Robinson and I reached 178 before Tim was out and Mike Gatting came to the wicket. Because it was spinning, we had a pact that we weren't going to push the ball off the front foot. If it was a half volley, we'd hit it, but the rest we'd just dead bat and stop. If you push at it, it just gives people catches. If either of us did that, the other one would go 'Oi!' It was calming really, because once you decide those balls aren't scoring opportunities, and you're not going to manipulate the ball, it's actually quite relaxing just to dead bat. Yes, you still have to pick the ball, decide which way it's going, but it takes away the pressure of trying to keep the scoreboard going. We were relying on them having to try something different before we did – and they did.

The shots we were looking for were either to rock back and square cut it, or just to clip it round the corner. I remember telling myself to bat for half an hour. And then I'd think: 'Right, bat another half an hour and then you'll get a drink.' That was always water with no ice. I didn't like cold drinks as they gave me stomach cramps. I wasn't drinking for pleasure, it was just doing a job to keep me hydrated.

It was a hundred degrees, and there was a fish-processing plant outside the gates, a gentle breeze bringing the smell wafting over the ground. It made my eyes sting, so every hour I had eye drops as well. The drinks, but especially the eye drops, were the reward for batting those half-hours. All the time I was accumulating, seeing what came along. It was just a matter of keeping going. I reached my hundred off overthrows. I was 97, hit a single, the fielder whizzed the ball in, it hit the stumps, and away it went for four. 'Yaaayyyy!'

By the last over of the day, I was 149 not out and Gatt was on strike. He swept the first ball and it went really slowly down to deep backward square leg. It was one of those long singles where you walk down to the other end. I got halfway and Gatt was just stood there waiting. I said to him: 'Gatt, do you not want a single?'

'You've done enough today,' he said, 'I'll take this over.' It was an incredibly kind and unselfish thing to do. The rest of the over, I didn't back up or anything. I actually had my eyes shut and my head down. I only looked up when I heard the bowler's footsteps. I was just counting the balls to the end of the day. I got to four and it was the end of the over – I was asleep for two balls.

When I got changed, my knees, which hadn't recovered, were stuck to the bandages, the bandages were stuck to my trousers, and my trousers were stuck to my pads. I remember peeling them all off, walking round the hotel with fresh bandages, and thinking: 'I only need one tomorrow and I'll get a round of applause.'

People were slapping me on the back. I had a beer, drank half of it, and was pissed. No one really knew about proper refuelling or rehydration then or gave a toss about that. I lost half a stone in that innings.

Next day, I got that single and told myself to carry on. I actually made a decision not to give it away. I had a rubbish bat. If you hit the ball exactly in the middle, it was fine, anywhere else it was like a chair leg, but that actually focused me. I thought: 'I can't hit it over the top. I daren't try, because if I don't get it exactly in the middle it's not going anywhere.' That altered my shot selection. Duncan Fearnley made me some beautiful bats, and this was the only time I had one that wasn't very good. As an opening batsman, you like a bit of meat higher up the bat, but this one wasn't going anywhere. On the other hand, it was beautiful for dead-batting the ball against spinners, so I suppose it helped. It was only when I was way past a hundred that right-hand off-break Shivlal Yadav came on and I hit him for three sixes. I was 170-odd by then.

Me and Gatt geed each other along. More than anything we told each other to keep on doing what we were doing. We were quite calm about it. All the times I've played best, I've been calm and composed within myself. There was nothing frantic about it, we were just chatting to each other, helping each other along.

What you talk about in the middle depends who you're in with. Tim Robinson didn't like talking. I'd walk down halfway at the end of an over and he'd still be standing in his ground. That's fine, but I thought he should have compromised a bit and met me in the middle. It's not just all about him. Others were as varied as their personalities. It might be they were frantic and want you to calm them down, or you want them to reassure you. They might not want to say much at all, or just talk about where they're going tonight.

These are things that I learned to pick up with people, and because I didn't necessarily have a preference myself, I would adapt to what other people wanted to do. With someone likc John Abrahams, we just had a laugh. Neil Fairbrother, meanwhile, would say: 'Don't leave me, don't leave me.' And I would reassure him he was playing well. Gehan Mendis would talk about where he was going that night, and I'd say to him: 'Stop pinching the strike, otherwise I'm going to run you out!' It didn't bother me at all what we talked about.

When I reached my double hundred, I remember getting to the other end and thinking two things: 'Well, they can't take that away from me,' and 'My dad will be happy.' It was something I was brought up with – whatever you achieve they can't take it away from you. It came from my dad. He'd say: 'Well, if you only ever play for Lancashire second XI, they can't take that away from you.' So the first thing I thought about was one of my dad's phrases, and then that my dad would be happy. But he had been such a major influence, not just in teaching me how to play cricket, but in philosophical ways too, without him even knowing.

Madras was a pay-off for all the hard work I'd put in to learn how to bat against spin. Back at Lancashire, a lot of players wouldn't bat in a net when it was worn, but it was Jack Simmons who pointed out: 'If we get on a turning wicket, you'll expect me to get them out. How can I practise if none of you will get in the nets?'

'I'll bat, Jack,' I said. 'I'll bat any time you want.' So Jack, Ian Folley and David Hughes would all bowl at me, the result being I got a lot of practice on shit wickets batting against spin.

Not that everything went well. Everybody has heard about how you need to use your feet against spin. I tried to teach myself how to do it. One day I told him: 'I'm going to try to use my feet, Simmo.' At one stage he went through his action and kept hold of the ball – I was halfway down the wicket. He burst out laughing: 'Fow, let me let go of the ball first!' I just could not get the timing right.

It was years later I found out I was getting in the wrong position to sweep, with my head behind my front knee. The position you should sweep in is the position you drive in, with your head right over your knee. Instead, I was in the wrong position, with too much emphasis on my weakest hand. Jack Bond was watching me make a mess of it one day. 'What are you doing? Don't bother with that. Hit the sightscreen, that's what you're good at.' And because that felt so nice, that's what I did. I learned I could hit balls there from middle stump, off stump, all the way out to 18 inches wide of off – and they never put a fielder in front of the sightscreen.

People didn't realise I couldn't sweep. Back when there were no leg-side wides in one-day cricket, Richard Illingworth used to bowl a foot down that side. I'd get down on one knee and try to sweep it, if only to get them to put a fielder in, because once that fielder was there it made me a gap I would like.

I also learned that, as a left-hander, if a ball landed in the rough that was nearest to me, I could smother that easily. If it landed in the rough furthest away, I had time to play it whatever it did, and when it landed in between the two patches, that was the ball that went straight back over the bowler's head. You have to be very good at judging the length, but that's your job. After a time I could tell within a sixpence where the ball was going to land. When I was playing well I could do it, when I wasn't playing well I couldn't.

The other thing I could naturally do was slog-sweep off spinners, with the ball spinning away from me, over straight midwicket. That then gave me options. If I hit a couple over long-off, they'd put the man back and that gave me space for singles. It opened up areas. As a batsman, you're constantly trying to manipulate the field.

Another vital element I discovered was never to play for spin unless I knew the ball was spinning. I know that seems a ridiculous thing to say, but you don't. Take the first time I played against Abdul Qadir, in my first Test match – I had not a bloody clue what was happening. I couldn't bat against Abdul, he made me look a right idiot. There weren't any leg spinners in county cricket. I knew I had to come up with a temporary solution until I could tell what the hell he was bowling. 'Right,' I concluded, 'I'm going to play each ball as if it's a googly, because that's going to be the most dangerous delivery for me. If it turns into me, I'll be able to hit it, but if it goes the other way I'm in trouble.'

At the same time I got my front leg really far out – in those days there was no DRS – so I wasn't going to be LBW, and I did that until I could see the subtleties in his hand, backed up by watching which way the ball spun. It might not have been graceful, or got me any runs, but it stopped me being out.

Once I'd learned to pick him, then I was all right. There were occasions I'd think, 'Christ, what's that one?' but again I'd play it as a googly. I don't know where that thought process came from, but I developed the strategy in the middle, at the time.

We had an interesting situation with Qadir in a one-day international in Pakistan. Again I was batting with Gatt and the sun was coming right over Abdul's right shoulder. He ran up, bowled, and I couldn't see the shape of his hand or which way it was spinning in the air. After the first over, Gatt asked what the problem was. 'I can't pick him, Gatt. I can't see to do it.'

So the next over, Abdul ran up, bowled and Gatt shouted, 'Legger!' I played it, and he was right. Abdul looked at him, Gatt looked ahead nonchalantly. Next ball, he ran up: 'Googly!' I played it, and again he was right. Abdul turned to Gatt to ask what he was doing. Gatt shouted for about four balls and all of a sudden, Abdul was going nuts. The umpire also had a word, but Gatt was having none of it: 'What's the matter? I'm not doing anything wrong.'

The captain joined in. Everyone was shouting at Gatt, Gatt was shouting back, so I walked down the wicket and told him I'd got the shape of Abdul's hand and wrist from the four balls he'd indicated to me. It had slotted back into my game. After that we swotted him all over. It must have taken a lot of guts for Gatt to do that – to read it and shout to me in enough time for me to be able to play it. But whoever the bowler, you have to be able to adapt.

It never worried me having fielders round the bat. Very rarely was I caught at bat-pad. Playing spin, you don't play directly in front of your pads; you play with the bat a short distance past your pads. I always thought of it as if underneath my eyes there was a groove that the bat came down. Play past your pads and if you nick the ball it will usually miss your leg. If your hands are relaxed too, it's not going to carry. Whereas if you play in front of your leg, the ball can then ricochet off it and go anywhere.

Some see having fielders round the bat as a cause for concern, but I saw them as four fielders out of the game, leaving more gaps. The one I certainly never ever worried about was short extra cover. It just seemed a nonsense to me. If someone put one in for me, I knew I could loft the ball over them or hit it two or three yards either side and it would be away. It's a very common position these days, although I can't see why. It would be better to place the fielder further back. Chances are the ball would still carry and they'd be able to cover more ground. Also, the presence of an extra cover stops the batsman driving, taking the slips out of the game. Whenever I was put there it felt like I was on holiday.

Sometimes, when playing on a good wicket, you have to make an instant decision about whether or not to play for any spin. If a really good ball is coming down, hits the middle of your bat, and drops down, you just think 'Thank fuck for that.' But usually they don't put string after string of those together, and they'll give you something to hit. What you are really trying to do when facing spinners is to get them to lose their patience, then they have to try something else. You're looking to play forward, but rock back if it's short. You've got more gaps then. It's patience, patience. And that was exactly how it happened in Madras.

However, I'm not sure I should even have had the chance to

be out in the middle. The way that tour finished was in stark contrast to how it started. We'd arrived at Delhi at three in the morning to be met by three Indians dressed as Mexican bandits on the steps of the hotel singing 'Home On The Range'. Our hosts put garlands round our necks – lovely, except they were full of bugs. Eventually we got to bed. Five hours later, I went down to breakfast to the news Indira Gandhi had been assassinated six miles away.

The hotel had a gym on the top floor. I have a vivid memory of Paul Downton legging it on a running machine with his Walkman on. Behind him, out of the window, were big plumes of black smoke. They'd set fire to Sikh petrol stations and schools, because it was the Sikh bodyguards who'd assassinated Gandhi. Paul Downton was running like a demon in preparation for a Test series as I was watching Delhi burn. It was bizarre.

Tony Brown was our tour manager. I found him unpredictable. I didn't know what was going on. The captain, meanwhile, was David Gower, who'd been on eight or nine tours by that point. After Gandhi had been assassinated, there was only one question: what happens now? We had a team meeting, but nobody had any idea what to do; we were all still trying to process the situation.

The following day we'd had time to think and we felt it would be best to go somewhere – Dubai, England, Pakistan, anywhere – so we could practise and then, when the games were rescheduled, we could come back. There was no point staying in Delhi as it was not very stable politically and we couldn't play or practise. Tony Brown then burst into the team room, went straight through into his bedroom where he kept the passports, and came out with them all. The one on the top was Lamby's. He threw it at him. 'Here,' he said. 'You're the ringleader, here's your passport.' This wasn't what I expected from the manager on the second day of the tour.

Lamby, to his credit, reacted calmly: 'No, not ringleader, manager. You asked us yesterday what we thought, and so we've all had a chat, and this is what we think now.' Lamby was really good, which was unexpected, but he was.

In the meantime, somebody had gone to tell Gower all hell was kicking off. Up he came to the team room. 'Er, manager, can I have a word?' He just defused the whole situation. 'Manager,' he said quietly, 'on all the other tours I've been on, this is how we deal with situations.' If it hadn't have been for Gower I don't know what would have happened.

Anyway, we went to Sri Lanka for three weeks while things calmed down. Soon after we landed back in India, in Bombay, Sir Percy Norris, the Deputy High Commissioner, was assassinated. A few hours earlier, I'd been stood next to him at a reception he'd hosted for us, talking to him about Accrington Stanley, and now we were going training, driving right past the spot where he was killed. Great idea. I'll put a big red hat on so they can aim at it.

This is why I rail against stupidity. Indira Gandhi had been assassinated, there was a load of anti-British feeling because we were seen to support the Sikhs, so we'd buggered off to Sri Lanka during a period of mourning. Then we came back just before the rescheduled first Test match, went to see Sir Percy Norris, left there at midnight, and the next morning he was machine-gunned to pieces. So what did we do? We got on a bus, drove past the exact point he was shot and went to practise. I was quite vocal about how stupid it seemed. 'What the fuck are we doing? Does this make sense to anybody?'

It was all the usual stiff upper lip. We got a message from Lord's. 'We think it is in the best interests of the England cricket team to carry on as scheduled to show the rest of the world that there is political stability in India.' Fuck off! You're not getting shot at. We weren't being shot at – but we didn't know that. We didn't know that at all. It was just lunacy.

But this is what happens in cricket. The players are left in the middle of horrendous situations that should be sorted out by the administrators. It was the same with Nasser Hussain and Zimbabwe, Gatt and the umpires in Pakistan when they just abandoned him. The people making the decisions should be the coach, the captain, and whoever's in charge at the ECB – it's not hard to make a conference call. And if there's any doubt, get on that plane and leave. You can always go back. It's not like you've gone on a ship.

What they always come back with is, 'Well nothing happened, did it?' Yes, but that's not the point is it? It doesn't matter that these people represent their country playing cricket. They are husbands, fathers, brothers, children. You can't mess about with somebody's life just because you want to be seen to do the 'right' thing. That's just wrong. What if one day something does happen, like it did with the Sri Lankans when they were targeted in Pakistan? More recently, another England tour of India was interrupted by the Mumbai massacre.

It's not for players to try to analyse the complicated politics of these situations. In India, it was like me trying to join in the last week of A-level physics having never done the previous two years. I had no knowledge of any of this and it was a bit too late for me to find out. I could perhaps understand why we returned after Gandhi was assassinated, but when Sir Percy Norris was shot, that was the point we should have come home. Not driven past where he was shot. In reality, the day after he was killed, the Test match took place.

CHAPTER 10

ESCAPE

I had no fear of travel. In fact, that was one of the big lures of being a cricketer. Even starting out, I loved going to new places, like Lincoln to play Minor Counties. Everywhere was a huge adventure to me. I was like a little lad on tour.

Travel was also a fantastic way to learn your trade. Before I toured Australia with England in 1982-83, I'd been there the three previous winters too. Mick Malone, the Australian fast bowler, took me over there the first time. He'd seen me batting in a benefit game and on the back of that I was headed for Scarborough, a coastal suburb of Perth. It was an inauspicious start – I was following two Englishmen the year before. One of them had run off with somebody's wife on New Year's Eve and the other one had left halfway through a game and gone home. When I turned up, not knowing any of this, and saw a bloke in an English county sweater, I said, 'Oh, nice sweater, where did you get that from?' His reply was, 'I found it under the wife's bed.' 'Oh God,' I thought, 'I've only been here eight hours.'

My first game in Australia was at the WACA in Perth. It was a weird experience. They had two games going on at once at either end of the square. If you were on the boundary in one game, you were only 30 yards off the batsman in the other. There was a fielder in front of me who was playing in the game behind so we had to help each other out. If the batsman in the other game smashed the ball, it could have hit me on the back of the head, so the fielder from that game, who was in front of me, would shout, 'Duck! Get out the way!' And vice versa. It was insane.

I was opening. I played forward first ball, and it whistled past my ear. I'd never played on a wicket like it or against a Kookaburra ball. I was all at sea, couldn't lay a bat on the damned thing. I quickly realised I didn't know what was going on. And then when I was fielding I had to work out what game the other fielders were in, as I didn't yet know my team. It was bizarre – and that was my first experience of cricket in Australia.

The second game I played was against Dennis Lillee. I remember thinking, 'I can't wait to get off and tell my dad.' It was incredible, and I ended up 8 not out. Lillee, if he wasn't playing Test cricket or state cricket, played for his club in grade cricket, which is how I ended up playing against him. The Australian pyramid is a great system. Everybody who plays grade cricket can potentially play for Australia. That doesn't happen in England – only around 300 players in county cricket can play for England. Australia have changed their system to make it more professional now – the Australian team is centrally contracted – but there's still the potential to make the step up from grade to state to Test.

I quickly realised I was nowhere near good enough to open the batting in grade cricket at that age, and they did, too. But because I kept wicket I stayed in the first team and batted six. If I hadn't been keeping wicket, I'd have been playing second or third grade cricket and wouldn't have learnt so much. They probably wouldn't have invited me back the next year. Although I was shit at it, it opened doors.

At the time, it was the hardest cricket I'd ever played and, without it, I don't think I'd have achieved what I did. I learnt three massive things in Australia: how to play the short ball, how to put pace on the ball by delaying your shot and accelerating your hands to spinners, and how to play very straight, because you had to hit it back where it came from.

Also, the Australians learn from an early age to really value their wicket. The way their cricket is organised, they play a match over consecutive Saturdays. If you bat on the first Saturday and get a duck, the next Saturday you might be fielding all day. The one after it'll be a new game, so you might be fielding again. It might be four weeks between getting a bat. That's a long time. If you have four bad knocks, you've had a bad season. The Aussies develop a hard mentality, because the game is hard. If you value your wicket, you end up with a stubborn, brutal attitude: 'You're not getting me out.'

All their wickets were prepared by the council. You had all these little old Aussie guys who loved making flat cricket wickets. They were rock hard, some of them were shiny, and they were the bounciest things you've ever played on – quick, true and wonderful. In England, the wickets can vary from session to session, ground to ground, week to week. It takes longer to build a technique because you have to play under different circumstances. The result is the Australians try to find ways to intimidate each other, because their wickets don't help them. It's a nation that speaks its mind. They have the view that you've got to be aggressive to be competitive. I didn't agree with that, still don't, but it's part of their culture.

This is how hard they were. Subiaco Floreat, a club in Perth's western suburbs, had their clubhouse broken into the night before a grade game against nearby Midland Guildford and everything had been taken. They had no stumps and couldn't get any in time for the start of play. Midland Guildford claimed the match – even though they had a set on their minibus. So these people aren't really playing for enjoyment, are they? That's win at all costs, not have a nice day's cricket.

They had another system one year where you got a fraction of a point for a run, so every run became vital. One team missed out on the top four (who then played off for the title) by four runs. We were playing against that team first match of the next season, and it was raining. In Perth, if it's raining, you call it off, but we hung around and played three overs in the entire game because they might have been important. It seemed ridiculous, but the attitude was that it could count.

Even the net sessions were tough. Every Tuesday and Thursday night at Scarborough, I had to face Mick Malone who played for Australia, Sam Gannon who played for Australia, Tom Hogan a spinner who'd go on to play for Australia, and Ken Lillee who was bloody rapid but nothing to do with Dennis. I approached each session like it was a game, because

I was playing against the best bowlers on these greased-lightning wickets. It was a big thing for me. Sam would say something in a jokey way, and I'd say something back, and next ball he'd bowl a short one and hit me. I didn't care, because I was learning how to play.

Up to that stage I'd never come across what I'd call a genuinely fast bowler. I'd never really been peppered, so I hadn't known whether I'd ever be able to cope with it, but I came back to England after that first winter and already I knew: 'I don't care how fast you are, who you are, what wicket we're on, you can bounce the shit out of me and I'm safe. I can get out the way.' And that attitude takes an element out of the game. It takes away that 'I wonder what might happen if he hits me?' feeling. I didn't care. They could bounce me all they liked, but I knew I was as safe as houses. It makes a massive difference to think: 'I know I can deal with it. I've got that in the bank now. I don't have to find out in the future. I already know if you bowl short at me, I'm fine.' As a young player, that's an enormous thing to have.

I've never ever been frightened on a cricket pitch. I wasn't before that trip, but it was an unknown quantity. Once I learned I could play the short ball, it took that uncertainty away. I could tick that box, I knew I could do it. It wasn't that I was frightened of the short ball, I just didn't know if I'd be able to deal with it. And then I realised I could.

Eventually, my team-mates at Scarborough forgot about those other two English blokes and I became part of the club. I worked there building bowling greens, working with the juniors on a Friday night, got stuck in, enjoyed myself. They gave me a nice little trophy for coaching the kids. I'd made a few friends, and so they invited me back the next year and paid my airfare.

I did a lot of growing up out there. I worked at a school from 6am to 3.30pm, two nights a week I trained from five onwards, and Friday nights I coached the juniors. I'd play Saturday, sometimes Sunday as well, and then on Monday I was back at work. I had to look after myself and cook in my apartment. Justin Langer's dad found me a car, an old beat-up Falcon, for the summer, and little Justin used to sit on my knee.

The following winter, 1981-82, a job came up to be the Tasmanian Cricket Association coach. I had a little Toyota car full of kit, went to four schools a day, and took a cricket lesson for an hour. I was using my teaching qualification, I was learning to put together coaching sessions, and I loved it.

Australia made me. After two winters in Perth and one in Tasmania, I thought I'd have a rest, because effectively, summers and winters added together, I'd had six consecutive seasons. And then I got picked to go on three England tours.

Heading abroad to play for a team for a winter while coaching and working is one thing. Touring is entirely another – a totally different mindset. On tour, you're with the same party of people, 16 players and four officials. It can become smothering, unhealthy, if you let it. When I was playing cricket, I loved it, it was what I did and I did my very best at it, but it wasn't who I was. If I was to maintain focus, I had to flick off and do something else to get away from it. Some found an escape by reading books, watching a film or sitting round the pool. For others it was golf. I didn't play golf, the reason being I didn't want to compete on a day off – because I would have had to compete.

On tour, if we'd netted in the morning and had the afternoon off, one of my ways of escaping was just to go out and walk. I had a little old Pentax camera and even if I didn't take many photographs, the mere fact I was looking at things in a different way meant that I'd switched off from cricket, and I found that incredibly relaxing. Today still if I pick up a camera it takes me to a different space in my head, so I forget what I was doing before. Even without a camera, simply going and walking would help. And I knew it was helping so I'd do it on purpose.

I used to like going to art galleries, and still do, to feed my brain by looking at something in a different light. I'd go to the cinema if I could, or the theatre. I remember watching *The Merchant of Venice* in Lahore. It was the most bizarre thing I've ever seen. And then the evening got even more surreal when I went back to the hotel and there in the team room was Engelbert Humperdinck.

Another time I went to see a palm reader. When he predicted I'd be surrounded by women, I didn't think he meant daughters. He also said I was bad at financial transactions, which is true, not that I believe any of that stuff. Just because the sun's over there and the moon's over there doesn't mean I'm going to piss in my pants in the morning.

Sometimes I'd go to the tourist places – the Taj Mahal, the Red Fort at Delhi. Other times I'd go off the beaten track. We were in Bhubaneshwar, on the banks of the Brahmaputra River, in north-east India, and I took some beautiful shots, not because I'm a great photographer, but because it was just beautiful. There were all these kids playing on the mudflats, and they were bowling hoops along with sticks.

The flipside was the darker things you see in India, little kids with disabilities, adults on boards, peddling, because their hamstrings have been cut when they were younger to make them into beggars. It really upset me at first. I thought, 'Here I am, I'm stopping in the best hotels, and all around me are beggars, and urchins, and I can't do anything about it. What can I do?' I came to the conclusion that the only thing I could do was play cricket to the best of my ability and hope it put a smile on their face. I couldn't change their circumstances or give them enough money, so I honoured them by playing cricket. Whether that's a poor justification, I don't know. But I couldn't run India, so that's just what I did.

The fact I enjoyed getting away on my own to see a bit of life did, I think, make me unusual. But I just wanted to experience life, see everything. When I was on tour and met somebody at a cocktail party and they asked if I wanted to come over for supper, I'd always agree to do so.

I've been in some incredible places just by saying 'Yes'. I ended up on a galleon at Sydney harbour with a Canadian gay a cappella group called The Nylons eating lobster and crab and drinking champagne. I'm sure at one point they thought I was the buffet. I'm lucky that I can never remember having the feeling, 'Jesus, what am I doing here? Get me out of here.' I've never ended up in dodgy places, in dodgy situations, with dodgy people.

The thing is, on tour, if you stay with just those 16 blokes, some of whom you might get on with and some you might not really like (though you find a professional way of dealing with each other), you get no respite. Even if you're not talking about cricket, you're still with cricketers, and it eventually comes back into the conversation. There are some, of course, who either don't want to or can't switch off. Jonathan Trott would appear to be, or have been, one, but he's not alone. There are plenty of others like that, and you wouldn't want to try to stop them either, because that's their mentality. In order for them to function as a cricketer, they have to be full time in it.

Whether that has any long-term repercussions, and they burn out quicker, get fed up or lose motivation, I have no idea. But I know that if I didn't get away from it and have a break, then it would get to a stage where it would be monotony. The only person I toured with who, when he was away from cricket, he was 100 per cent away from it, was Beefy. Like me, when he wasn't playing, that was it, he was off. There was no thinking about what would happen the next day.

The truth is you need a happy medium with free time. When Goochie was in charge for a tour of the Caribbean, they didn't have a single day off, because that was how he liked to be – I don't think he understood that some people were different from him. Gower, meanwhile, gave people freedom to decide if they wanted to practise or not, trusting us to make our own decisions. But he got a lot of stick for that, so basically you can't win.

In my experience, successful sportsmen know what they can and can't do. I've seen people who weren't going to be good players, and when it dawns on them they're not going to get anywhere, they decide that wherever they go they're going to enjoy themselves. I've seen second XI lads do that certainly. But you can't be a professional sportsman at the top level and not have some personal discipline. You can't just go off drinking and be a drunkard. At the World Cup in 1983, the format was quite simple: drive to the venue, have a net, check into the hotel, eat, and have an early night. Next day, play the game, get pissed. Following day, drive to the venue, check into the hotel, eat, and have an early night. Day after, play the game, get pissed. It was a brilliant format. But there were rest days between games; there was no way anyone would be drinking the night before a match.

As a young player, you fit into the era in which you're brought up and play. When I played for England, there were rest days in the middle of the match. You didn't play on Sunday, so Saturday night was party night, and nobody thought anything about it or suggested we shouldn't be doing that because we were international sportsmen; it was accepted. At the same time I briefly got to know the Olympic hurdler Shirley Strong, who used to like a fag and a glass of vodka. I also used to drink occasionally with some of the Manchester United players, and they could stick it away too. This was a cultural thing at the time, it wasn't just cricket.

I wasn't drinking like that in the middle of games, but my reputation followed me around. Jack Bond, for instance, would tell me off for being an idiot having heard all sorts of stories. I used to think that if I was doing what he thought, how the hell would I be able to play cricket? And why would I jeopardise my career by doing those things? But I've always been guilty of a lot of things I haven't actually done. I seemed to be a catalyst for excess, so people's partners would say to me: 'He's not coming out with you – every time he does he gets mortal.' It wasn't done on purpose, it's just how it was – a love of life, an exuberance, a love of mischief.

But you can go too far the other way. I once told Lancashire manager Alan Ormrod that I probably got drunk twice a season when it was not appropriate. He came up to me later in the year – I wasn't doing very well at the time – to ask if I'd had one of those occasions, which I hadn't, so he said: 'Well, have one tonight; you're batting like an idiot.' I knew where he was coming from. He was actually giving me permission to relax.

There isn't that casual drinking culture at the top any more. The way the game is now, people have warm downs and massages. If you're an England cricketer, you don't leave the ground until about eight o'clock at night. A lot of them then go back to their room and have room service. Also, the way journalists are on tour now, if Alastair Cook was seen in a pub at 10pm it'd be front-page news. So the players go back and lock themselves up. I don't know whether that's healthy, it's just different.

Because people don't have a drink every night, they just wait and wait and then have a release. When Ben Stokes won the Ashes, he tweeted the next day, 'Well, I'm alive at least!' And I thought that was brilliant. Ben Stokes is a proper bloke to me. He wears his heart on his sleeve, he always makes something happen with the bat and the ball, he's full of life. I don't know the circumstances that led to him being sent home from the England Lions tour of Australia for late-night drinking, but discipline can be way over the top.

One of the worst things I ever saw was when David Gower and John Morris got bollocked for going up in a biplane and buzzing the ground while their team-mates were playing Queensland on the Australia tour of 1990-91. That tour was a nightmare, England were doing so badly and they were just trying to lighten the mood. To me, what the establishment should have done is privately bollock the shit out of them and fine them, but publicly say: 'What a great thing for the lads to do, to try to lift morale, give everyone a laugh at a really tough time. Although we may not approve of what they did, we applaud the motivation behind it.' Instead they bollocked them publicly, fined them publicly, and John Morris never played again.

People who love life are always going to go a bit too far. I speak from experience. There were a couple of times in Australia I climbed up the outside of hotels. Another time I climbed out the window on to a concrete ledge that ran round the side of a hotel in Bombay. I'd got half way round when I suddenly panicked – it occurred to me that maybe these things weren't built to take a person's weight. And I was 23 floors up. That's three incidents too many. I might not have the suicide gene, but I've put myself in some risky situations.

Truth is, though, for every story of high jinks, there's 25 nights where nothing happened – you had a couple of pints, a crap curry, and went to bed. There's also the times when you've got the opportunity to let your hair down and you're not anywhere that you can, there's nobody to do it with, and you're sat there watching telly. Don't get me wrong, though, if there was an opportunity I was in there. I wouldn't be shy. And I'd be lying if I said I'd never exceeded my limits.

I wouldn't say the attitude of the TCCB really affected my off-pitch behaviour. On the other hand, if you're making a lot of money, or a reasonable amount of money, like players are now, and are well supported, then obviously you have to abide by the rules of the system you're in. But we didn't have a system; there was nothing – it was just turn up and play. And when you left that game you didn't know if you were going to get picked for the next one.

You were playing for your country and they didn't offer you any assistance, so one of the perks was to be invited to parties or taken on nice days out. In New Zealand in 1984, when myself and Graham Dilley were left out of the first Test match, Bob Willis told me he had a job for me (I thought my job was opening the batting, but obviously he thought differently). 'I want you to keep Graham happy. He gets homesick. I want you to room with him and keep him happy.' We had eight o'clock nets in the morning during the Test match, after which Graham and I would run back to the hotel, kip for a couple of hours, and be up all night partying. So I kept him happy.

From a lifestyle point of view, as a tourist eventually you find out who suits you. On that same New Zealand tour, Vic Marks, Chris Tavaré and myself would eat together most nights, and we were three completely different personalities. They'd been to Oxford, I'd been to Durham. We were not alike. We'd eat early because Chris would want to go to bed early, Vic Marks sometimes went to bed, sometimes came for a beer, and I wanted to eat early so I could go out, because I went out every night. It suited us to eat together, even though we had three different outcomes. You have to find a way to mould yourself into a particular set of circumstances, be adaptable with those around you. It turned out that Vic Marks and Chris Tavaré were fantastic company, I love them dearly, and we had a fantastic laugh. And we all got something we needed from the arrangement.

I loved being with Derek Randall. He was totally eccentric and, for me, totally loveable. His mannerisms and how he conducted himself were unique. Some cricketers, if they're in a dressing room, like things to be just so. He was a scatterbrain, all over the shop. While that upset some people, I found it entertaining. Because I could switch on and switch off, I didn't mind all his distractions, but those who wanted to maintain more focus couldn't deal with it.

Derek, known as Arkle or Rags, just said and did things in a completely different way. We were in Pakistan playing three one-day internationals and had a team meeting in which up popped the subject of Abdul Qadir. Bob Willis, the captain, asked: 'Arkle, you play him quite well. How do you look to play against him?'

And Derek said, 'I swipe him.'

'What?'

'I swipe him. Every now and again I just swipe him. He doesn't like that. Just swipe him.'

Bob was looking at Derek – that's not what he expected to hear. I was pissing myself laughing. An international meeting had descended into comedy because the best advice one of our senior batsmen could give us all was just to 'swipe it'.

Again in Pakistan, we were playing in a one-day international with flares and smoke bombs going off. I'd just got out, twelfth man Nick Cook had brought me a drink, and Derek was sitting opposite me reading a book, and he's the sort of bloke who when he reads a book, he molests it, bends it, twists it. He was next in – there was a big roar, so there was obviously a wicket. Derek started shouting, 'Cooky! Cooky! Get in here!' Nick charged down the corridor, by which point

Derek had picked up his helmet from here, his bat from over there, and his gloves off the floor.

'What do you want, Arkle?'

He gave Nick the book. 'The hero's in the shit,' he said. 'Read a few pages and get him out of trouble.' And then he walked out to bat. Nick Cook stood there, bewildered, and I thought that was fantastic. He hadn't done it for an audience, because there was only me in there. It was just him being him. It encapsulated him perfectly.

Rooming with him? Jesus. 'Do you want a cup of tea, youth?' he'd ask. 'Do you want a cup of tea? I'll make you a cup of tea.' It didn't matter what you said, he'd make you one. Then you'd realise he'd brought you a coffee. 'Oh sorry, youth. I'll make you a cup of tea. Make you a cup of tea.' And he'd have poured it away before you could do anything.

I roomed with him in Sydney, and I'd been out and come back late. I was creeping in about two in the morning when he sat bolt upright in bed. 'Whooh! You're pissed. You're pissed! Want a cup of tea? Want a cup of tea?' And he jumped straight out of bed and made me one. I rang my old Lancashire mate, Bob Ratcliffe, in England. Derek grabbed the phone off me, and for the next 20 minutes I was talking to Derek Randall talking to Bob Ratcliffe in England. Cost me a bloody fortune.

Another time in Pakistan we were in a hotel – well, to call it a hotel is a bit of a misnomer really – and we had a big phone on the wall in our room. The bathroom, meanwhile, was so small you could actually shit, shower and shave at the same time. The plughole was on the wrong side of the slope, so all the water went into the bedroom where our beds were like a divan but with the fabric of an doctor's old waiting-room sofa.

You had one blanket and a sheet. How do you make a bed out of that? But that's what it was.

First night, the phone rang. It was just somebody ringing the hotel. I put it down, but it rang again. Every phone call that came into the hotel rang on this phone. I left it off the hook, but Arkle fretted about the hotel not being able to get calls coming in. 'I don't give a toss,' I said. 'I want to go to sleep.' And it still rang! How does that happen? I was now at my wits' end. I couldn't unplug it, because there was no plug, so I ripped it off the wall. There was plaster, wires, everywhere. I'm not proud of it, but I wanted to sleep. And that was hard enough given his snoring. The great thing about Arkle, though, was that when he snored you could literally get out of bed and beat him half to death with a pillow and he wouldn't wake up.

This was after the so-called 'sex, drugs, and rock 'n' roll tour' of New Zealand. It was a turgid time in Pakistan, and the papers were on our backs. They sent out this blonde bombshell to sleep with one of the players. She stuck out like a sore thumb in Pakistan.

There was all sorts of crap going on. It was the tour when Ian Botham flew home with a bad knee and told everyone, 'It's the best place to send your mother-in-law all expenses paid.' The upshot of that was the hotel refused to cook for us.

After all the press we'd had in New Zealand, that tour was the hardest. Communications were difficult, as we'd book phone calls then get cut off, so husbands couldn't talk to wives. There were a lot of marital situations that were strained by what partners had read in the press. Whether it was true or false, it still put couples under pressure and the atmosphere was horrible. I'm sure it must have left a massive strain on many relationships.

The sadness was that a lot of what was in the papers was simply made up. Half of what was written about the players was actually done by the journalists. They were writing about each other as if it was us. Everything became mixed up – something they'd done, at a place we'd been. It was incredibly difficult to find the thread of truth as to what had actually happened. One story mentioned that one of the players was sitting up in bed with a woman, other players were smoking dope, and I was at the party but I wasn't doing either. Why would I be mentioned as being there but not doing anything? That made it look like I'd sold the story. And let's be honest, who goes to a party and is found sitting up in bed with a woman? You don't sit up in bed with somebody, do you? 'Oh, this is a jolly nice party, isn't it?'

Relations between the players and press had never been good, but clearly stories were being leaked to the newspapers. Beefy and Bob Willis had an idea who was behind it. 'Right,' said Bob, 'I'm going to give him some false information.' It was given to this one specific bloke, and ended up in the newspaper, so we found out who it was. That was the first tour where off-field activities had really been written about, and cricket was never going to be the same again from a journalistic point of view.

By the time we'd finished in New Zealand, we'd been away 12 weeks. If you're winning it's different, but we were losing, and everything had gone wrong. Then we had to go to Pakistan for another five-and-a-half weeks. In Pakistan, you've nowhere to go, so you stay in the hotel. We were all registered as alcoholics so we could have a drink. In the middle of all this, one of the only bright parts was Arkle. When he got down, I hated it. It upset me to see him like that. With somebody who's normally so bubbly and effervescent, you tend to forget that he has feelings, too. Why should he always be up?

I preferred to think of him a few weeks earlier in New Zealand. It was windy and freezing. I was at cover and he was at extra cover. Derek didn't like to walk in, he ran – so I did the same. Essentially, there were two idiots in the covers. Bob Willis ignored us and let us get on with it. He was at the end of his run-up and we were 80 yards away, supposedly saving a single. As Bob ran in, so did we. In fact, we sprinted. It was done for a number of reasons: because it was cold, because it was funny, and also because the batsman didn't have a clue what was going on. Sometimes we'd stop, sometimes we wouldn't. Sometimes we'd both run up to him, stop three yards away, and go, 'Hello!'

Arkle would start off at cover, I'd start off at extra cover and we'd swap. Sometimes I'd run in to stop the single and if I couldn't get it he was behind me. Sometimes it was the other way round. It's really disconcerting as a batsman to look round and not know where the fielder is. But it highlights an important point: with fielding, it's not where you set off from, it's where you end up. At Lancashire, David Hughes would want to move me a yard or so, and I used to try to explain to him that he just needed to tell me where he wanted me to finish, because I could set off from anywhere. He didn't get that, but Arkle and I did. We knew the batsmen didn't know where we were going to finish up, so we had a lot of fun confusing them.

Derek's anatomy was amazing. I'm 5ft 9½in, at least I was, but 6ft 2in from fingertip to fingertip. Derek is 5ft 9in, but when I stood in front of him, both of us with our arms out, my fingers came up to his wrist. He had the longest arms in the world, size 10 or 11 feet, massive hands, short legs. He used to cut the bottom off his pads because they were too long. Rather than just get them made shorter, he'd hack the bottom off. It was typical him, and that's why they always used to slide round his legs. He didn't have that curve at the bottom that sat on his shoe because he'd cut it off. Everybody thought it was a mannerism, but it was because he hacked his pads to pieces. Because of his span, he could reach things other people couldn't get anywhere near, way better than Jonty Rhodes, who was massively overrated in my opinion. Every time Jonty stopped the ball, people were saying how incredible it was, but he'd simply stopped it.

Derek was very athletic, very flexible, a bundle of nervous energy. We played in the World Cup at Lord's and he took an amazing catch at deep extra cover, threw it up, and because he'd caught it in an unorthodox way, with his hand the wrong way round, hit a bloke in the crowd right on the head. He took another catch at long off one day and caught it behind his back. Then, after he'd had six ducks in a row in first-class cricket, in the seventh innings, he hit one down to long leg, got halfway down the wicket and did a cartwheel. I absolutely loved all that about him.

You had to be so alert when batting with him. He was so quick, but his running was really iffy. The way you should judge a single is whether both batsmen can get in. He didn't see a single like that. He judged if he could get in, but his partner was on his own. He'd hit it straight at a fielder and scream 'Yes!' and I'd yell at him to go back. He'd then come down to me to apologise; 'Sorry, Foxy. Sorry. You'll have to do all the calling. I'm rubbish. You do it. You do it. You do it.'

He always liked talking to people in the middle, so one day we decided to do this daft thing at Lancashire and not speak to him. Anyway, he came in: 'Morning, Foxy. How are you? All right? Morning. Morning. Morning.' I just looked at him and stared. 'What's up? Are you not talking to me?' He looked at the umpire. 'Why's he not talking to me? Are you talking to me? Is nobody else talking to me?' I began to think it wasn't going to work. It didn't. He got 150, though David Lloyd said to me afterwards: 'That's the worst hundred and fifty I've ever seen in my life.' I'm not sure how you score a bad 150.

I found him so wonderful, so exciting, so fantastic to be around. But while I felt that if he went out and scored runs, it didn't matter what he was like, I think his quirkiness counted against him sometimes. Back then, though, man management wasn't even an expression. And you only have to look at how Kevin Pietersen was handled to see it's still a myth to some people today. When I got dropped by England, the selectors didn't keep coming round to my house to tell me that I'd been dropped again. Why keep re-sacking him? Who thought it a good idea to reopen that can of worms?

I don't know Kevin, but I can see why they got rid of him after the Australia tour of 2013-14. On tour everything is accentuated even more. I'll give you a hypothetical scenario: you have an unbelievably talented person who's also a nuisance and you have to keep an eye on him the entire time because of poor discipline or what he says in the press, or whatever the problem might be. If he's getting shedloads of runs or wickets, he's worth the effort, but if the balance tips and he ends up being more hassle than the value of his game, he's got to go, even if this value is still higher than some of the other people in the team. I've been in dressing rooms with players like that. They suck up your energy and use up 90 per cent of your day. All you do is talk about them, and how they're a nuisance, and they become – what's the expression? – mood hoovers. I've had a couple of lads in the centre of excellence who were the same way, and I had to get rid of them.

I played with one very talented lad at Lancashire, who was a lovely bloke, but he just consumed everybody's energy. In our dressing room we used to say, 'In six years, he'll either be playing for England or he'll be down the road.' And he was down the road. Every conversation was about him. We actually got to the stage where people would say, 'He's not here, can we actually stop talking about him?'

You get sick of it, but that sort of thing has its own momentum. It's on the tip of everybody's tongue so it keeps coming out. There were times ten of us would have a team meeting, and leave him out. We used to do the same with Beefy, because if he switched on we were going to win the game anyway, so there wasn't any point including him in the discussion. We'd tell him we were going to have a meeting, but he wouldn't care and didn't want to come. It was OK with him, but then he wasn't like anyone else.

While I wasn't averse to speaking up and certainly never just went with the crowd, I wasn't the sort who would separate myself from what was going on. I was too busy embracing the whole experience of playing for England. I always felt it was a privilege for me to be playing for my country, to be put up in lovely hotels, and to be in some incredible parts of the world I was never otherwise going to get to. As a bloke who appreciates being somewhere different, I tried to make the most of it, soak up as much as I could, enjoy the culture and have a good look around, because I might never be there again – as I was about to find out in the starkest of ways.

I always was a snappy dresser – my first school photo, at Peel Park School, Accrington.

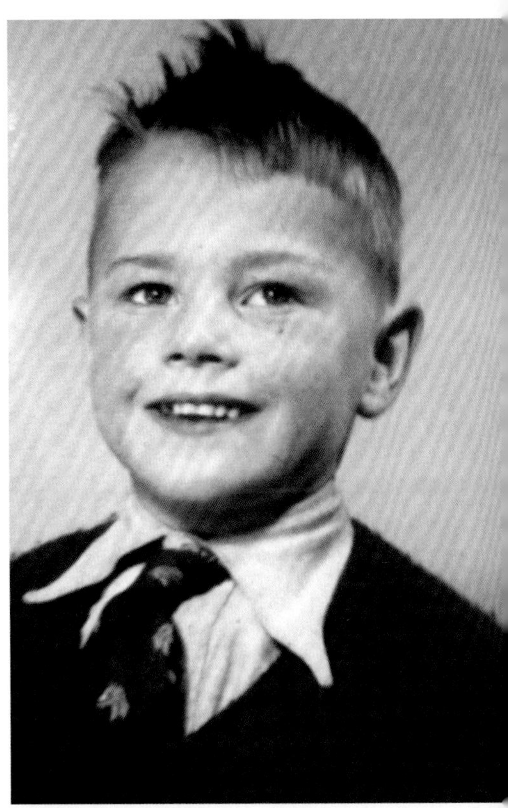

My dad, with the only pint I ever saw him drink.

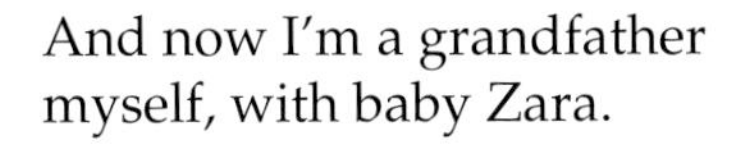

And now I'm a grandfather myself, with baby Zara.

With Bumble looking on, I'm ready to pounce during the 1981 NatWest Trophy semi-final. He was such a help to me early in my career. *(Mirrorpix)*

A decade later, and my time at Lancashire was coming to an unhappy end – though it couldn't mar the great times I'd had there. *(Getty Images)*

I almost felt I was being set up to fail when I made my England debut at Headingley in the final Test of the 1982 summer, but when I top-scored with 86 I booked my way onto the Ashes tour that winter. *(Getty Images)*

I followed it up with another good innings at Brisbane, when I decided to ignore all those who were telling me how to bat and to trust in my own instincts and ability. *(Getty Images)*

The squads line up for the 1983 World Cup. Even the Queen noticed that England were the only side not to have team blazers – we looked a shambles. *(Getty Images)*

The problems continued on the pitch, where we had very little in the way of strategy, so even though I hit four consecutive half-centuries in the tournament, I could have done even better. *(Getty Images)*

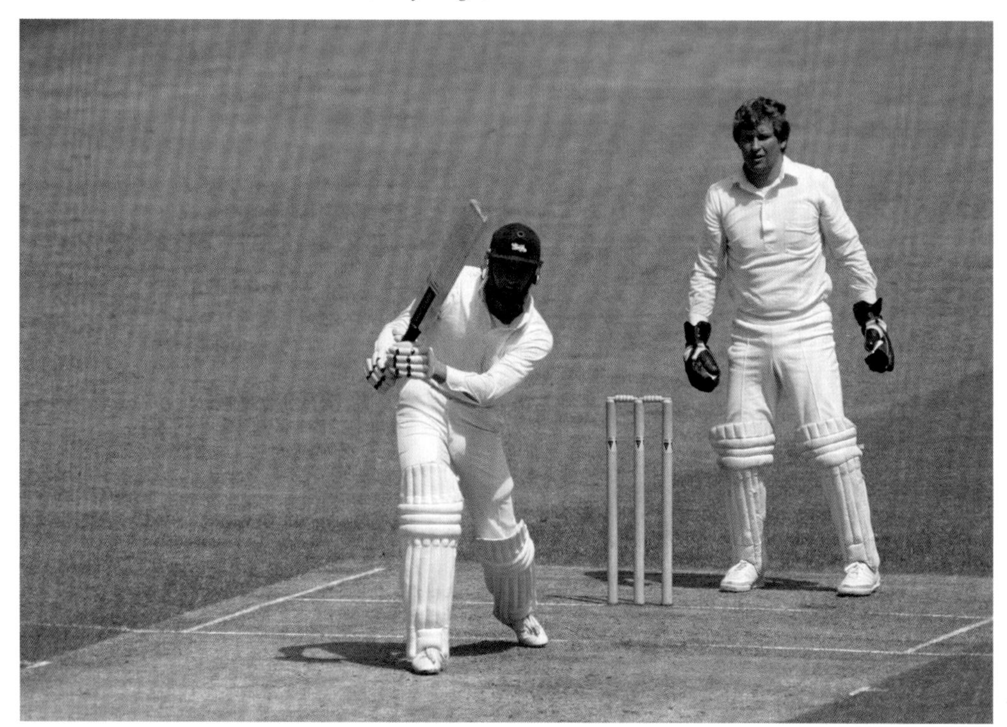

Two highlights of my career: (above) West Indies skipper Clive Lloyd brought on Roger Harper just before I reached my century at Lord's. After the barrage of pace, he came as something of a relief. By contrast, my double century in Madras was more about dealing with their spin attack on a bone-dry surface. Having batted through the day, I actually fell asleep at the non-striker's end for the last two balls.
(Getty Images)

Catching practice with the students – middled it!

On the last day of the season at Durham University, we always warmed up in fancy dress, with the lads picking the theme. This time it was wife beaters and Y-fronts.

Over 60 former students gave me a surprise party to celebrate my career at Durham – there was at least one person there from every year, and I was overwhelmed by their support.

Sarah and I toast the memory of Richie Benaud – and naturally we wore beige.

Georgina and I head off shopping.

Katherine's favourite photo of us.

Alexa-Rae, Katherine and Georgina during the summer of 2015.

With Beefy just before he dragged me off to the barbers to be shaved.

A committee meeting, with Stephen Atkinson, Joseph Neenan, Jim Pearson and Ian Botham.

CHAPTER 11

CRASH

I had a good number of Tests under my belt, was the senior opening batsman, felt comfortable playing, and had shown I could perform against the best bowlers in different conditions. That combination of factors, those stars aligning, had produced my double hundred in India. And that was my last series. It had just reached a situation where I could handle it, was good at it, and yet I'd never play a Test match for England again. And the reason could be traced back to something that had happened a few years before.

In 1978, towards end of the season, the Lancashire bowler Peter Lee went back home to Northamptonshire and left behind his sponsored car. The Austin Princess was given to me. At the time, my girlfriend was a teacher from the north-east. Unbelievably, she got a job in my home town of Accrington, so just before the start of term I went up to collect her in readiness for the new school year.

I was driving along the A59 between Skipton and Gisburn, a road I'd used frequently over the previous three years going to and from university in Durham. It was about ten at night. The road had double solid white lines in the middle and was wide enough for two cars. On either side, it was lined with trees and steep banks. I was coming up to a left-hand bend and knew a vehicle was coming in the opposite direction – I could see the headlights shining in the trees. I dipped from full beam and went round the bend at about 50mph – and I really mean 50mph – to be confronted with four headlights across the road. A car had crossed over the double solid white lines and was on my side.

'What the hell is he doing?' Before I reached the end of that sentence, my world had slowed right down. A head-on collision was inevitable.

I had nowhere to go. Rather than hit completely head-on, I lined up one headlight with his, as I reasoned the impact would be less. The impact, in fact, was enormous. I was thrown forwards, my head going towards the gear lever, and I did not bounce back. If I passed out it must have been only for seconds as I can remember hearing glass crystals from all the broken car windows and windscreens landing on the road like rain. I remember hissing, probably from the radiator hoses and tyres bursting.

My head was resting on the gear lever, my eyes were closed. I sat up and mentally scanned my body to see if I was badly hurt. I wasn't. It was then I opened my eyes, trapping glass crystals between my upper eyelids and eyebrows. I gently wiped them off and spat them from my mouth. I looked at the passenger seat, but it was so dark I could see no one. 'Are you OK?' I asked.

'Yes, but my stomach hurts.'

My next thought was to get both of us out of the car, just in case it caught fire. The seatbelt came free, but the door wouldn't open. It was smashed inwards, the roof was bent upwards, the pedals and floor were a lot nearer my seat than they should have been. I pulled myself through the driver's window, or where it should have been, and walked round the car. The passenger door opened, just, and I made sure my girlfriend could get out.

My behaviour then went haywire. The car was trashed, written off. The radiator was wrapped around the engine like tinfoil round a chicken. The driver's side front wheel was at least two feet further back than it should have been. It was the wheel that pushed the floor and pedals closer to my legs. I noticed a foot-long gash in the tyre. I thought: 'Fuck, I've got a puncture.' The bonnet was pointing skywards, the front of the car was gone – in fact it was curved like a banana – and the roof was deformed. Only the back passenger doors looked normal, and I was annoyed because I had a puncture!

As my eyes were becoming used to the countryside darkness, I spotted something curved and shiny on the road. It was part of the bodywork belonging to the car I'd hit. I instantly became angry. I was going to find the other driver and smash his face in for being so idiotic. He could have killed us all. The sight that greeted me was bizarre and horrific. Somehow, on impact, my car had either smashed past or gone over his gold Vauxhall Viva. He had been on the wrong side of the road, overtaking a cattle truck up a long hill. He obviously couldn't wait.

Because I lined up my headlight with his, the impact was half and half head-on. This slight out-of-square alignment had pushed his car under the cattle truck, and it was wedged between the front and rear axles. It did not look like a car. I stuck my head through what was once the driver's door window and screamed: 'What the fucking hell were you doing?' No reply. As my eyesight adjusted, I saw the pedals level with the base of the driver's seat. The long steering column had been pushed so far that the steering wheel was resting against the roof beyond the back of his seat. I thought the driver had gone through the windscreen and decided to find him.

Then a North American voice groaned, and I could clearly see a middle-aged woman in the front, all battered and bloodied from hitting the dashboard. You have to remember that wearing seatbelts was optional at the time, and I only wore mine in the Princess because an annoying light flashed and clicked on the dashboard if you didn't. In the back seat behind the passenger was a younger woman, and lying across her was the driver. The impact from the floor and the steering wheel had propelled him with such force between the two front seats that he broke the upper arm of the woman in the back. He was knackered: no shoes, tattered trousers, covered in blood. He looked like he'd been in an explosion. I just stood and stared in shock, helpless.

Eventually, I was moved out of the way by the rescue services. They put all five of us in one ambulance and took us to Keighley Hospital. I remember shouting at the driver and being told to calm down by the ambulanceman. I did and spent the entire journey looking at this smashed-up man. I don't know and never did know his name. The young woman in the back had recently flown in from Canada. They were on the way back from Blackpool Illuminations.

At Keighley Hospital, they told me I had broken the tibia in my left leg – the clutch pedal must have hit it. They gave me no treatment or painkillers, telling me to go to my local A&E in the morning. I had to walk back to the main reception area, but they didn't give me any crutches.

The next morning, the Victoria Hospital in Accrington put a cast on my leg. Two days later it broke, so they replaced it with an identical one. Two days later that broke. Only then did I phone Lancashire. I was a little naïve and didn't know I had health cover as a Lancashire cricketer. They sent me to have private treatment. That one didn't break. Although I'd been in a head-on car crash, neither hospital X-rayed any other part of me and when I then went private, they simply put on a better cast and didn't ask me how I'd done it. The fact that my neck wasn't X-rayed was to have massive consequences in my life.

Eventually, my leg healed and the cast was removed. Within a week, though, I was in a hospital in Manchester where all the nurses were nuns. It was here I had bone removed from both big toes. When I was at university studying PE, we had a lecture on hurdling and the lecturer got us to jump over a fixed bench. I absolutely cracked it with my left foot, and then did it again with my right. God, they were sore. What I hadn't realised was chips of bone had gone into the joints and calcified. So in 1978, my first year out of university, playing for Lancashire seconds, my feet were killing me.

Surgeon David Markham told me he'd have to shave some

bone off the joints of both big toes. He made it sound so simple, but the upshot was agony. I went down to nine-and-a-half stone from my usual 10st 4lb. From September, when I had the car crash, I didn't have shoes on again until February. Because of the operation, my big toes are tiny, so I don't have big-toe strength like most people. If you stand behind me and push me I'll just fall over. To this day, I still have no balance walking on a moving train or boat. My daughters think it's hilarious how I stumble from side to side.

In 1979 and 1980, I had to learn to walk and run again, to balance properly. Pre-season training was painful. The slightest knock on my toes almost made me cry, but as is customary in sports teams, there was no sympathy. I was still a second XI player in 1979, after all, having played only one first-team game at Chesterfield in the Sunday League, and I hadn't even batted in that match.

The operation resulted in the joints between my big toes and feet becoming very unstable. It became a matter of course that while sprinting for a ball one of my big toes would dislocate. If I kept running, I learned that I could put it back into place. It took a long time to master and was uncomfortable, but, as months went by, it became less painful. I managed to play in 1979 because my dad made me metal toecap-like items that protected the side of my feet. People would ask what they were, but I didn't care how they looked.

Because of the redistribution of weight throughout my feet, until my body adapted I had further problems, including a stress fracture, a tendon sheath that needed splitting, and a Morton's Neuroma, a condition that affects the nerves between the toes. For years I was petrified of being hit on the foot, stood on, stubbing my toes, all manner of things, such was the resulting agony.

So my early career was physically painful: operation, recovery, operation, recovery. I remember when I was told about the operation to remove the Morton's Neuroma from my right foot, I went home and cried. Not because of the pain, but out of frustration, knowing how much rehab I'd have to go through again. But I never thought of giving up – it never entered my head. Not once did I question any of it. It wasn't even stubbornness – that's when you dig your heels in and won't be moved. In my case, it was a complete lack of any thought process about the situation. I just did it and got on with it as if it was completely normal. My feet and balance were getting better and better – until Jeff Thomson at Brisbane. That hurt.

Apart from the problem with my feet, from 1979 onwards I occasionally had a sharp pain underneath my left shoulder blade. Physios said it was a trapped nerve, and it would come and go. Over time it happened more frequently, taking longer to go away. By the time of the tour of India, this trapped nerve was becoming a nuisance. Strangely, it was OK when I looked over my right shoulder, but hurt when I tried to look over my left. Thankfully, being a left-handed batsman, I spent most of my time looking over my right shoulder. I also noted that my fingers were often different temperatures, with my little fingers often being much colder than the rest. This coldness was sometimes replaced by pins and needles. It was all a bit weird, but because it had happened slowly over a long period of time, without knowing it I had built up ways of dealing with it. Most of the time I wasn't aware how much I was compensating.

Arriving back in England after the tour, I picked my bag up from the airport carousel and a searing pain shot through my shoulder blade. I rang Lancashire. They booked me in again with David Markham, a man I knew well and trusted after the surgery on my feet. In his rooms, we discussed my painful shoulder blade. It was then he asked about my arms and fingers, and he discovered how my head movement was extremely limited.

After my head was X-rayed from every conceivable angle, he asked if I had ever had any head trauma or fallen and landed badly? I couldn't think of anything. Then he said: 'You have an old injury, probably six or seven years. Can you remember anything major?' I told him about the car accident, and after I had explained the collision in great detail, he sat back.

'That's when you did it. You crushed two bones in your neck.' I was numb. 'You've been lucky,' he continued. 'Ever since, one jolt in the wrong way could have caused damage to the spinal column.'

'Meaning?'

'Best-case scenario, paralysis. Worst, death.'

It was hard to think straight, but questions kept coming as I wanted to find out how I could fix it, and whether I would still be able to play. His advice was a progressive course of treatment: 'We start with physiotherapy, then traction, manipulative surgery under anaesthetic, then invasive surgery.' I had no words.

I had played from April 1979 until March 1985 ostensibly with a broken neck. I went home and sat in a daze. I didn't know what to do. I did make one decision, though. I wasn't going to tell anyone who didn't need to know. I told only the Lancashire manager, Jack Bond, captain John Abrahams, and my room-mate Paul Allott. In my life I have made many bad decisions. That was one of them.

My logic was this. In my last two Test matches, I had made scores of 201 and 69, so I was in top form. My neck was broken then, nothing had changed, so I'd just carry on. England would only have told me to get it sorted at Lancashire, so why even tell them? But something had changed. My neck was getting worse – and now I knew about it. I felt like a little boy who had fallen over and starts crying only when he sees the blood running from his knee.

I noticed how poor my head movement was. Most blokes, when they're putting trousers on a coat hanger, at some point will trap them between their chin and chest. I couldn't do that. I could look right, but moving my head to the left caused a sharp stabbing pain under my left shoulder blade. If I tried to tilt my head backwards and look at the sky, I would feel pain accompanied by dizziness and the sense I may pass out. The pins and needles were worse. I was a physical mess. Alongside this, my first marriage was dissolving before my eyes. The only things we seemed to share then were a house – and arguments.

I carried on playing but couldn't score a run. I couldn't coordinate, and here's how I knew. For all the time I'd played, catching a cricket ball was easy. With the exception of slip catches, I can't remember dropping more than two outfield catches in my career. But in 1985 if a fellow fielder threw me the ball, I had no idea which part of my hands it would hit. One day I was standing at cover and one of the lads threw the ball to me and it hit me on the wrist. I realised I couldn't get my hands where I wanted them. It was as if my hand/eye fuses had blown. Dr Markham told me the condition had affected my coordination centre. 'With someone with your level of coordination,' he told me, 'even a one per cent decrease is going to mess you about.' This inability frustrated me. But that was only the beginning of it. Within four months my international career had ended. I'd lost my place in the Lancashire first team. I was lost.

My mood was awful and I became verbally acidic to those around me. I was particularly harsh with John Abrahams. Here was a guy who had helped me grow up in cricket for years, a great friend, and I was being horrible to him. Even now I regret how I treated him. Abey, I'm sorry.

I was losing the plot, and then it completely disappeared in mid-June against Derbyshire at Old Trafford. I was facing Geoff Miller for the final over of the day. I'd known Dusty for years, having toured Australia with him on the 1982-83 Ashes tour, and he's a good bloke. With one ball of the day's play left, I was 21 not out – believe me, it felt like 121. All I needed to do was play out the final ball and I'd be not out overnight, a lovely feeling. Happy that you're doing your job, you can have a lovely relaxing evening and know exactly what you have to do the following day. I knew my team-mates wanted me to be not out as well. They had not liked my misery. They also wanted the opening batsman back scoring runs.

Dusty bowled the ball slowly at least two feet wide of off stump. 'Just leave it,' I should have told myself. I found out years later he bowled so wide on purpose so that I would indeed be not out overnight. I have no idea why, but I hung my bat out and edged to slip. I imploded silently. Walking into a completely silent dressing room, I put down my helmet, gloves and bat, took my car keys, and left without a word. I had no thoughts, no anger, no feelings. Inside, my head had died. As a singular ball, that was the worst thing that ever happened to me in a game. I was in a terrible, terrible, terrible place.

At the time I lived in Accrington, 20 miles and 45 minutes from Old Trafford. I drove an MGB soft top, pageant blue. My house had a short driveway. I pulled up, turned off the engine, and opened the door. I couldn't get out. When I looked down, I was still wearing my spiked cricket shoes. And yes, I was still wearing my thigh pad, box and pads. I couldn't get out because my pads had become wedged under the dashboard. In the back of my mind I knew I should have found the situation funny, but that was a whole universe away.

I unlocked the front door, still padded up, and went inside. I must have looked a right prick. I stood there. I knew I had two crushed vertebrae in my neck. I'd lost coordination to such an extent I couldn't function. I'd gone from scoring 200 in a Test match to even playing games in the Lancashire second XI. So when I nicked that last ball I had no idea what to do. In my head, at that point, I was gone. I can't fix my neck. I can't coordinate. I haven't told anybody. I'm stuck. I'm numb. I didn't know what to think. Looking back, now I know what suffering from depression is, I don't think I was depressed, but I do think I was in a state of shock.

Not telling anybody was the biggest mistake. The idea that, having made a Test double century with the injury, I could cope and do it again was totally misplaced. It had got to a stage where it was trapping nerves, pinching things, and I'd lost a lot of movement. Being warm in India, it was OK, but when I came back I was knackered. It had gone past that tipping point.

The thing is, if I'd told people, I don't know what would have happened. England's set-up at the time wasn't like today. They wouldn't have looked after me. Peter May, the chairman of selectors, did send me a beautiful letter, saying how well I'd played in India, how I'd find my form again, how one day a bowler was really going to cop it, and that was lovely. Norman Gifford, the former England spinner, said to me: 'Don't worry. You never lose it. It just hides in funny places.'

I had lots of advice, people telling me what to do, what not to do, but none of them knew the truth. I got fed up of people giving me advice. It was well meaning but it was nothing to do with form, being out of nick; it was my neck. It got to such a stage that I didn't dare tell anybody the real reason because it would look like I was making an excuse. How stupid is that?

Even if I had told everybody, I'd still have had to go through the various stages of physio. The difference is, instead of waiting for the end of the season to have an operation, I'd probably have had it mid-season. But it's easy to see what I might have done differently looking back.

The final straw came against Hampshire at Aigburth. We'd been doing some fielding practice and I was just coming off when somebody hit a ball to me. It was above me, but I knew I could get it. I jumped up, twisted to catch it one handed, and felt something go in my neck.

I lay there on the ground. At that point I was thinking:

'This is it. I've had it.' John Abrahams and Paul Allott came over, the two who knew about my injury, and I told them I couldn't move my left side. An ambulance came and had to drive on to the pitch. I was scooped up on to a stretcher. I'd pulled the muscle off the vertebrae that were crushed, so my body went into complete spasm. David Markham said to me: 'You're a very lucky man. Your strength has stopped you having serious damage. The way you move, the way you jump around, you could have dislodged your vertebra and damaged your spinal cord.' But I didn't.

I carried on playing, but it was futile. As soon as the season ended, David put me in hospital for the next phase of treatment – traction. This meant lying in bed with a harness round your head attached by a thin rope around a series of pulleys and then finally a big polythene bag with graduated lines to determine the amount of water and therefore the amount of weight. If you've had traction on your neck, you will understand it is the most boring thing ever. You feel well but are made to lie on a bed motionless.

In order for me to watch TV, which was on the wall at the foot of my bed, they gave me a special pair of glasses. Instead of having lenses, they had prisms – a clever idea but unless I was perfectly lined up the picture was massively distorted. Prisms are magical and beautiful how they split the light into all colours, but not when you're bored. I wanted to watch telly without the news presenter looking like he was broadcasting from a pigging rainbow. The other problem with these glasses was that as soon as any guests came in, they took them from my bed, lay on the floor, and tried to watch telly. Thanks. Allott found another way of amusing himself – gently swinging the bag of water from side to side. This caused me to look as if I was watching tennis at Wimbledon. Again, thanks.

While I was in hospital I was invited to go to Grand Cayman for two weeks on the Fred Trueman International XI Tour. I chatted with David and he said I should do it. At least I'd have a bit of a holiday, and I could come straight back into hospital on my return. Among the squad were Trevor Bailey, Jack Hampshire, Colin Milburn, Robin Hobbs, Frank Hayes, Richard Hutton, Brian Close and Farokh Engineer. Some of the players took wives, and the cricket was obviously social. Billeted out across the island, our hosts were magnificent. Wherever we went they paid for every meal, every drink.

On the middle Saturday, a big dinner was organised. Fred was the speaker. This was a huge event for the cricket lovers and our hosts. Halfway through the speech, Fred stopped, produced a bat, and raffled it. The money went into his pocket and was never seen again. Our hosts, quite rightly, were not best pleased.

Later on the tour, the Governor General hosted us at his official quarters for a 'Welcome to the Cayman Islands' drinks reception. We were instructed on the protocol upon meeting him. 'He speaks and shakes hands, you reply. Do not start a conversation.'

I was at the back with Frank Hayes, Colin Milburn and Robin Hobbs, drinking very cold refreshing lager. The MC announced the Governor, using his full and very long title, who made his entrance wearing a white ceremonial military uniform. He had more medals than anyone I've ever seen and it was all topped off with white gloves and a white topee, out of which protruded an enormous feather. It's fair to say it wasn't what we were expecting. There was some disrespectful giggling and the odd comment. Frank Hayes was crying.

The Governor stepped forward and welcomed the Fred Trueman International XI to the Cayman Islands. It wasn't inspirational, but it wasn't a long speech either. He stepped back and the MC then called upon Fred Trueman to respond on behalf of the visitors. What happened next I shall never forget. Fred walked to the microphone. 'Thank you,' he said. 'Before I start, Ollie, where are you, son?' He was referring to Colin Milburn, swilling lager at the back with us. On the rotund side, he was nicknamed Ollie after Oliver Hardy.

Ollie walked from the back of the large room through the guests all dressed in their finery. As he reached the front, he looked at Fred. 'Ollie, give it to 'em son!' Without a second's hesitation, Ollie turned round to face the audience and started singing the Tom Jones classic 'Green Green Grass Of Home'. The Governor looked as if someone had shoved a poker up his arse. The guests were stunned, and we fell over laughing at how bizarre, unexpected and ridiculously funny it all was. It ranks as one of the most surreal moments of my life. Ollie was in full stride and, to be fair, didn't have a bad voice. He finished the last note – and then immediately launched into 'Delilah'. By this stage I was laughing so much the back of my head was killing me. I thought Frank was going to have a heart attack. When Ollie got to the chorus, he managed to get all the guests with their hands in the air swaying and singing to 'Why, why, why, Delilah?' It was true comic beauty.

Meanwhile, the Governor stood to attention, rigid, with an expression that suggested he was being rogered by something invisible. When 'Delilah' finished, he legged it, Fred said a cursory 'Thank you', and the drinking started in earnest. The locals, buoyed by Ollie's exuberance, were now in a party mood, and the polite chit-chat was replaced by raucous laughter. Everyone refused to adhere to the 7pm deadline and eventually we were thrown out – but only because we'd drunk them dry.

During that trip I had to lie flat on the floor for a day as my neck was playing up. Upon returning home, I went straight back into hospital. When I saw David he decided we needed to go to the next level of treatment: manipulative surgery. I had crushed vertebrae C4, C5 and a little of C6 in my neck. Because over time they had started to recalcify, the resultant growths of bone were preventing me from moving my head properly, and trapping my nerves. As I understood it, manipulation under general anaesthetic would break these little pieces off.

Lying on a bed in the pre-op room feeling a little drowsy due to an earlier injection, the anaesthetist said: 'Mr Fowler, I'm going to inject the anaesthetic into your arm and I'd like you to start counting to ten.' He was looking worried at nine and was flabbergasted when I got to 15. When he asked how I felt, I told him I was fine, so he gave me some more. I didn't start counting. 'That's it, bye,' I said, and fell under. It turned out that due to my fitness level and metabolism I'd needed as much anaesthetic as is generally used to knock out a 23-stone man. It was a hospital record.

When I woke up, it was incredible. I felt like someone had turned all my life switches on. There was no pain, not even slight discomfort. My head moved freely, with no more pins and needles in my hands. I felt lighter and brighter, and full of life. I felt brilliant. I had got myself back. I was alive again.

I stayed at home for the rest of that winter. Indoor nets at Old Trafford were a delight and I couldn't wait for the season to start. Pre-season matches were very important. I knew I had to play well and regain my place in the first XI. No one ever owns their spot in the team, they only borrow it while they are playing well. I wanted to borrow the opening spot again.

I was batting like myself again. My neck, hands and fingers were fine and I was selected for the first championship match of the season at Hove, v Sussex. John Barclay won the toss and stuck us in. At lunch I was 27 not out, but it felt as if I'd scored a hundred. I couldn't remember the last time I'd batted a full session. In the end I scored 180 and we won by nine wickets. I was off and running again.

Obviously I wish the accident had never happened. There are times I'm a little bit frustrated that my neck interfered with, and basically ended, my international playing career just as it had started. Before England went to Pakistan, Australia and New Zealand in 1987-88, I was the leading English run scorer that summer until Graeme Hick pipped me in the last game of the season. The selectors sent out 30 letters and I didn't get one of them. Neil Fairbrother was picked to go. Gehan Mendis came up to me and said: 'I'm sorry, Fox, they've taken the wrong left-hander from this club.' But I just realised that was it. The way I looked at an England recall was it either came along or it didn't. Yes, it would have been nice to play again for my country, but I wasn't going to dwell on it. They didn't take me, they took someone else. England had gone. The selectors had changed, the captain had changed, and there was a view that turning to me would have been a backwards step.

If the hospital had X-rayed my neck at the time of the accident, I doubt I'd have been allowed to play cricket at all. I was a qualified PE teacher, and I wouldn't have been allowed to do that either. What on earth would I have done with my life? So actually not X-raying it and playing 21 Tests and having the career I've had, I'd take that any day.

OK, the injury ended my international career, but at least I had one. I actually think I'm lucky. It could have ended my life. After 20 Test matches, I'd scored more runs than any other English opener at the time, including Boycott and Gooch, but so what? I might have played rubbish after that. Just because you're on an upward path doesn't mean it will keep going. You can't think about that, instead you must enjoy what you've had, and get on with it. The accident was out of my control. He was on the wrong side of the road and that was it. It's a bit like carrying regrets – I don't. I can't see the point. Why carry regret around? Bloody hell, can you imagine having depression and regrets? It'd be a fun day every day. At least I did have a taste of international cricket and all that came with it. You take the hand that you're dealt. If somebody gives you a sweet, enjoy it, don't ask for two. I enjoyed it. Great. Move on.

The only thing that irks me slightly is when people say that I only had a career with England because Graham Gooch was serving a ban for going to South Africa and didn't play when he got back. My answer is quite simple – there are two openers. When he came back, I opened with him in two one-day internationals. If he'd been around, I'd like to think I'd have been picked as the other opener. I had loads of different partners. For a while I was the senior opening partner, so I'd have been with Goochie. But it's all ifs and buts. As it was I was just settling into Test cricket when my neck gave up, and that was perfect timing: 'Goochie's back, let's get rid of Fowler.'

While I had no problem with people going to South Africa if that's what they wanted to do, there were occasions when they made comments about putting England first, and I thought: 'Well, you didn't.' I got an offer to play out there myself. Ali Bacher, the managing director of the South African Cricket Union, who organised the rebel tours, rang me up to be captain of Orange Free State, but I turned it down. I didn't agree with it. I'm not a hugely political person, but apartheid was horrible. I've always had the same view – there's good people and bad people. I don't give a monkey's what religion, colour, creed, race someone is. To treat people completely horribly because of the colour of their skin doesn't sit in my mind. I'm not someone who's going to walk down the street and demonstrate, but in my own personal life, and how we've brought up our children, there's no such thing as colour, there are just people.

Whether I'd have struggled to look a black team-mate in the eye didn't come into it, because I was never going to go. I couldn't justify the way they were in their society, so it didn't even enter my head. Obviously, I'd have liked the money as much as anyone else, but there are some things you just don't do.

Thankfully, all the time I was playing for England, I still loved playing for my county. So that first year I had just playing for Lancashire, in 1986, was great, actually making a contribution to the team, compared to before where I was nipping off to England, coming back for a bit of practice, and then heading off again.

At the start of your career, you have that hunger to play well, but you're not equipped to do so. But when you get to that place where you can actually play cricket and you just enjoy being good, there's nothing better. That was the stage I'd reached. Up until then, whatever I'd been doing was not playing cricket, I'd just been hitting a ball. It's the same with a bowler. Until he can run up and put it exactly where he wants it, he's just letting go of the thing and letting fate take over. Once he can put it where he wants 99 times out of 100, then he's bowling. When you get to that stage of playing, it's wonderful.

When I was playing my best, and obviously it doesn't happen that often, it was as if I wasn't doing it. It was like I had a screen in my head, and as the bowler let go of the delivery I could see the shape of the ball and which boundary board it was going to hit. People call it being in the zone. In my experience, it doesn't last very long. It might be just 20 minutes, but for those 20 minutes you can't remember what you've done. I've come off, looked at the scoreboard and I've got another 40, and I couldn't remember any of it. At those times, there's no thought process, no little man on your shoulder chirping in your ear. It's a dream. I probably experienced it only five or six times. Something happens in your head and you just go into it. I've never been hypnotised, but I would imagine that's what it's like, as if you're watching yourself, you're not doing it. You don't have a bat in your hand. As the ball's coming down, it just happens. The only thing you'd like is for it to last forever, because most of your career you're either out of nick or trying to get to a situation where you're scoring runs. But on those rare occasions when you get in that zone, it's bliss.

I knew 'the zone' was a rare occurrence – you can't expect that all the time – but in my head, after England had gone, I was going to play as well as I could, enjoy myself, make a contribution to the team, and see out my career at Lancashire. In reality, it wouldn't quite happen like that.

CHAPTER 12

END OF AN ERA

Bob Bennett, Lancashire chairman, was an ambitious man. I think he had designs on being the England manager, and wanted to be seen as a strong man in cricket. There'd been an incident when Wasim Akram had got frustrated during a game and started ranting in his native tongue. It was highly unusual for Wasim to do this, but the upshot was he was reported for it and fined something like £3,000, a lot of money considering this was the first time he'd ever done anything.

Wasim couldn't understand it. 'Foxy,' he said, 'if I was shouting at a batsman, I'd shout in English. If you're having a go at somebody, you don't do it in a language they don't understand. I was shouting at myself in pure frustration.' It was all over the papers. We appealed on his behalf, but that was that.

At the time, a guy was writing a book about Wasim and Waqar and he came to my house in Manchester to interview me. He was there for three hours. I mentioned this, about how I thought Bob Bennett wanted to be seen as strong because he wanted to be the England manager, and as we finished I said: 'You can edit this any way you want, but out of courtesy, before you publish it, I want to see it.' Anyway, somehow, instead of the draft coming to me, it went to Old Trafford. I'd never seen it, but Bob Bennett clearly had. We were about to start a game at Lord's against Middlesex when the dressing-room attendant came in to say there was a phone call for me. It was Bob, and he wasn't happy about what he'd seen. I pleaded my case.

'I had this bloke sat in my house for hours,' I told Bob. 'I don't know what he's written because if I had I wouldn't have allowed it to be sent.'

It was clear to me that Bob wasn't happy with my explanation and I was hitting the panic button. I rang up the author and got hold of a draft and the stuff about Bob Bennett wanting to be seen to be strong was all it said. But obviously it seemed he didn't like it, so I told the author to take that bit out, and he did. It was never published, but I was put on a charge of gross misconduct.

I was given a letter, and had to go to see the committee. I was talking to one of my mates about it, and he knew a solicitor who had just represented Jackie Collins against a tabloid newspaper and won. This bloke looked at what had happened with me. He was a cricket fan, liked the way I played, and offered to represent me for nothing. We went into the meeting and within two minutes he'd got the charge reduced from gross misconduct to just misconduct, which mattered because with gross misconduct you can be sacked. In the end, they fined me £1,000, but said I wasn't allowed to tell the press how much the penalty was.

I went outside where the reporters were waiting and kept quiet on the details, but the front page of the *Manchester Evening News* speculated 'Fowler Fined Five Grand'. I had people sending me money – one chap sent me a grand. Some students sent me a fiver in an envelope and said: 'We know this won't contribute very much to your fine, but at least you'll be able to get your hair cut!'

Lancashire never put any of this down in writing because, my solicitor said, if they did, we could sue them and he thought I could get thousands. I didn't want to do that. I didn't want to sue the club that had given me a living. I never paid the fine, and that was the end of it. Except, of course, it wasn't. I felt my days were numbered and that my card was marked.

I played the next year and got a message to go in one Saturday morning to meet the chairman. I rang up the manager Alan Ormrod to see if he knew what was happening. 'It's probably the same thing they've just done with me,' he told me. 'They've sacked me. They sacked me yesterday and they're going to do the same to you and Paul Allott today.'

I went in, and was told that I had never supported any Lancashire captain and had been a disruptive influence in the dressing room my entire career. Essentially the same message was given to Paul Allott. Yet Walt had been vice captain, I was a senior pro, and there had been times when, along with the captain, we did selection, so I didn't understand this complaint. I don't recall my ability was ever mentioned.

I had served under David Hughes for most of the latter end

of my Lancashire career. He was captain when we won the NatWest Trophy and Benson & Hedges Cup in 1990, and by that time he was aged 43. In both competitions he'd barely bowled and scored hardly any runs – because he batted at number nine and didn't bowl. We'd developed such a team that we hardly needed a captain, as we just knew what we were doing. We were doing brilliantly. Well, ten of us were. He wasn't. Walt and I had fended off a lot of pressure from the other players, who questioned why he was playing and believed someone else, such as Graham Lloyd, should have been playing instead. Our explanation was: 'If he does his job – if he gets an extra ten runs out of every batsman, if he gets an extra wicket out of each bowler – then it's worth it.' We were defending him. We were stopping what could have been a mutiny.

At the end of the season, Paul Allott and Hughes always played golf. 'I'm going to have a word with Yozzer,' Walt said. 'I'm going to say to him, "Why don't you retire at the top? You've just won two competitions, call it a day, you'll retire a hero."'

He planned to raise it with him in the bar afterwards, but Walt couldn't wait. He told him on the first tee, so they then had a stony silent round of golf. Yozzer didn't retire, carrying on into 1991, when we lost in the NatWest in the second round and the Benson & Hedges in the final. By that stage it was obvious it was the end. He knew it, we all knew it. We played a game at Somerset and he took Neil Fairbrother out to look at the wicket. When asked, Neil said we needed another bowler, because what we had was five batsmen, four bowlers, a wicketkeeper – and David Hughes. He twigged what Neil meant. I don't imagine he was happy, but he did actually drop himself for that game.

I believed that the situation with Hughes might have been one of the reasons I was sacked, as he must have been one of the captains I had supposedly not supported. So when it came to going in that Saturday morning, I just sat there and listened. I was in a leather jacket and jeans because I knew I was going to get sacked. I thought: 'Fuck it, I'm not going in a blazer and tie. I'll go wearing what I want.' I was told to clear my locker out and go. I went outside and sat on the boot of my car. I decided I didn't want any of it going in the papers, because why be bitter and twisted when I'd had such a great time at the club? Instead I thanked Lancashire for the career I'd had, thanked all the members, and said how I'd enjoyed every minute of it.

Internally, though, I was hurting. And the most hurtful thing was I felt it was done in such a nasty way. They'd just decided they were going to get shot of me. There was no consultation, nothing, but I already knew that nobody I'd been at Lancashire with had left nicely, not Clive Lloyd, not David Lloyd, John Abrahams, Peter Lee – you name any of them, none of them left nicely. So if that's what they'd done to them, they were going to do it to me, weren't they? There was always the attitude of 'us and them' between the players and the committee. It felt like they treated us like naughty schoolboys and eventually they expelled us from school. We created problems for them because we had brains and thought of how we might change things for the better, and it probably disturbed their lunch while they were drinking nice red wine.

A few years later I was working on *Test Match Special* at Old Trafford and I saw Bob Bennett in the marquee at the end of the day and went up to him. 'Bob,' I said, 'can I just tell you my side of the story? Don't walk away. If you do I'm going to shout at you at the top of my voice in this marquee because I'm not embarrassed about what I have to say, I'd just like you to listen to me.

'All those things you told me when you sacked me, did you really believe them? Did you really think I'd never supported a captain for seventeen years? If I never supported any captain at this club, why would I bat in a match with thirty stitches in my mouth? Why would I have cortisone injections to keep playing? I've never gone to the press and told them anything because I loved playing here. But you never asked me the truth of any of it.'

We didn't say much more, and we've not spoken about it since. The stupid thing was I liked Bob Bennett and got along with him. We used to have a laugh and a chat; I still have nothing against him. If I saw him now I'd go straight up to him, shake his hand, and go and have a beer with him. If he felt that was what he had to do as chairman of that club, fine. I might not like it, but that doesn't affect my opinion of him as a bloke. I'd be really disappointed if he did it through malice, but I don't think that was the case so I have no problem with him at all. I suspect somebody wound him up, but I wish he'd given me more of a chance to put my version of events at the time.

As I've said, I don't believe in bearing grudges or carrying stuff around. It would have been nice to have played one last game at Old Trafford, knowing I was going so I could wave at everyone, say thanks very much, but it didn't happen. Being sacked was just an episode, not life or death – it's just part of life. So I'd go and stop at Bob Bennett's house if he asked me.

I've no problem with David Hughes either. After I left, I went with MCC to Amsterdam for a week and David Hughes was captain. I walked up to him – he must have thought there was going to be all hell on – shook his hand and said: 'Captain!' And after that we got on well.

Although in my head I had seen myself playing out my days at Lancashire, and had no desire to go anywhere else, those final couple of years had become less enjoyable. Some people get better with age, I wasn't sure I did. I got a bit lost. It wasn't as if things became clearer as I got older, it was almost that I was best when I was more naïve. Then it was exciting and new, but once I got to understand the game more and what was necessary to play it, I noticed there were a lot more things missing from my game than I thought. The more I understood the game, the more I realised I wasn't that good. It's always a bit disappointing to realise you're not as good as you might be.

Even so, once Lancashire had sacked me I still wanted to carry on. I wasn't ready to give up. It was in all the papers that I'd gone from Lancashire and I got a couple of phone calls, one from Somerset, and one from Geoff Cook at Durham, who I knew having played international cricket with him. He offered me a deal, and I was happy with what was offered, but I told him what I was really interested in was helping their young players. 'When I've finished, if there's an opportunity, I'd like to coach the second team.'

Durham had been given first-class status only a year earlier and it was fascinating to be there at the start of a new county. One of the lovely things was a lot of the younger players were local. It was great to see the exuberance they had, and the naivety. I was brought up in a very strict regime at Lancashire, knocking on doors and all that, and here that didn't exist. At Lancashire you thought twice before saying anything, whereas at Durham they were encouraged to contribute. There was no fear factor created by the senior players, as there shouldn't be. Some of the things they came out with were brilliant because they were so fresh and hadn't gone through the treadmill of an old existing club. It was brand spanking new. When it came to results, finishing bottom the first couple of seasons was inevitable. Everybody knew it was going to take time, but the feeling was: 'We'll get on with it – we'll get there in the end.'

Clearly there was a liberal sprinkling of older players – Phil Bainbridge, David Graveney, Beefy, Simon Hughes, Wayne Larkins, me. But it wasn't like we'd gone there to die. We'd gone there to help. They wanted senior players to develop the youngsters, bridge that gap, and we were more than happy to do so. Other people might have thought we were a bunch of old-timers seeing out our careers, but we certainly didn't.

Beefy was the figurehead, there to put the place on the map. My time at Durham included one year with him. His last game was at the Racecourse, against the Australians, and thousands turned up, because they all knew it was the end of an era. We were fielding and when we all walked off at the end and went into the changing room there was just silence. 'Well,' said Beefy, 'that's that.'

Somebody asked if they could have his bat. 'Yes, just help yourself.' He left the changing room with nothing. Not a thing. He walked out a civilian. About three weeks later, Kath said to him: 'Have you got some cricket stuff to wash?' He thought about it, and eventually he twigged that everything had gone.

When the 1994 season came round, our first match was at Cambridge University. I asked Geoff Cook if I was going, but I'd not been picked. In that case, I wanted to captain the second team, but he didn't seem to think there was much point in me playing second XI cricket, although he still wanted me to be a squad member. I couldn't see how I was going to get in the first team if I didn't play in the second team and score some runs. And if I was drafted into the first XI, because there'd been an injury, and I'd not been playing in the second XI, how was I going to perform?

So basically the message I took from it was: you're out the door here. But I'd already made my mind up it was my last year anyway as things hadn't been looking good for a while. We were playing one game and before it started Geoff told me he was going to play Robin Weston instead, the explanation being that he was a better player than me.

'Geoff,' I said, 'I have no problem with you turning round to me and saying, "You're on the way out, you're old. He's up and coming. I think he's going to be a good player." But don't tell me he's a better player than me, because you know he's not, I know he's not, and history will say that he wasn't. So don't do that to me. Just tell me you don't want me to play.'

Later that season, the first team were playing South Africa, Allan Donald and all. I had hardly played for weeks, and then I got a phone call to say I'd been called up in place of Robin. It seemed to me I was almost being picked to fail. As it turned out, I top scored in both innings with two sixties. But that was about it. I knew I was gone and that's how it turned out to be.

My final first-class innings was on 1 August 1994, against Yorkshire at the Racecourse. Caught Kellett, bowled Silverwood 0. You'd think I'd have a clear memory of such a landmark moment, but the truth is I don't. In all honesty I can't even remember it. No big deal. No raising of the bat to the crowd, taking it all in. I must have been out and that, as they say, was the end of it.

CHAPTER 13

SARAH

'Weasel-faced love cheat' – that was my favourite description. It was February 1994, and I'd become front-page news.

By now, it was completely obvious I'd finished with the game, and the game had finished with me. I'd just had a shoulder operation and couldn't bend down. As well as that, I don't think the Durham chairman Don Robson was over enamoured I'd been on the front pages of the tabloids for a week. 'Foxy Fowler Faxes For Divorce' wasn't a great headline.

I've had two failed marriages. The second one, Nicole, I don't know why I married her. The whole thing was just ridiculous. When I came to Durham from Lancashire, it was obvious things weren't going very well because she wouldn't come up to visit me. She said the garden needed watering. It's always a warning sign when you're coming second to a watering can.

In the meantime, Sarah was the marketing manager at Durham. She was the go-to person in the club to find out what was happening, what time you had to be somewhere, where it was, how many people were going, which hotels we were in. She knew everything. At the same time, I had a club car, whereas she used to drive a Transit van towing the club shop to whatever ground we were at, which meant she had no transport home. At the end of the day, I liked to have a couple of drinks in the bar so she'd drive us both back in my car and then pick me up in the morning. It worked well for both of us, and that was how we started to be mates.

Weirdly enough, all through that time when I was struggling to get on with my wife, she used to give me marital advice. She used to spend time with Nicole, tried to talk to her, which is a bit ironic really considering how we ended up. But then again it was all a bit mad. I remember we had a conversation at one point where I said I'd love kids, and Sarah answered: 'I'm going to have one next year.'

'Hang on,' I said, 'don't you need a boyfriend first?'

'I'll find somebody,' she answered, and then we had a conversation about it, the upshot of which was me saying, 'Well, I'll be the dad then.' It got a bit serious: we actually worked out details, and how I'd support it. We made a mental agreement.

While this was going on, I went home to Manchester one day and found Nicole had left me. She flew back to Australia and sent me a 23-page fax which basically said I was a bastard. She wasn't very concise. I replied saying: 'OK, it's obvious the marriage is over. I'll file for divorce.' But I'd used that magic word 'divorce', at which point the story appeared in the press. Hence 'Foxy Fowler Faxes For Divorce'.

She flew back to England and her story appeared first on the front page of the *Manchester Evening News* and then in every tabloid for the next week. I went from Foxy Fowler to Faxy Fowler in a matter of days. By now I was living with Sarah and our phone was red hot. The fax machine never stopped. There were photographers camped outside our house. It was ridiculous. One morning we went to a Durham CCC membership drive in Billingham. The press chased us, but we lost them. The next day the headline was 'Foxy Fowler And Blonde Divorcee Flee Lovenest'. The whole thing was absolutely crazy. It was the world's biggest non-story, but it just went on and on. Eighteen months later, there was an article in *Marie Claire*. 'Divorce by fax,' it said, 'is no longer the domain of the rich and famous, including Phil Collins, Sylvester Stallone and Graeme Fowler!' Illustrious company but I could have done without it.

At its worst, the phone rang again. I said, 'Leave it,' thinking it'd just be another reporter, but Sarah answered it. A voice quickly said, 'It's Kath, don't put the phone down.' It was Kath Botham. 'Come and hide at our house. They won't pester you here.'

In the *Mirror* on one day our story had occupied the first nine pages. 'How did you manage that?' wowed Beefy. 'That's better than one of my efforts!' He almost sounded jealous.

Beefy and Kath took us to a quiet restaurant and we stayed the night under the Botham roof. It was a wonderful thing to do. It was Kath who said: 'We didn't have it as bad as this. We just had the Eighties.'

My mum and dad were on holiday abroad at that time. They passed a shop selling the English papers, glanced across and saw the headline. 'Eeh,' said my mum, 'what's he been up to now?' 'Weasel-faced love cheat' was just hilarious. And this is it, I laughed at it. It didn't upset me at all.

The thing is, when Sarah and I got together, we had two or three uncomfortable days where I went through my history and she went through hers. We decided to start with a clean sheet, and I told her what I'd done and where I'd been, and she did the same. So then when all this crap started coming out in the paper, Sarah would go: 'I know about that and I know about that. What's this? I didn't know about that.' And I'd say, 'Sarah, if I've told you about that and that, and I haven't told you about that, it's because that didn't exist. That's untrue. That's a lie, because otherwise I'd have told you.' That was an absolute godsend.

Sarah was thrilled. She was described as a 'stunning 25-year-old blonde divorcee'. 'Who the fuck's this?' she said.

Sarah and I made each other laugh from the start. The way we got together must have been seamless because I don't particularly remember it. Wayne Larkins was having a surprise 40th birthday party, so I went back up to Durham in the autumn. Sarah was there, and I think that was when it happened. Round about that time, the chairman's wife, Jenny Robson, who was good friends with Sarah, took me aside and said: 'If you hurt this girl, I will make sure your life is not worth living.' So every time I ever bump into her I remind her of what she said and how long we've been married.

To be fair, I was not exactly a great prospect: married twice, reputation for being an idiot. But Sarah's parents Sam and Pam were great. When we told them we were together, Sam turned round to Sarah and said: 'Won't be long. He'll want kids.' He wasn't wrong. Sarah soon got pregnant. We went round to their house. 'I'm not telling them,' she said, so I did it.

'I've got some news for you,' I said. 'You're going to be grandparents.'

Sam paused. 'That didn't take long. Anybody want a cup of tea?'

There was no trepidation about getting married for either of us. Sarah had been married before as well and we had a great conversation where we said, 'Look, this is it. You've done all your leaving. I've done all my leaving. Whatever happens from here on in, we stay together. There's no fucking off. That's it.' Once you've got that in the background, you get through everything. I said: 'If you leave I'm coming with you. And if I fuck off I'm taking you with me.' So that was it, done.

Kate had been born by the time we got married. In fact, by then Sarah was pregnant with Georgina. I said I'd marry her when we had three kids and compromised on one and a half. Sarah's parents used to book a holiday with a firm which, if you went to Spain, offered a free weekend at Linden Hall in Northumberland. It was coming up to Valentine's Day in 1995 and Pam offered us the weekend break while they had Kate. 'Well, we might as well get married then,' I said when Sarah told me. 'We'll get married and then we'll go to Linden Hall.' Call me an old romantic if you want.

Because the press had been hounding us, we didn't tell anybody. We didn't tell Sarah's mum and dad, we didn't tell my mum and dad. The only people we told were Sarah's brother and his wife. We had good reason to think the press would give us grief. When Kate was born at hospital in Durham, there were photographers climbing over fences, pushing cameras through windows. The matron said to Sarah: 'The *Sun* are on the phone asking if you want to do an interview.'

Sarah looked at her: 'Tell them I'm dead.' And that's what the matron did. She picked up the phone – 'She says she's dead' – and put it down again.

On the morning of the wedding, I took Kate down to Pam. 'It's a lovely day for a wedding, isn't it?' she said. I was a bit taken aback, and asked what she meant. 'Well, it's a nice fresh day, sunny, great for pictures.'

We went to the Dun Cow pub in Durham first, and then to the Register Office next door. When the registrar did the 'I now proclaim you man and wife' bit, I turned to Sarah and said: 'Do you know, that's the best wedding I've ever had.' The registrar looked like she was going to kill me. But I meant it. It was sweet, it was simple – but again, probably not the right thing to say.

The following day, Sarah said I'd better tell her parents, so I rang them up and said to Pam: 'You know how yesterday you said it'd be a nice day for a wedding? Well, it was. We got married.' She was furious – for one reason and one reason only. I'd denied her the opportunity of buying a new hat.

I always wanted a stable family life, but in the past I wasn't very good at picking the right women. Sarah and I have been married for more than 20 years now and have three beautiful girls.

It's funny, when Kate was born I remember a transition. I thought: 'I am no longer Graeme Fowler. I am Kate Fowler's dad. I've done lots of things in my life, it's now my place to help her do stuff. I'm here to facilitate her. You've had a good run, Fowler, you've had a great life. Your life now is looking after her.' I come second now. And I quite liked that as I felt the pressure was off me now.

It's helped being an older dad in that I'm not as much of an idiot as I was in my early twenties. I'm far more philosophical and laid back. The flipside is I didn't get to run around with them as much as I'd wanted. I think, though, it's more beneficial to them that I'm a calmer parent rather than haring around a village green. It's like you're babysitting them until they're old enough to go off on their own. It's like coaching – you can only help them be what they are. Encourage them not to go in a certain direction. Encourage them to use their assets and go the other way. 'Don't' is a very dangerous word when you're talking to your kids or coaching somebody, because immediately it puts hackles up. You have to remember what it's like at that age.

I've always said to Sarah, you're prepubescent and then you're an adult, and that bit in between is awkward. What we have to do is make that bit as smooth as possible. If they want a drink, I'll teach them how to drink. If they want boyfriends, no matter how uncomfortable it is for me, I'd rather they were with them here than behind a bus shelter. If they want to smoke, I'm not going to encourage that, but I'd rather they did it openly. There's a beauty in honesty.

One of the things I've always said to them is: 'We all do stupid things now and again. We all get in trouble. That's a fact. But whatever you've done, don't lie about it. Be honest, and we'll deal with it. But if you lie, I'll know you're lying, and you'll get in more trouble for that than you ever will for what you've done.'

I have those memories of my mum in my head. Why be confrontational when you can just ask? As a child, I never liked the response, 'Because I say so.' That's unacceptable. We've always talked to our kids as people, and we've always allowed them to speak. The only time we've ever tried to discipline them is if they were going to do something dangerous, like stick something in a plug socket.

I thought as a parent you'd be able to influence your children, but I'm not sure you can. You just guide them and help them. But there's a difference between helping your child and pushing. My dad said to me: 'I'll buy you any sports equipment you want on two conditions. One, you use it. And two, you look after it. The day you don't use it or don't look after it you don't get any more.' We weren't rich, we didn't have a lot of money, but that was an agreement I had with my dad and he stuck to it. If my dad had been pushy, I'd have pushed back. With my personality, I'd have rebelled against his authority.

There's nothing worse than pushy parents. My dad taught me how to play, but as soon as I reached Lancashire second XI he backed off and let me get on with it. It was fantastic, because from 11 to 16 he'd pretty much been my coach. The problem comes when people try to live their dreams vicariously through their children. You see it all the time. All three of my girls played football with varying degrees of success at primary school. I used to go and watch but I'd get so angry I had to go and stand on the other side of the pitch to move away from parents screaming at their kids. Leave them alone for God's sake. There was one occasion where this bloke was shouting at his son when he was in front of goal. The boy turned round to his dad and the goalie picked the ball up. I thought: 'That serves you right, you bell-end.'

I find serenity in my family; they're everything to me. Having a family was everything I expected, and more. Back at the start, a lot of mates were having a go at me because I was already divorced twice and thought I was ruining my life. Now they're all on their second marriages, someone else bringing up their kids, or they're raising someone else's children, and I look at it and know which way I prefer it. I have great solidity here. I'm half of a whole. I couldn't be without Sarah on many different levels. We're symbiotic really. We just know each other so well, and the great thing is the more time we spend together the more fun we have. We don't get fed up of each other, we just get more into each other.

We have a relationship where we have our own areas. This sounds rather glib, but she once said to me: 'What sort of curtains should we get?'

I said to her: 'Look, if I asked you what sort of CD player we should get, you'd say I should sort it out. I'm saying the same thing to you about soft furnishings.' And after that, when something cropped up, either I'd say to her, or she'd say to me 'Curtains!', so we both knew who'd look after it.

It would be an absolute lie to say we've always got on brilliantly, because we haven't, but we're getting on better the longer we go on. I think the main reason is we're so comfy with each other. I know Sarah better than she knows herself, and she probably knows me the same. And I love it. We've always said all we need is each other. Why go to Tenerife? We can have fun sitting in a bus-stop.

It was very hard for Sarah when I first became depressed.

It took her a long time to comprehend that I wasn't doing it on purpose. It took her a while to realise it wasn't personal, and that I didn't hate her. It was just a thing that happened. First time it occurred, I wasn't aware of how much it affected people. Now I do know, so if I'm not careful I could start feeling guilty about being depressed, and that's the last thing you want – feeling guilty because you're affecting other people's lives. But that's an emotional choice, and I can get rid of the guilt by saying: 'It's not my fault. I don't have anything to feel guilty for. Just keep going and get yourself well again, and then we'll go and have some fun as a family.'

I've got a great back-up team in this house. Alexa-Rae had three mothers for a while when I was unwell, and by the time she was old enough to remember things, I was much better. They all understand and we make a joke of it. 'How much of a loony are you today, Daddy?'

'I'm a twelve.'

'Oh, you're a happy loony!'

It's just accepted that how I am is their normal dad. I think it's brought us closer as a family in a weird sort of way, more understanding and more communicative, even if it's just that single number on my mental-health scale.

We have daft family events, such as Eurovision or the darts. Kate makes numbers and we all wear silly hats, like we're in the audience. We also have what we call 'music night', where we turn off the telly and play songs that Sarah likes. They have to be ones she likes because if she doesn't, she'll just tell us to turn it off. Sometimes we'll get drumsticks out or we'll push the sofas back and dance, other times we'll sing. We do daft stuff. And obviously when my numbers are above ten we have a lot more of a laugh than when they're not.

The really bad periods of depression are immensely difficult. Sarah and the kids have to amend how they are around me. They have to tip-toe sometimes. When I'm a five, I'm incapable of analysing it. That's all there is. When I'm a seven, I know I'm a seven, and I know that I feel terrible. So in some ways a seven is worse than a five. But if you asked me I'd still rather be a seven because at least then there's some activity going on in my head.

Sarah would often ask if I was all right, and then she'd say: 'You've no words, have you?' When I've no words, it doesn't mean I've got nothing to say. There is nothing occupying my head. It's just blank. It's almost like sensory deprivation – just nothing. Seven is still not good; I couldn't go to work as a seven. Eight or nine I could just about go to work – some of the time. I might have managed a training session or a net session, but I've given all I've got for that day. There's no more left, so then I'd come home and be like a vacuum again. It was as if I had a tiny bit of mental health to use, and once I'd used it I was back to the bottom again.

What stops me being a 20? You have to bear in mind this scale is something I thought up out of nothing, and I needed something that could expand at both ends. The first time I ever saw a ten in gymnastics, I was disappointed. What happens if the next girl comes on and performs better? If you've got a system like mine, to say I'm a 20 would mean I can't ever feel any better. If I operate between five and 15, there's a chance for it to be a four or a three, but there's also a chance for it to be a 16 or 17. Some people have criticised me for having a numerical scale, believing that I'm limiting every day I wake up if I give myself a number. But they obviously don't understand the system. They think if I wake up a 12 and announce it to the family, that dictates the day. That's not what happens, and I don't know why they'd think it would operate like that. I've had days where I've woken up brilliantly and ended up on the floor. And that happens to anybody.

Background noise gets me if I'm not good. Also, when I get anxious, I get butterflies in my stomach and start to prickle inside. I have to keep going outside. I feel boiling hot. I don't get cold if I'm anxious. I can walk round the village in the middle of winter in a T-shirt. Mental health does weird things to you. I used to be incredibly robust, and now I'm not. Sarah has said she can tell when I'm on the edge of an episode of depression because I become more animated about things, get angry, maybe at someone or something on the television. I've recognised that in myself now. This house is a tip. When my MH is good, I can live with it and laugh about it. When my MH is bad I get absolutely furious. I just want to throw things and shout.

I began to notice that if my MH was about to go down I'd get OCD about the towels upstairs: they all had to be folded and face the same way. It's bizarre, but it's like a trigger or warning to tell me I might be going. It can also just suddenly explode, so if I'm with Sarah I might suddenly shout: 'Shut up!' It comes as a shock to both of us, but we know we can work around that.

We don't give a toss. People seem to chase things that don't enhance their life. What matters in this house is what we have together. The rest I couldn't care less about. Having Sarah, and the family we have together, has been at the very centre of everything. Whatever I've done, whatever decision I've made, I couldn't have done it without her – and that was certainly true when it came to taking the next step in my career – a step I think outweighed anything I achieved as a player.

CHAPTER 14

A NEW START

Three-quarters of the way through my career, I thought: 'When I finish playing I'm never going near another cricket ball.' But then towards the back end, when I was batting with Graham Lloyd and other youngsters, I enjoyed helping them. I'd turned into Bumble – a worrying thought!

Also, what else did I know about? I'd seen other cricketers finishing, they'd have a sports shop with their name above the door, and because they knew nothing about business they'd get ripped off. All I knew about business was I knew nothing about it, but I did know quite a bit about cricket, and I enjoyed teaching. I think it's a wonderful thing. Teaching someone something new, or coaching someone to make them better, really appeals to me. So when I'd finished, first at Lancashire, then at Durham, I wanted to stay in the game. What I hoped to do, and there was half a promise of this at Durham, was take over the second team. Once I'd had a domestic change of arrangements and run off with the marketing manager, however, I think that chance disappeared.

I'd become an advanced coach in 1979 and enjoyed the coaching I'd done in Australia and Tasmania. When I left cricket, I coached in public schools and I could do it, but it didn't give me a lot of satisfaction. I began to think about running coaching clinics in the area and the obvious place to do so was Durham University. I wondered if they'd let me use the nets to coach the first team. And there it was, the seed of the idea: if we did it properly we could get the students on training programmes, video analyse them, work with them one on one. The outline of what became a centre of excellence was taking shape.

I spoke to Sarah's dad Sam about it – at the time he was on the English Sports Council – and he told me how the government was looking for centres of excellence in higher education. He asked me to put my thoughts down on paper and offered to turn it into a document. I wrote out some bullet points and little sentences and gave it to him, but the document I got back was a work of genius. It said everything I wanted to say in a far better way than I could ever have said it. He explained that the TCCB would have to ratify it, otherwise he feared I'd be seen as 'just a talented loose cannon'. He always thought I was anyway.

We went down and saw TCCB chief executive A.C. Smith. He loved the idea but had no money, and the university liked it but they had no money. Fortunately, though, John Major was prime minister at the time and the government came out with a White Paper about sporting institutes in higher education. Sports governing bodies were invited to Downing Street and the only one who had any clear suggestions was A.C. Smith who spoke about our idea of a scheme at Durham University.

Nothing happened for a while, but then the National Lottery started, with its aim of funding sports with some of the money raised. Before they did so, they wanted to see a complete development plan. The TCCB's charitable arm, the Cricket Foundation, secured grants for 26 regional development officers and another to Durham University to start the centre of excellence. That's how the centre came into being. And it was through Sam shaping it, guiding it, and taking it to Lord's, that it happened. He ended up being on a committee to select the next five centres of excellence. Without him, one of the best men I ever met in my life, none of it would have happened. And he was proud of me being his son-in-law.

It also wouldn't have happened without Sarah. When we had Kate, we were more than skint as Sarah wasn't working; like me she'd left the club. I decided I had to get a teaching job, but she wouldn't have it: 'No, you will not, because if you get a job teaching in a school you will die. You'll hate it. And I won't like the fact that you're not happy. You've got this fantastic idea of the centre of excellence – keep going. You'll get that going one day, because that's what you need to do.' That was an incredible thing for her to say.

Finally, on 1 September 1996, I was there, at the start of the centre of excellence – shirt, tie, trousers, sat at this desk, in an empty room. I had one thought: 'What the hell do I do now?' It had taken me 18 months to get it going, I'd finally done it, and now I didn't have the faintest idea what to do. I almost started giggling.

All we had indoors was one net, with a four metre run-up, and a multi-gym in the corner. That was it. Then there was the other small problem – no players. How do I get hold of the lads? They didn't come back until October, and then of course the cricket season had gone. There were no university emails at that point, so I couldn't try to let them know what I was doing that way. In fact, I ended up driving round the colleges putting notices on the boards and trying to get hold of people through the University Athletics Union.

Part of the problem was the situation with the university team as it existed was pretty shambolic. Basically, they just turned up and played. They had nets but didn't have a system of training. Games themselves would mainly be friendlies. It was ten weeks of basic cricket. Players didn't progress because they were playing for Durham University. When we were at Durham and it came to playing proper cricket, Paul Allott and I would jump in the car and travel down to Lancashire to play in the county second XI or the Under-25s. The organisation, the focus, wasn't there. It was a university cricket club, nothing more.

Eventually I rounded up the lads. 'The aim of the centre of excellence,' I told them, 'is to help young players finish their education and progress their game into first-class cricket and beyond.' That was always the remit, pure and simple. The priorities were education first, cricket second, social third. Some academic departments worried the centre would take people away from their studies, but what we actually found was the more organised they got with their training, the more organised they became with their academic work.

I told them: 'If anybody doesn't want to do it, that's fine. It's not compulsory. But anyone who does want to do it, stay, and we'll start talking.' My recollection is they all stayed.

I explained to the lads what we were trying to achieve: 'A centre of excellence is not a building, it's an attitude. It is us. We are the centre of excellence. How we train, what we do, is the excellence part. No matter what you're doing, press up, sit up, stretch, you do it to the best of your ability, with good technique. If you train sloppy, you play sloppy. If you're sloppy in your physical strengthening, when you try to reproduce that strength in a game situation, you'll be sloppy. I've always been a big believer in "whatever you do, you do to the best of your ability, with excellence". Ten minutes of excellence is better than three-quarters of an hour of mediocrity.'

It sounded great, except the sports hall was fully booked – there were 21 hours of staff badminton scheduled – so I asked for some of that time, but was told it was a long tradition. So I opened and locked the sports hall myself on Sunday night.

I always wanted to be the sort of coach I'd have liked to have had. Most times you need to be encouraged in cricket because the game flattens you; it's cruel at times. Usually you need more support than criticism, and what you also need is analysis of what parts of your game are going well and what needs to be improved. The only time I'd have a go was when their preparation was poor, their attitude was poor, or they weren't thinking. I wanted to be hard but fair, with far more carrot then stick. I'd had a lot of stick, from senior players or whoever, and, although it helped to some degree, it's a cruel way of doing things, and I didn't want to be like that.

I also wanted there always to be a purpose to what we were doing. When it came to nets, for instance, I was never a believer in 'last six balls, twelve to win'. Instead, I'd say to them: 'Before you have a net, batsman or bowler, you need to think: "What am I trying to achieve?" It's not a social afternoon. If you want to talk, do it when we're finished. We're here to do business. There's no point wandering in, having a bat, and coming out and thinking: "I don't know what we're doing."'

I also wouldn't let them go in the nets too early. I didn't want them to have nets before Christmas and to develop a nets mentality. I wanted them to be hungry. And anyway, you get some players who are brilliant in nets and hopeless in games. I tried to learn from what had and hadn't worked for me during my career.

As a player, if there were no nets available, I never saw the value of knocking up on the outfield, patting half volleys back into the advertising boards. Instead, at Lancashire, I used to get our wicketkeeper Warren Hegg to hit me short catches, to get my reactions, hands, balance and eyes going, and then I'd hit him some. I remember one day when we were playing Hampshire and I'd done what I needed to do – the stretching, the group fielding, my session with Warren – and I was watching Malcolm Marshall warm up. He was unusual, Macko. He came on to the pitch later than everybody else, signed a few autographs, did a bit of stretching, and then he'd call over Bobby Parks, the wicketkeeper. Bobby, obviously used to this, left what he was doing and ran over to Macko who bowled to him on a wicket at the end of the square. Macko ran up really slowly, and when his arm came over, it was that fast, and his legs that slow, that he bowled off the wrong foot. He walked back, and he ran in a little bit faster, still off the wrong foot, and what happened was, over several minutes, his legs got quicker, until his legs and hands were at the same speed. He bowled a dozen balls at full speed and went off.

While that was going on, David Hughes, our captain, offered to give me some throwdowns, but I didn't want any. He started having a go at me: 'You've got to be part of a team. You've got to prepare yourself properly. You can't be just standing there doing nothing.'

I thought he was completely wrong. I knew what I needed to get myself ready. 'Yozzer, why would I want you to throw me half volleys at sixty miles an hour that I can pat back at the boards when that is not going to be anywhere near what I'm going to face at eleven o'clock?' I just didn't need to do it and I didn't know why other people did it. Maybe when you're 18 or 19 and you're still trying to groove your swing, but I was in my late 20s. Yozzer didn't like it, but why would I practise something that doesn't happen in a game? And in a coaching environment I took the same approach.

So when it came to fielding practice, I used to hit proper boundary catches, not 40 yards with one hand, proper ones you're going to get in a game. The second and third years would say to the first years: 'Just you wait till Foxy starts hitting catches.' I'd hit them 80 or 90 yards.

When I coached British Universities at The Parks in Oxford against Sri Lanka, Guy Jackson, who managed the universities team, saw them practising high catches with me. 'You know what?' he said, 'I don't even have to know who the players are taking the catches, but I can tell which ones have come from Durham University.'

If you're going to practise high catches, make sure they're proper high catches. The scoreboard at Durham University is on top of a really high bank, and the last day of the season, when we always used to warm up in fancy dress – black tie, the lot – the players asked me to go up there and smack these massive catches. I was about 20 metres up. The lads were miles away. It was fantastic. They had a great time doing it. I'd introduce little quirky things like that to keep it fun, because if you get everybody laughing and joining in, it works. Everybody puts more in if they're having fun.

As well as group sessions, there was specific one-to-one training, batting, bowling, whatever. We had club nets twice a week and a big centre net on a Sunday. After a Sunday net, we'd often have a lecture or seminar where I'd give them scenarios. Early on, I'd give them one about time management, for instance. Other times I'd get them to work out who their favourite player was, what made him their role model, and ask them where they saw themselves in comparison to them, and what they needed to do to get to the same level. If they picked someone like Shaun Pollock, I'd ask: 'Well, how do you think he started? Do you think he started like you? I'm sure he did. So how did he get there? What did he have to do?' It got them thinking, and because they were bright lads, they responded to it. I'd ask them about their role as a player, how they would achieve it, what they needed to improve and what their role was within the team. They were all questions to get them to start thinking.

I'd have a wagon wheel with speed, strength, power, deep catching, short catching, sprinting, all different shots. The further out on the wheel they were, the higher the score. I'd say to someone, 'You've scored yourself an eight for fielding on the boundary. Are you being serious? You're the slowest boundary fielder I've ever seen. Do you really think you're an eight?' I'd have a go at them like that, but I was always careful who it was and that my relationship with them meant it would work.

I wanted them to be realistic. I used to say: 'Look, if you stay as you are, there isn't one of you good enough to make a living at first-class cricket. I'm not being harsh. When Andy Strauss was here, he wasn't good enough either. He had to improve as well. So you're in the same position, and you've got the same opportunity to improve as anybody else. It depends on you. It depends on how hard you work, how much commitment you put it in. I can't do that for you. I'm here, but I'm not your father, I'm not your headmaster. I'm not here for your pleasure. If you knock on my door, I'll answer it. But if you don't turn up, I ain't going to come and get you. And if you don't turn up you ain't going to be in here very long anyway.'

Once you've got that culture going, then they add to it and contribute just as much. It's the same as I saw our dressing room. I liked it to be more of a cooperative, with me having the casting vote.

I didn't let them relax and think they were in a routine. Sometimes they'd ask what we were doing and I'd say to them, 'No idea,' so then they'd have to think and come up with ideas themselves. Or we'd have an open-ended training session, because when you're fielding you have no idea how long you'll be out there for, and I wanted to get them out of their comfort zone and into an area where they could mentally cope. That's a way of building up mental strength. I'd get people to sprint up flights of steps, but not tell them how many times they were doing it. Then you see how various people adapt. I'd make them tired before we started. I'd make them run for 20 minutes in their pads, because you can bat for a long time, and you're not always going to feel fresh and energised. Get people out of their comfort zone, get them working hard, because if you can do that in your training, if you then get a difficult situation in a match, you can feel you've done this before.

In coaching, I would always encourage my lads to understand their limits. How much sleep they needed, how much they could drink. I took British Universities to Cape Town, and they had only one free night, and that was the last one. They then had to be up at 6am for the flight, so I taught them how to stay up all night. 'It's not complicated,' I said, 'drink until midnight and then have water. But you can't quit at three am because you'll never get up.' Second night's harder!

As a coach you have to be realistic. You can't pretend that people haven't stopped up all night. The lure of the opposite sex means you're going to stay up later than planned some nights just on the off chance you're going to get lucky. Every bloke I know has tried it. So I taught them how to do it.

I had to get used to the way young people drink – and find ways to counter it. The first time I played for Lancashire seconds, the twelfth man had to go round and collect a drinks list for the team. Everybody had pints – lager, bitter, mild, whatever. I was brought up in a cricketing environment where at the end of a day's play everybody had an alcoholic drink. Very rarely did anybody have an orange juice. I was educated that way, to drink with the opposition, the sponsors, as part of your job. To all intents and purposes, I was raised in a pub culture. And I didn't find that arduous.

The difference was our process was to drink throughout the evening and if you got a bit tipsy towards the end, fine – but that wasn't the aim. In fact, I remember being told as a kid at Accrington when I'd got a bit drunk: 'If you want to come out with us, you either drink less or you learn to handle it, because we're not going to take you out if you're going to get drunk.'

It was the same at Lancashire. Bob Ratcliffe said to me the day I started as a professional cricketer: 'Right, now you're a pro, wherever you are, wherever you go, you do so as a Lancashire cricketer. So if you get drunk in public, you are getting drunk as a Lancashire cricketer. How you behave is a reflection on the club.' It taught you to drink in moderation. Most of the time anyway.

My students at university were different. They might not have drunk for a fortnight and then they'd all decide to go out. They'd gather at someone's house for pre-drinks and then get absolutely plastered downing shots and playing silly games. When they went out they'd be absolutely mortal. We never did that. That was just a completely different social convention to what I was brought up with. It was just bizarre. They couldn't remember what they'd done. They'd fall over.

The two big nights at Durham were Monday and Wednesday, and I could tell whether my lads had been part of them or not. Two days later they were still looking rough, so I said to them: 'You're just a bunch of talented binge drinkers. And if you can't change your way of life, I'm going to change it.' I paused. 'Next Tuesday, seven am, on the running track.' When they protested, I added Friday morning to the list, and it operated until the day I left. That did a couple of things: it stopped them getting hammered, and it also changed their perspective. Obviously they didn't like getting up at 6am, but they liked the fact they'd done their training and had a whole clear day afterwards. It became part of a routine. It's mental toughness. If you can get up at 6am, middle of January, twice a week, and go outside training when it's freezing and pouring down, then fielding all day is nothing. If you get them out of bed at 6am and then they go away on tour and have to do the same, they'll be OK, as they've done it for years.

I did have to have words with people. I had one lad who wasn't going to make it in first-class, but he'd have been a good minor counties player, and he was getting in such a pickle. Every time he went out he was getting in a fight, falling over. I had to take him on one side and ask him about it, and to his credit he said: 'Foxy, I've got a problem. One drink is too many, and fifty is not enough.' Once he'd started, he couldn't stop. I kept it quiet, but I got one or two people to keep an eye on him and asked counsellors within the university to help him with his drink problem. He was honest and straight up about it. He caught it and eventually became a successful businessman.

I liked having that give and take with the students. I liked the fact they felt they could talk to me and I think it encouraged communication, on serious matters as well as otherwise. When it became common knowledge that I'd had mental-health issues, lads would talk to me about their problems. A few of the students had issues in the time I was there. They were bound to – it's one in four of the population. One lad in particular I spent quite a lot of time talking with. I never got him to use my number system, because I didn't want to put anything on him, but I'd sit and chat with him.

I also used to talk to basketball players and rowers when their coaches sent them to me. I was OK with that if they were, but I didn't want them to be sent to me to discuss something deeply personal if they didn't want to. What I normally did was tell them about my mental-health issues and what had happened to me. Then they would usually join in – maybe what they were experiencing was similar. I'd explain that I was just sharing my experiences, and if they had anything similar, or slightly different, they should go and sit down with their GP. I'd never position myself in terms of specific advice as that would have been dangerous. By telling them about my depression, though, usually a conversation developed, and that stayed between me and them.

I'd also keep an eye on students. If something arose I was concerned about I'd have a chat with them. I'd do things by stealth rather than anything as obvious as telling them I was worried about them – I'd never start with that. You'd just watch, and then if their behaviour changed slightly – 'he's been quiet the last three weeks, he doesn't look like himself' – I'd take them on one side and ask how they were and if their degree was going all right. But I wouldn't keep asking questions, I'd explain that they'd been quiet for the last couple of weeks and that I wanted to check they were all right. Usually, they would come back to me with something. There'd be people who had issues at home, issues with a girl, or they'd run out of money – there were a million things it could be apart from MH, so I'd never assume that was the problem.

There were always issues to deal with, because it's incredibly difficult to be a professional cricketer. Mentally, emotionally, physically, it's hard work. The idea of the centre was, after all, to prepare them for first-class cricket. Not all of them were going to make it or be good enough. I remember one third-year student, who I could see wasn't quite going to get there: 'Look,' I said, 'if you want to leave, and concentrate on your degree, then that's fine. No one's going to blame you, and if you're playing well enough you can still get picked for the team.' I told him he could have a couple of days to think about it.

'I don't need two days,' he said, 'I can tell you now. Foxy, I want to stay. And the reason I want to stay is I'm learning more about life in the centre of excellence that will stand me in good stead than I am in my degree course.'

I often described it as 'helping them grow up', but using cricket as a model. Above all, they had to think for themselves.

'What shall we do next?'

'What do you think we should do next?'

'I don't know.'

'Well, we're all going to stand here and wait for you to make your mind up. When you do know, let us all know what it is and we'll get on with it. I'm not here to think for you. You do that bit.'

We wouldn't start nets until four on a Sunday. Sometimes, deliberately, I would arrive 20 minutes late, just to see what they were doing. Of course, they'd all be standing around, so I'd whistle and say: 'Er, can I ask a question? What have you come down here for?'

'We're having a net.'

'Doesn't look like it, does it?' And I'd walk out. And then they'd get the nets out. Players have gone from not doing anything to being told to do everything. What I do is a happy medium. I want, not just for me to educate them, but for them to educate each other.

I've always felt that the worst type of coaches are those who just tell you what to do. I don't like people who tell. The other coaches I hate are the little empire builders at age groups, where they want to win every match, rather than looking at the best prospects and picking them instead.

I remember one time at Durham University, when we played a 50-over game, starting at 12.30, away from home. We got to the match an hour and a half before the start, and the opposition had been on the pitch since nine, fielding, doing drills. They were going to be knackered before they started.

We had two left-arm seam bowlers who absolutely hooped it, and bowled them out for 80. We knocked off the runs very quickly, and afterwards their coach came up to me to ask if I minded them having another practice on the square where we were starting a two-day match the following day. So he made them have naughty-boy nets because they'd got bowled out by two superb swing bowlers – and they weren't even practising against what got them out. What sort of coaching is that? Those lads were going to be absolutely pissed off. And if you're angry and don't think you should be doing something, firstly, you're not going to be doing it to the best of your ability, and secondly, because of that, you're learning bad habits. That's the worst coaching you can ever have. If your players don't respect you, how on earth are they going to learn?

You have to work out with them how they approach the game, what areas they want to work on, which areas they need to work on, and facilitate them getting better. Once you do that, then a natural culture builds up where everyone is happy with what they're doing. They like the way it's being done, but they're also being pushed and challenged, the trick being to get them to challenge themselves. You can only do that by giving them the freedom to think for themselves, because when you're in a game situation, you're on your own, whether it be bowling, fielding or batting. In that split second, you're making those choices. You have to have a background of being able to think for yourself, other than just being a robot. You only need to look at the England one-day squad. After yet another poor World Cup in 2015, all of a sudden there was a massive sea change in attitude, and I honestly think that was because Paul Farbrace and Eoin Morgan went: 'Come on, you don't need be told – play how you can play. That's what got you here.'

If you have a coach who just works on science and data and who doesn't allow people to use their abilities, their art form, you're not going to get results.

CHAPTER 15

THE STICK

It's a tricky balance between coach and player, but it's one you can get over by having relationships. I always used to say to the lads at university: 'I don't care if you've played badly. I'm not going to bollock you for playing badly. What I am going to do is have a go at you for lack of preparation, lack of effort, or lack of thinking. If something doesn't work, that's the game of cricket. But if your attitude is wrong, your preparation, then I will have a go at you.' And I did.

I had lads who did not show up for a week or two. If they let me know before training they couldn't come, I was quite happy with that – but not afterwards. They're not complicated rules.

'So you're all right, today?'

'Yes.'

'Well, funnily enough I'm not happy with you being here today, so you can get your stuff and go home.'

Take Essex batsman Tom Westley, and Leicestershire and Nottinghamshire opener Greg Smith. At Durham, they were two good players, but in the second year they were coasting it, a common mistake at university – and if you coast in your second year, you're up against it in your third.

The one thing I had absolutely no time for was people being late. I think it's unprofessional, it's rude, and there's no need for it. I explained to my players that if the bus was leaving at eight in the morning, and they arrived at eight, they were late as that's when the bus was leaving and they should already be on it. On the occasion I took British Universities to South Africa, we left at eight on the dot and left one lad behind. He had to get a taxi and pay for it. He wasn't very happy, but that's by the by. You have to be punctual.

With Greg and Tom, two talented players, I could tell they'd lost a little bit of focus. We'd start training at three o'clock in the downstairs gym, but they came in at five past and apologised for being late. The next week, they came in at ten past. I'd seen them in the week and could just tell they were giving it the big shot as professional cricketers who knew what they were doing. Once again, they apologised for being late. 'Doesn't matter. Just get your stuff and fuck off.' They were astonished. 'Get out of here, now. And make an appointment to come and see me. I'm not having people swanning in ten minutes late. If you can't be arsed getting here on time, I can't be arsed to have you in here. Fuck off.'

I had spent a long time thinking about what I was going to do. I'd never done it before, and I've never done it since. What I was about to do was extremely risky. They came in individually and as they sat down I said: 'Right, what's going to happen now is I'm going to speak. You are not going to say a single word. I don't want to hear a single word come out of your mouth.' I told them what I thought they were doing. 'You think you're a good player, fooling about, being lazy. You are not good enough to play first-class cricket full time yet, but here you are, cock of the walk.' I went on and on. 'Unless you change your attitude, you're going nowhere, and that is just a waste of talent. That is how I see it. That is how I feel. So buck your ideas up otherwise you're going nowhere. Get out!'

I did that to both of them. Neither of them said a word, and that's a really risky strategy. What if I'd been wrong? But that's what I did, because I wanted to shake them up. About four weeks later, Greg asked if he could have a word as we were walking round the ground while a game was going on. We talked about batting and when we finished, I said: 'You know that meeting where I wouldn't let you speak? How was it?'

And he just went: 'You were spot on.' That was when I thought, 'Thank God for that,' because I'd laid it on thick.

Only once did I really lose it. It was a final at Lord's, my students were batting second and we knew from the radar it was going to rain at four o' clock. Twenty minutes before, we were three behind on Duckworth Lewis. I sent a message out to the batsmen Laurie Evans and Nick Lamb: 'Get in front of Duckworth Lewis!' At ten to four, we were eight behind on Duckworth Lewis. I was starting to bubble, but still nothing happened. They didn't make an effort. By four o'clock when it rained – and it wasn't going to stop – we were a dozen behind.

I'd sent two messages out and they hadn't done anything. I went absolutely nuts.

'What were you doing? What were you thinking of?' What really kicked me over the edge was when one of them said it wasn't their fault. Boosh! 'Well, whose fucking fault is it? There are very few occasions where you can actually blame somebody for losing a match, but I can blame you two.' The dressing room emptied as everybody ran in the showers and I went absolutely bananas.

There were times I used to pretend to be angry to make a point. Sarah and the girls say that when I speak sternly I'm frightening. If I did have to give the students a dressing down, I could act, but I wasn't actually full of inner rage. More usually, I'd prefer to say: 'Come on, let's have a walk round. Why did you play that shot? What were you thinking when you bowled that ball with that field?' That's far stronger than: 'What the hell were you doing?'

Everybody's different. Some people you need to put an arm round them and encourage them, some you need to talk to in an emotional way, others in a logical way. Very, very few people get better with the stick. The carrot is far better.

I never bollocked anybody for playing a bad shot. If they did it three times in a row, I'd take them on one side: 'Three times you've done that now – do you think it's worth pursuing that shot so early in your innings? Or do you think if you stayed in for another half hour it would get easier?' I'd only bollock them if I thought they weren't applying themselves.

I knew what it was like to be on the end of a bollocking. I'd had a few come my way, often born out of frustration for what people could see in me. 'Wake up, Fowler! What are you doing?' At Lancashire, Bob Ratcliffe used to dress me down, but it was all done for a reason and I could appreciate that at the time. I might not have liked it, but I could see where he was coming from. Most of the bollockings I had made sense. Then again, I was brought up in an educational environment where you got hit by the teachers. Christ knows how many times I had a leather strap smashed round my arse or got slapped across my face, so to have a verbal dressing down was almost a relief.

When you make a mistake as a coach, you have to admit it. And I've been wrong many times. I'd quite happily admit it to students. You've got to be honest. You can't coach people without occasionally making mistakes. It's just part of life, and in all parts of life we don't get everything right. It would be very naïve of me not to think that I'd made mistakes, the same as you have to hold your hands up occasionally and admit there are some players you just can't connect with. I've had players I've been a complete failure with because I could never quite get through to them somehow. And that's frustrating.

I completely and utterly failed, for example, with Holly Colvin, predominantly a bowler, who plays for the England women's side. I tried to help her by asking questions: 'Do you ever use the crease? Because if you do it gives you different balls.'

'I don't bowl like that.'

I quickly realised I wasn't going to have an influence on her. All I could do was facilitate what she needed. At the end of three years when she was leaving, she thanked me and shook my hand, so I said to her: 'You haven't learnt a single thing off me in the last three years, have you?'

'No.'

'And that's because you didn't want to listen, did you?'

'No.'

'OK – and by the way, I don't mind.' But I did regard it as a failure, because I know more about the game than she does.

Personality clashes can come into it, but it was my job to ensure I didn't clash with a personality. It was up to me to change, not them. As long as they were respectful, and as long as they were working within boundaries, that was fine. Often, challenging people could be the greatest fun, but it was up to me to accommodate them, not them to accommodate me. They were there voluntarily, they didn't get paid for coming every week. I was there to help them fulfil their potential. But I wasn't there for them to just use; I wasn't there for their pleasure.

Some students would openly challenge me in front of the others – which I liked. It showed a different side to them, and also it meant we could have a dialogue. I wanted them to think for themselves. I didn't want them to be little sheep and just follow me. I never thought that I was above them and they were underneath me. 'I don't employ you. I'm here to help. But don't take the piss out of me and presume.'

They'd quickly learn, like one lad who'd been to Eton who asked me for the time – a lot of people who've been to Eton believe the rest of the world is at their disposal. 'Have I got "Speaking Clock" tattooed on my head? Have you not got a watch?'

'No.'

'Have you not got a phone?'

'Yes, it's in my bag.'

'Well go and look at it. I'm not here for you.'

The first years occasionally would say something stupid, and all the second and third years would know what was coming. I remember telling one guy that he could bat first in the nets. Everyone else was running round the field, and he started padding up without doing a warm-up or anything. So I stopped the other lads, pointed out what he was doing, and they all started laughing, in a knowing kind of way. I let him get completely padded up then asked what he was doing.

'You said I could bat first.'

'What about a loosener?' He still didn't twig. 'Have you got A-levels?'

'Yes.'

'Did you win them in a raffle? How long have you been coming down here? You come down here three times a week, and yet you haven't done a loosener? It's all right, get your pads on, your gloves, your helmet, pick up your bat.' He started walking to the net. 'Where are you going?'

'To the nets.'

'No. You're going to do a loosener with all your kit on. Off you go.'

Two weeks later, this same lad turned up, and he stank. 'Look,' I said, 'I don't mind anybody smelling of sweat by the end of a session, but some of you stink and we haven't even started. That is unacceptable. Anybody can wash and dry a T-shirt. I'm not asking you to iron it, but don't come smelling.'

The Students' Union had got a sponsorship deal from a deodorant company – I had a pack of 12. I took them into the gym, gave them out, and we emptied all 12 cans of anti-perspirant on to him. The lads kept stopping, but I told them to keep going until he'd had the lot. We could hardly breathe in the gym after we'd done it, which I hadn't thought about, but he never came back smelling again. Nor did anybody else.

I did have to throw people off the course. I had one lad who wasn't getting any runs or wickets in the first team and so I told him I wanted him to play in the second XI, who were about to play in a semi-final. He said he didn't want to play in the second XI, but I explained: 'You probably don't, but look at your facts and your figures. You're not getting any runs. I need you to go and play well.' He didn't turn up. Instant dismissal.

Another thing I wouldn't tolerate was remonstrating when you'd been given out. People talk about the spirit of the game – if there is such a thing – and it's not within that spirit to complain about being given out. Just get off. I've said to a couple of my students down the years: 'If I ever see you do that again, I shall walk on this pitch and drag you off.'

There are two things I've never believed anybody saying: 'I didn't see it' and 'I don't know whether I hit it'. I've never believed that last one, no matter how fine the nick is. I always walked; I was told to. In the first game I played for Lancashire second XI, when I was 16, there was a big appeal by the wicketkeeper for a catch, but I knew I'd hit my pad. After I was out, John Savage, the second XI coach, asked if I'd hit it and I told him what had happened. 'Oh good,' he said, 'because if I ever find out you've hit it and not walked, you'll never play for us again.'

Walking was the right thing to do at the time. If I was playing these days, there's no way I'd walk. Not just because nobody else does, but because umpires have had a change round as well. I've heard umpires actually tell people off for walking: 'Oi! Don't you walk off. I make the decisions, not you. That's why I'm here.' You have to respect the umpire. It takes it out of your hands.

I felt so sorry for Stuart Broad against Australia at Trent Bridge in 2013 when he nicked it and it hit somebody's leg and went to second slip. Yes, he stood there, but he did that because he was waiting for the umpire to give him out. When he didn't give him out, Stuart must have thought, 'You're joking. I've smashed that. You're making me look an idiot.' He got a load of stick for it, but nobody ever worked out it was just because he was waiting to be given out.

I said to my students: 'I've got no problem whether you walk or whether you don't. But if you don't walk, don't ever shake your head on the way off if you haven't hit it. You take the rough with the smooth. No indicating to the umpire that you've hit it when you're LBW, nothing. Just stand there and accept the decision.'

Nasser Hussain used to be terrible for that. You can't nick it and stand there, and then when you get a bad decision complain about it. Remonstrating with umpires does appear to happen more these days, but a lot of it's easier to see because there are so many cameras. Bowlers used to walk past the umpire all the time, and ask why they'd been turned down. Now there are 20-odd cameras at a Test match so it's highlighted more.

I always wanted my team to have standards, but we came up against some teams – they're young men and they think they're being clever – and they behaved like idiots. If that happened, when my team came off, I'd say: 'I know what they've done, you know what they've done. We do not behave like that. We play hard, we play fair, we do not behave like idiots. They've made themselves look stupid. We do not go down to their level. Keep your dignity.'

Generally, though, there was no need. I never found that the young people I dealt with were anything like the portrayal of people that age as arsey and unwilling to listen. You'd get the odd one, but the culture we created was one of cooperation. Everybody knew the rules. Break them and you were going to get the piss taken out of you – or you were going home. They didn't have to stay and do the course. There was a door in and a door out.

Sledging is not something I ever went along with. People talk about it as if it's a way of getting inside the opposition's head, but in my experience having a go at somebody usually just peps them up. Take Curtly Ambrose, he always had wristbands and a little towel tucked in his trousers when he bowled. He was playing against Australia at the MCG in a one-day game and Dean Jones, being Dean Jones, demanded he took them off. Now Curtly hadn't been bowling very fast at the time, and he wasn't bowling very well, but there was a big kerfuffle and in the end he was forced to remove them.

Dean Jones's team-mate David Boon was interviewed afterwards. 'Curtly wasn't bowling very fast,' he said, 'until Deano wound him up. He bowled two yards quicker then and the game changed.' You have to be wary of what you say. If somebody gave Viv Richards or Ian Botham a mouthful of abuse, they needed to be careful. They were unleashing a beast that could change the game. So what was the point of that?

I did get the full verbal treatment off people, but not very often. I got it when I first went out to Australia as a kid, but it worked in my favour, because I became used to it. When I returned to England, I felt people could say what they wanted, as I didn't care. In fact, if sledging intimidates you, you shouldn't be out there.

I don't actually like the word 'sledging' (Steve Waugh called it 'mental disintegration'), but there is almost an art form in distracting the opposition and getting them to lose concentration, which is when you then get them out. I used to say things to batsmen, especially if we were away from home. 'I had a drink with your sister last night.' You know that's now going round in his head.

At the end of the next over, he'd either say, 'How do you know my sister?' or 'I don't have a sister.' Either way it didn't matter, it had lodged in his head. If he said: 'How do you know my sister?' I'd reply: 'I've known her a long time.' If he said: 'I don't have a sister,' I'd answer, "Well, that's strange, she swore blind she was your sister. She looked a bit like you as well, although obviously she was nicer looking.' And then I'd just walk off.

Similarly, if I was at silly point for the spinners, or leg slip, and Warren Hegg was keeping wicket, I'd start to tell him a joke, but I'd be making it up. It could never be a joke the batsman had heard, because I hadn't heard it either. 'This bloke walks into a butcher's . . .' And I'd make that last an entire over, and at the end of the over, as we were walking down the other end, I'd say to Warren: 'After three, just burst out laughing. One, two, three . . .' And you knew the batsman was just dying to know what I'd said, but I hadn't said anything.

Some would ignore you, others would insist we told him. It worked, but more than that it was a great way of making life fun, making the day fun.

I absolutely loved playing the fool. It suited my character. OK, you get a reputation of being a bit of a joker, but then you can do it even more. I realised early on it distracted the opposition, that little mind games like that were far better than sledging. Geoff Lawson used to swear at me all the time. In return, I used to patronise him. 'Too good for me, Henry. You'll have to bowl it straighter than that for me to nick it.' He'd go nuts. Tony Pigott used to blow up too, but I could always make him laugh and he'd have to turn away.

The people who gave the most abuse were usually the ones who shouldn't, and they used to do it at the wrong time. David Capel was a classic. Play and miss a couple of times and he wouldn't say anything. Smack him for four and he'd have a go at you. I said to him one day: 'I've just hit you for four. Why are you having a go at me? You should be having a go at me when I play and miss.'

Jonathan Agnew was the funniest. I used to watch the bowler run all the way up to the crease to time my backing up. I was doing this with Aggers and he stopped: 'Will you stop staring at me?' I'd got him now – without even doing it deliberately. I said to him, and I don't know where this came from: 'I'm just watching your cheeks wobble when you run in.' I found out a long time after, when I started working with him on *Test Match Special*, it messed him up all day. Even when I wasn't batting he was conscious of his cheeks wobbling and was sucking them in. Now that is brilliant – far better than calling someone a string of names or threatening to hit them on the head. When Michael Clarke said to Jimmy Anderson, 'You'd better get ready for a broken fucking arm,' there was no need for that. It wouldn't bother Jimmy him saying it; it would have just shown him what type of bloke he was. As so often in cricket, it's all about understanding the psychology of those around you, and of your opponents.

CHAPTER 16

IN THE HEAD

Peter O'Toole bent down and kissed me on the forehead. It was Bill Wyman's 60th birthday party. Robin Smith, the England batsman, commonly known as the Judge, was there, talking to the acting great, and he asked me over to sort out an argument about cricket. I listened to both sides. 'Right,' I said to Judgey. 'If you're to agree, he needs to think this, you need to think that. And for him to think that, you need to think this.' They thought about it for a minute, then the Judge turned and shook my hand. Peter O'Toole took the more intimate route. It was a big moment for me, and not just because I'd been kissed by Lawrence of Arabia. It was the first time I realised I could solve human situations.

I seem to have the awareness to understand different personality types and the interplay between them, and getting inside people's heads is something I like doing. With the students, I'd prod them, take the piss out of them, watch them, see who were the quiet ones, the lively ones, ask really serious questions, silly questions, find out what made them tick, who trained with who. It was so easy to do. I'd see one of the lads at the centre of excellence, and I'd know immediately if he'd had a big night out, and the reason I did was because he'd looked at me in a way that said: 'Can he tell I was pissed last night?' I just love all that.

You'd get answers from students without them even noticing, and then you could work out if they were emotionally or logic based, which would then affect how I coached them. I worked out with Greg Smith, for instance, that if I explained things in a logical sense – like how he was getting stuck on the crease, not getting forward properly, not transferring his weight – in biomechanical terms it was like a cold fish to him. But if I said to him: 'Do this and you'll get a sense of your movement, and it will feel a lot better – you'll get a lovely flow going through and that will fill your head with joy that you've actually done it,' that made sense to him. Because he's a feeling sort of person.

Effectively, being a good coach is like being an amateur psychologist. I have learned how to see games and tactics, and how to talk to people. You have to bear in mind I'm a qualified teacher and I've been an advanced coach since 1979 – I'm now a Level 4 coach. I played for Lancashire seconds from when I was 16, I then had 17 years there, two at Durham, played 20-odd Tests, 20-odd ODIs, a full World Cup, so I have all the bits – a lot of bits. Those bits can then be adapted to help players, whatever their personality or character.

Take wicketkeeper James Foster. He was another unbelievable talent, picked for England far too early and then,

I felt, treated badly by Duncan Fletcher, which ended his international career. Right from the start, Fozzy would catch things you shouldn't get anywhere near. He hated dropping the ball – you could see him getting angry on the pitch – and I thought this could be a problem, so I asked him one day: 'You know when you tell yourself off when you've done something wrong? Do you ever congratulate yourself when you've taken a blinder?'

'No,' he replied, 'because I'm not supposed to.'

'Hang on a minute,' I said. 'If you drop three balls all day, you're three-nil down. And if you do that the whole time, you're in the negative. Over a period of days, weeks, months, it's going to weigh on you. You cannot live in the negative. So what you have to do is congratulate yourself every time you take a good one. At the end of the day you might have taken eight good ones and missed three bad ones, but you're eight-three up. Overall, you haven't had a perfect day, but you've had a good day. If you don't congratulate yourself on the good ones, every day you've had a bad day. You need to do that over a period of time to keep your head in a good space, otherwise you're going to go downhill.'

All the time I was focused on helping to fulfil the students' potential. I never wanted to make them into anything. I just wanted to them to be themselves, explore their limits and boundaries. If you chase perfection as a coach it's pointless. If I'd have made Andy Strauss bat like me, or think like me, he'd have had a Test average like me. But I didn't, I encouraged him to be himself. Why put a limit on anybody? Be yourself. And if you can fulfil your potential, no matter what it is, even if it's only county second XI, then, as my dad taught me, you can always hold your hands up and say you made the best of yourself. You can be a proud man. But if you only play county cricket and your potential was international cricket, then you should be disappointed.

One of the most talented lads I ever had was Robin Martin-Jenkins. I thought he could have been an international batsman and bowler, a striking all-rounder for England, but he didn't, in my view, have the ambition. He appeared quite happy playing for Sussex, and enjoying his family life. He probably doesn't view it the same way, because he had a good career at county level, but to me he could have been playing instead of Andrew Flintoff, because he was a better batsman and a better bowler. It makes me a little bit frustrated, because I could see how much ability he had. It oozed out of him. I took him to one side and actually spelled it out to him in the indoor nets once.

I said: 'MJ, if you go back to Sussex and you get forty-odd, fifty wickets in the summer, you're going to go on an A tour and you're one step away from playing for England. But that doesn't start in the summer. It starts now, in these nets. I've just watched you bowl six shit balls. You have to focus. You have to pretend you're playing in a game. You have to be professional even in this indoor net in January. Now come on, get your arse in gear.'

He half took it on board. Perhaps it's not for me to say, but he seemed like he was only a cricketer when he put his boots on. He never spent any time working things out. And I can sympathise with that. He made his choices, and did what he's done, and if he's content and happy then brilliant. But to me, I could see so much in him.

Straussy was different. I didn't see him play for the first two years, because it was before the centre of excellence started, so I didn't know what he'd been like. What I did know, I liked. He had a dry sense of humour, was quite quiet, and was always considered in his speech. I didn't look at him and think he was going to captain England, but I knew he had massive hand-eye coordination and talent. I saw him play in goal one day for his college football team. He had his rugby boots on, Middlesex tracksuit bottoms split from ankle to groin, a 1970s goalkeeping jumper, and his gloves were a pair of yellow Marigolds. He took a goal kick, scuffed it, and it hit their centre forward straight in the chest on the edge of the area. The forward let it drop, half-volleyed it back towards the goal, and Straussy leapt miles in the air, got his hand to it, and tipped it over for a corner. It was unbelievable. He got everything wrong but they couldn't score, because he just had this natural agility.

He could play golf with a single-figure handicap, be in the first XV at rugby. He was a ball player. Anything like that, he'd got it. You could see it in him, but nobody knew how good he was going to be. Far from it. One day, we were sitting in the pavilion at the Racecourse ground at Durham. I was telling some story, and he was padded up because he was next in. A wicket fell, and out he went. First ball he hit straight at mid-wicket and set off running. He was run out by eight yards. He just kept going, straight past the stumps, straight off the field, through the door, into the pavilion, and sat down on the very same stool where he'd been two minutes ago. 'Sorry about that, Foxy. I don't think I was switched on.' It was absolutely hilarious.

But that was what he was like – he needed to wake up and focus. But in the end he did that himself. Eventually, he realised there was more to being a professional batsman than he first thought. I explained to Straussy it was no good playing six great shots and then getting out. That wasn't his job. His job was to occupy the crease and accumulate, then eventually he might be able to score six fours in an over. But it was not what he was there for; he was there for the long haul and needed to play high-percentage shots – shots that 99 times out 100 are going to be good – and even 99 times out of 100 is not good enough because it means you have faced only 100 balls. If your strike rate is between 40 and 60, as it generally is in first-class cricket, and you've faced 100 balls, you've only got 40-odd. You haven't got a big score. Straussy was receptive to this kind of advice, and he said it started him thinking about his game. I never wanted to tell people how to play, because that's their performance, but I wanted to give them the science bit behind it, and for them to use some logic and a little bit of thought as to how they could do it.

In some ways, the person who is a reasonable cricketer but not a great is probably more likely to be a better coach. David Gower was a beautiful player but while he worked on his game, I don't think he could deconstruct it for anyone else. I, however, although I had natural talent, am not a Gower – I knew what I had to do but I couldn't always do it – and so I've always had to break things down, analyse everything, and build them back up again. I can look at the game, especially the batting side of it, and tell what bits aren't quite right. I can tell how to take those bits apart, make them OK, and put them back together so that person can then play their game.

In many ways it's a perfect fit for me. I love helping other people. I love teaching. I love coaching, and I like watching people get better. It's a pleasure to work out what they may need and to sit down and discuss it with them. Hopefully, we can then progress together.

It's for the same reason that I think the most important coaching position in a county club is the second XI, taking people from being good amateurs to being good junior pros, teaching them, helping them to understand what they need to do and achieve. A first XI coach, on the other hand, isn't a nuts-and-bolts coaching job, it's being more of a facilitator. But you need the whole structure in place. I did once get asked by a county, and told them I wanted to be director of cricket, and that I'd want a first XI coach, a second XI coach and an academy coach, and that they would all have to coach my way, so it'd be seamless all the way up. I was told it would be too expensive, but six years later, that's exactly what they put in place.

One of the issues that was never resolved on a permanent basis at the centre of excellence was a sports psychologist. We'd get one for a couple of years and then they'd go, and we'd get another one. There just weren't enough around who understood cricket. You need to understand the game to understand the problems that come with it.

The way it operated was that we'd do an introductory session and then if the students wanted to go to see that person, they'd do so. I didn't want to know whether or not they'd gone or what they'd talked about. I didn't want the psychologist telling me they'd got anxiety issues, confidence issues, motivational issues, because if I knew it would probably influence my decision and I didn't want that. It's not appropriate for me to know anyway. It's their head, their territory. I felt it was like doctor/patient confidentiality.

A lot of sports psychologists say you need to feel confident to perform. I disagree. You don't need to feel confident at all, especially playing cricket, because the game breaks down so easily that all you have to do is play each ball as it comes along. You just need to believe in your ability because you've done it so many times before. But that belief is not an emotion. It's just something you have at the back of your mind. There are days when you wake up and think you don't want to play, because you're batting like an idiot, but you can put that out of your head, focus on each ball, and get a scratchy 50. You can wake up, feel on top of the world, get a quick 25, and then smash one to long-off. How you feel is not necessarily a reflection of your performance.

For me, a lot of the psychology of cricket surrounds a basic question: how do you put yourself in a comfortable place? I don't believe you have to be massively confident. You simply need the ability to be yourself, not get wound up with things. I remember for a while I couldn't get past 26. One day I got to 24 and I had this stupid thought about making sure I didn't hit a two. And then I realised: 'Don't be a fucking idiot. The universe does not care about the number twenty-six. It is not influencing your life, your cricket, it is just a number. Stop it.' Because your head plays tricks with you like that.

It was like I'd gone back to being a kid again. Back then, I used to count number plates; I'd read a number plate on a car and say it to myself three times. I don't know where that came from, but it got to such a stage it became an obsession. I can remember saying to myself: 'I am not doing this anymore. Ever.' It wasn't that I thought something bad would happen if I didn't, it had just become a habit. Immediately after I had that thought, a car went past and I shut my eyes so I wasn't tempted to look. I did that for a bit and eventually I was able to look at cars, and number plates, without repeating them. Now I can look at a number plate and it's simply a number plate. But it's amazing how many people do things like that and they escalate.

The only superstition I had was not to have any superstitions, because they are pointless. They don't impact on anything – they can only be negative. I've seen superstitions destroy people. Don't have them. If I heard someone saying they couldn't find their lucky shirt, I told them there was no such thing as a lucky shirt! It's a shirt. It doesn't possess powers.

I saw it with team-mates, too, who felt they had to have the same spot in the changing-room to get dressed there. What? No, you don't. And all the business about not moving from your seat because it'll make something bad happen out in the middle, I never had any of it. People would tell me to sit still, but I'd say: 'No, it's completely irrelevant. If you want to stay in the same place, fine. But you're not forcing your stupid superstitions on to me. I'm not doing it. Why do you think the universe cares? It doesn't.' You can put superstition on the same level as religion – and fairy stories.

But then cricket is a game that seems forever destined to believe that real life can be affected by made-up concepts. Take this idea of 'momentum' – there are popular phrases that I really don't like, and that is one of them. I don't believe in momentum at all. What is it? The thing about cricket is every day is a new session, and every game is a new game. Just because you played well in the last game, there's no guarantee you're going to play well in this one. In fact, if anything it can be a distraction, because you can believe that because you won that one, you're going to piss this one as well.

As an individual, I think you can have momentum through an innings or through a bowling spell. If you're batting, you can get into a rhythm and your timing is good; if you're bowling, you can be in a good rhythm and putting it exactly where you want. You can have momentum like that. But as a team, that's a load of nonsense. It just doesn't work. If momentum is such a big thing, how come you can lose a Test match, win the next one, and then lose the next? It's just crap. To anyone who believes this stuff about momentum, I'd simply ask them to break it down and explain what it means and how it works. If something doesn't make sense and you can't define what it is, don't use it.

Another phrase I cannot stand is when someone tells a slow bowler to 'get it above the batsman's eye line'. Can anybody tell me what that means? Matt Maynard, the former England batsman, now Somerset coach, a man I love to bits, uses it, and he had it from Duncan Fletcher. But getting the ball above the batsman's eye line doesn't mean anything: the ball is just there. Was Joel Garner above the batsman's eye line? Does anybody under 5ft 9in ever get it above the batsman's eye line? It's an expression that simply means nothing.

Then there's 'he's hit it on top of the bounce'. No, he hasn't, because the top of the bounce is usually eight yards past the stumps. 'He's hit that nicely on the rise.' They're all on the rise! The ball's always coming up when you hit it.

These are expressions that nobody has ever actually thought through what they really mean. I would never use such terms in coaching because they don't make sense. I think maybe I might have mentioned this a couple of times at the centre of excellence. Sometimes I'd sit on the grass bank at Durham and watch my players, and occasionally one of them would say to me: 'Good shot that, Fox. He hit that on the up.' Just to wind me up!

I liked having that sort of relationship with my students. When I went back to work after my first serious episode of depression, I never wondered what they were going to think of me – not that I thought they would be judgemental. As a cricketer you get used to people having opinions of you. A lot of cricket writers thought I couldn't bat, but I didn't care about their opinion. Even when team-mates told me in the dressing room that I'd played a shit shot, in my own mind I could say: 'Well, hang on a minute, when did you ever open the batting?'

I've never bothered what people thought about me. In my younger days I would wear clothes that other people would view as ranging from ridiculous to garish, but I was always my own person. My attitude was: 'What's it got to do with you? I don't really like how you dress, but I'm not saying anything.'

I still have two pairs of PVC trousers, a pair of leathers, and a pair of suede. I've got some furry, black and white cow pants too. What I cared more about was when other people's opinions put barriers in the way of my coaching. Especially ones that were unhelpful, unnecessary, and made very little sense to anybody.

CHAPTER 17

UNLEVEL

Right from the start, I've always believed in the value of qualifications, be they as a cricket coach or otherwise. I finished at Durham University in 1978, and a year later, at Bisham Abbey, they did the first coaching course just for cricket professionals. Bob Ratcliffe asked if I'd go with him. I wasn't sure, but it was only for a week and he persuaded me it would be good. One thing that swung it for me was I realised if I had a qualification, when I went abroad I was qualified to coach kids, and then I could earn some money.

I turned up to find myself among all these gnarly old pros. There were quite a few murmurings, as some thought I'd only been in the game two minutes. But I'd just qualified as a teacher, so I knew what I was doing better than anyone, like how to get the kids to sit down: 'Stop. Face me. Put the ball on the floor.' Simple. Funnily enough, once they'd seen I could do things like that, they all wanted to talk to me about how I got the kids to do what I wanted, and how to write a lesson plan. It all changed round.

So when the ECB came up with its elite Level 4 qualification, it was by no means my natural standpoint to find myself dead set against doing it. The idea of Level 4, in the words of the ECB, was to 'equip coaches working in, or aspiring to work in, the high-performance environment'. It fits in with this idea that there should be a career path in coaching; that's where Level 4 comes from, so that those who achieve it can have a good job. And that suits some people – but it doesn't necessarily make them good coaches. There are great coaches who have done Level 3, which is more hands-on and actually about playing cricket, who are totally unsuited to Level 4 because it's all pen on paper. Not everyone is academic. There are people in cricket from all backgrounds, but Level 4 made no allowance for that. All the centre of excellence coaches had to do it. There were people there who wanted to do it, and that's fair enough, but it's not for everyone and there should be some acceptance of that.

You don't need Level 4 to be a coach at a county, but there are some in cricket who see it as the way to go, a pathway to the top. The problem with that is it ignores knowledge accrued over time. All too often experience counts for nothing. Instead there's this insistence that you have to have the right qualifications to coach. Michael Holding once agreed to come and do some bowling coaching for me. When it came to it, though, he couldn't, because he didn't have the relevant qualification. Ian Botham can't coach, or Viv Richards, because they haven't got the necessary qualification. Truly ridiculous.

Level 4 was based on the Australian system. For a time,

anything Australian we copied. If the Australians stood in a bucket of shit at the end of every day, we'd have done the same thing. So that's where Level 4 came from – except of course then the Australians went and scrapped theirs.

By the time Level 4 came along, I'd been coaching at Durham University for ten years, had thought of the centre of excellence, was a qualified teacher, and had my cricket career. I felt I had sufficient experience that I knew what I was doing. Then, all of a sudden, head of cricket at the MCC John Stephenson told me I had to do Level 4. To say I was unenthusiastic would be an understatement. I said to him: 'What about grandfathers' rights? Why should I have to do it? It's taking me away during the winter when I should be coaching the lads.' But there was no escape.

It soon became apparent I'd have quite a few issues with Level 4, as the course had many flaws that meant I thought it was entirely unsuited to the job it was trying to do. For example, one of the first sessions we had was to identify different learning styles. We worked out there were 16. And then, for the next two years, we got just one – lectures.

We were also told if you can coach one sport, you can coach any other. I inherently disagree with that, but we had to go and coach somebody from a different sport. For me it was a rugby player, kicking. I worked out that his problems stemmed from him not extending his thought process to the follow-through. It was a principle I could apply from batting. His foot was like a bat. It had to come through consistently and have a follow-through. But that was not an example of me coaching rugby, I was dealing with a specific issue, looking at the mechanics. Of course there are some transferences between sports – man management for example – but can you imagine me teaching someone how to serve at tennis? No idea. Or football? It's like me talking about the intricacies of fast bowling. Nine times out of ten, I coach fast bowling from the point of view of the batsman: 'This is what I wouldn't want you to do.' Because I realised I lacked in that area, I wasn't going to intrude. Instead I'd bring in Alan Walker from Durham CCC during the winter.

These bits of nonsense cropped up again and again. At one point, Kevin Shine presented a three-day module. His first sentence as ECB fast bowling coach was: 'Over the years my coaching of fast bowling has evolved. I now coach completely differently to how I coached four years ago.'

'Hang on a minute,' I said. 'Does that mean there are Level 4 coaches out there who are using the method you taught four years ago which you now no longer agree with?'

He was stuck now, wasn't he? Matt Maynard added: 'So why should we believe a word you say now? You might change your mind in six months.'

It wasn't the way to start off, not with our group anyway, because we had some very inquisitive people. We developed a reputation as being really awkward, but I saw it differently. We weren't awkward, we challenged. We weren't there to be spoon fed. How do you improve if you just accept everything you're told? I've always told my kids the same thing, and the lads at the university: 'Don't believe what I say. Think about it, question it, let's have a conversation.'

So we challenged everybody that came along, and highlighted any inconsistencies. We asked Kevin Shine: 'Do you need to get off the back foot as quickly as possible in the delivery stride?'

He said not, so Matt Maynard piped up: 'Well, that's not what the biomechanics bloke said. He said you have to get off it as fast as possible. So which one is it?' They put themselves in some corners. You can't be dishing out contradictory information.

Another problem with Level 4 is it's very wide-ranging, and it gets broader the higher up you go. I don't know any other profession where that happens. The way it generally works is things get more specialised. If I was a doctor in orthopaedics, for example, I'd specialise in knees or shoulders. A solicitor would specialise in certain areas of the law. And yet in cricket they made Level 4 broader. We had assessments on everything – biomechanics, coaching styles, the works – and not one on batting, bowling or fielding.

A friend who was on the course pointed out: 'Anybody who's just done a sports degree would piss Level 4, and they might never have picked a bat up.' And he was right. You don't need to know anything about cricket to pass it. It is all about managing players, situations, how to embrace coaching styles. Some of it's useful, but a lot of the time I wondered what the point was. I'm not saying I didn't learn stuff on it, I did, like the personality profiling of the Myers Briggs assessment system, but if you've got a structured pathway, surely you should have a specific goal at the end.

In one session we were told, right at the beginning, in order to understand biomechanics you need to do a three-year degree. We then got two days. Then, at the end of one of the assessments, they told us: 'You're not qualified to do this, but we want you to put together a twelve-month fitness programme.'

I put my hand up: 'But you've just told us we're not qualified to do it.'

'Well, get your strength and conditioning coach to help you.' I didn't understand why my strength and conditioning coach at Durham should be given some homework when it was me doing the course. Then someone else put their hand up to say he hadn't got a strength and conditioning coach, so how was he supposed to do it. Clearly it was flawed.

But it had happened before. When I was studying for my Level 3 we had a course on 'How To Bat Against Spin'. Mike Gatting was there at the time so they asked him to demonstrate, and he did. It was bloody brilliant, as you'd expect. When he'd finished, the bloke in charge said we should break for coffee. But Gatt said: 'Hang on, that's only one way of playing spin. Foxy played a completely different way.'

'Yes, but we haven't time now.'

Phil Simmons, the former West Indies all-rounder and coach, spoke up. 'But I want to hear how Foxy plays spin.' He was told to have a drink with me in the bar that evening. Really? In the end, I never got to tell anybody.

I don't know why these things have to happen like this. It's like the answer is too bloody obvious for anyone to see. The stupidity is that both me and Gatt got double hundreds against spinners in India. They'd listened to one side, but they hadn't listened to the other. And that's without going into the intricacies of there being two sorts of left-handed batsmen. Gower was a right-handed left-hander, so was Clive Lloyd. Allan Border and Neil Fairbrother were left-handed left-handers who cut and pulled and swept. It makes such a difference.

I'd been having these thoughts about the system for a while.

When I was doing Level 3, I had a conversation with two other blokes, one who was head of sport at a school, and another who coached Under-15s. 'This is why it's wrong,' I said, 'because if us three applied for a job in a school to coach junior cricket, who's going to get the job? I am, purely because I've played Test cricket and it's a name for the school. But they're making the worst choice possible. I'm not very good at coaching young kids. You two would be brilliant. That's why this system is wrong.'

The best way to work it, in my opinion, would be if someone can reach Level 3 in either an ability range, or an age range. If they then go up to Level 4 as a coach, it should be as someone who specialises in something – in my case, it could be left-handed batting. Others might get Level 4 in left-arm spin, or whatever. If somebody wants to run a camp within their school, or an emerging players' programme at an academy, or a county, and they want a specialist, they should be able to look down a list of Level 4 coaches and pick out who would be best suited to their needs. For me that is an inherent flaw in the system we have.

At the start of the Level 4 course, everybody should identify which direction they want to go in. I would be a left-handed batting coach, but the bloke sitting next to me might want to be a wicketkeeping specialist. We would do the general stuff together and then my dissertation would be about being a left-handed batting coach. He would lead the wicketkeeping section, with the coaches, and his dissertation would be about his specialism. That way you would have people working in specific areas. At the end of that course, you would have 12 unique dissertations which would add to the body of knowledge that everybody has. So, as a coach, if I'm stuck on something like left-arm spin bowling, I'd be able to go back to the Level 4 archives and get a dissertation done by a left-arm spinner so I can pick his brain by reading it.

To me that makes far more sense than everybody doing everything, with no actual work on cricket. Why should I have pieces of work to do on psychology, strength and conditioning, learning styles, and not one piece on batting, bowling or fielding? That didn't make sense to me. There needs to be a lot more talking about the game, how to play the game, the intricacies of it, and how we can help teach those to people.

On the course with me were people like Grant Flower, Matthew Maynard, John Morris and Steve Kirby. Mark Lane was the coach of the most successful England team that we had at the time – the women – and they were making him do Level 4. We should have been listening to him. We had this fantastic group of people and yet we never had an open forum. They never came to us and asked how they might improve this. They looked at us as a naughty group, who would challenge them. They didn't look at us as a really exciting opportunity to get some insight. We ended up behaving like naughty kids. We used to draw cocks on the board.

Back in the day, when I was learning how to be a teacher, I was told that in every class there's probably somebody more intelligent than you, the only difference is you have more experience, and I believe that. By contrast, on that course it was obvious that we had more expertise about the game than 99 per cent of the people who were talking to us. There were never any discussions in class between Grant Flower, John Morris, Matthew Maynard, me and everybody else. We were viewed as a rebel cohort, as a difficult group – I suppose I was one of the main reasons. In the end, all Level 4 really did was confirm that most of the stuff I was doing was right but I'd just done it from a different angle.

So we now have a lot of people who are Level 4 coaches, but they haven't had to do any analysis of cricket to get their qualification. It's like saying someone's got an O-level – totally meaningless. When it comes to cricket coaching, there are people trying to reinvent the wheel.

Next time I saw John Stephenson, out of mischief I said to him: 'You realise I'm the most qualified coach in England now? Well, who else is a qualified PE teacher, had my career, and got Level 4? Nobody. Are you going to make the other Level 4 coaches become teachers as well? How long have you been running MCC? Are they going to make you do an MBA?' I was just winding him up. Point made.

In the end, it would make no difference. Level 4 or not, my coaching days at the centre of excellence were numbered. In the background they were planning a change there was no way at all I could countenance.

CHAPTER 18

SHUTDOWN

They closed the centres of excellence in 2014. To my mind, that's a disaster for English cricket.

The beauty of the idea was that it allowed students to take a degree and progress their cricket at the same time. They didn't, as I did, have to make a choice, facing the possibility of sacrificing one for the other. A lot of my desire to set up a centre of excellence was born out of the fact that, even by the time I'd finished my career, nothing had changed. I'd had to go through this situation in the 1970s, but why, in the mid-1990s, did other people?

The thing is some people don't get the concept. Mike Gatting's belief, for instance, is if you're good enough to play cricket, you should go straight to a county. But times have changed! When it comes to these lads, some parents have paid a lot of money to give them the ability to go to a high-class university, get a qualification, because you can't even apply for a lot of jobs these days unless you've got a degree. What happens if you've got a really bright lad, and he's good at cricket, like Andrew Strauss? Do you think he should just abandon his education and go and play cricket? What if he doesn't make it, or picks up a bad injury, and he's 24, 25, what's he going to do then? He's missed the boat. He's at the back of the queue. Is he really going to take that risk? I've seen people fall out of love with cricket and I've seen people not get where they want, but if they'd been to the centre of excellence they had a degree behind them, so they weren't lost. They went and did something else.

Somebody once complained that there was quite a high failure rate from cricketers who'd been to universities. I was baffled; they'd totally missed the point. They often don't stay in the game long because they have options! If they didn't have a degree they'd have to struggle along as a journeyman for as long as they could. And also, if they aren't going to achieve what they want, they do the game a benefit by not clogging the system up. How many ways do you want to have it?

Alex Loudon played one-day international cricket, moved from Kent to Warwickshire, and got to a point where he just had enough. Fine. What's wrong with that? Neither Michael Brown of Surrey nor David Brown of Gloucestershire and Glamorgan quite got to where they wanted to go. David said to me: 'I've retired, Fox. I'm just hanging on. I want to be an accountant.' Brilliant. Good luck to him. They both went as far as they could with their cricket and moved on. That's the whole reason I set up the centre of excellence. What it did was safeguard people's security for the future. If you take Mike

Gatting's view that you should leave education at 18 and go and play cricket, David and Michael Brown would have been knackered at 26. But, because they've got degrees, they were able to go and get the job they want and have worked for.

It is so sad to see that option has realistically gone. It's taken the game back 19 years and more, but there'd been hostility to the idea from the start. Initially, all TCCB chief executive Ossie Wheatley appeared to do was pull it to pieces. Eventually, I did what I did with Barry Wood and absolutely blew up at him: 'All you can do is be negative about this. You rip everything apart, don't offer anything constructive. Do you know how to make this centre of excellence better? No. But I do.' At which point I stood up and walked out of the meeting.

I went outside the hotel where we'd all gathered, absolutely fuming. Terry Bates, a former teacher who worked at Lord's for the National Cricket Association, came outside and calmed me down. He agreed with me, if not my approach. 'I'm not quite sure that's the way to go about it,' he said. I went back in, but I didn't apologise. However, something must have clicked somewhere. At the same time as Durham started, they decided they were going to set up five more, at Cambridge, Cardiff, Leeds, Loughborough and Oxford.

A lot of the counties didn't understand what I was doing either. There were even some who objected to Durham University getting money for the centre. I wrote to one chief executive: 'We've got one of your contracted players. Would you care to contribute to what we're doing with him? Because we're trying to prepare him to play at your county.'

I was a bit naïve – I got a letter back saying not only would he not contribute but we'd had money given to us which should have gone to the counties anyway. Oh, right OK. Thanks very much. Weirdly enough, three years later he thanked me for what I'd done with the self-same player.

I tried to organise practice fixtures against Durham for my centre of excellence, because they were next door, but it was the ECB who, when we had six centres on board and they had all reached the necessary standard, announced three first-class matches each against the 18 counties. It wasn't something I supported. I said to ECB director of operations John Carr: 'We don't want to be first-class. It's going to cause a lot of problems. Why don't you create a level and call it A Class, like they used to do in South Africa? Then everybody knows what it is?' No. It had to be first-class.

There'd been arguments ever since I can remember that Oxford and Cambridge shouldn't be considered as first-class. This was a perfect opportunity to take that status away from them and start again with six centres playing practice matches against counties. But instead they eventually made us all first-class. Instead of getting rid of the problem, they made it worse. So people started talking about that rather than what the games were all about.

We played one game, the first time we were first-class, against Durham at Chester-le-Street on a green one in April and were bowled out for 67. We hadn't had any practice matches. They, like most counties at that time of year, had a full team out. Everything was stacked against us.

After a few years, when all six UCCEs were first-class, the ECB then did something really bizarre. We had three three-day games, but only two of them were first-class and the last one wasn't. The reasoning was that the last game was later in the season and the counties wouldn't be putting out a strong side. Really? They're still a first-class county.

It was a bit of a nonsense, but it was still an absolute thrill for my lads to play first-class cricket. The funny thing was we often performed better in the first-class games than we did against the other universities. I used to say to my lads: 'The only difference between their team and you is experience. Mark Chilton of Lancashire was playing here three years ago. So was Will Smith at Durham, Luke Sutton. And we've got younger legs. We know we're fitter than they are.' All my lads used to go back to counties and come top of the fitness tests.

All that's by the by now. They're not centres of excellence anymore, and to me that comes down to finance: it was always a battle to get the money. There were always a lot of old boys at the MCC querying the expense. No matter how much they were told what was happening, their response was always to look at the cost. It was really iffy getting the scheme through the finance committee – John Stephenson worked tirelessly time and time again – and in the end someone decided it was not worth it. The reason behind it, I suspect, is that the redevelopment of Lord's is going to cost £120 million.

Funding for the centres came originally from the Cricket Foundation, the charitable arm of the ECB, as part of a three-year pilot. Then they decided it was going to work, so they gave us funding for a further year while we organised the other centres. I managed to persuade the MCC to put some money in as well, so for a while we had a joint venture between them both. But as soon as the MCC put some money in, the ECB withdrew the equivalent amount. Eventually, the ECB said it couldn't afford it and so the MCC took it on. It was their largest single expense in this country, adding up to three quarters of a million a year, but the centres of excellence gave the MCC a purpose in the UK. There was a connection with them – the MCC ground staff, if you think about it, was essentially the first centre of excellence.

I got local sponsorship too for a while and the university used to put some money in. What should have happened is that the ECB should have funded the scheme from day one. It should have been an established pathway. Those who don't want to go into higher education go one way, into the counties, those who want to go to university go to an ECB-accredited university. In the end, the MCC changed the system, making it more community-based, diluting the excellence and reducing the funding. The only way the scheme has carried on is by altering it so it falls into line with the ECB's expansion of participation programme. The MCC decided they wanted to make it more broad-based, and overall what that's done is kill the top – the part of the programme that is going to produce players capable of playing first-class cricket.

When I put the scheme together in 1996, it had one aim – to help produce English cricketers for first-class and beyond. I ran it that way, and that's what it was. From Durham University alone we sent more than 60 players into first-class cricket. Several went on to play for England, including Alex Loudon, James Foster, Andy Strauss, Nick Compton, Caroline Atkins and Holly Colvin. It just pigging works, to the extent that two years ago 23 per cent of all county cricketers had been to one of the six centres. Of those, eight per cent had been to Durham. Nineteen players from the centres of excellence have gone on to be county captains, six from Durham University, including Will Smith who captained Durham to the county championship, and Strauss who captained England to a first away Ashes win in 25 years.

That's without mentioning the cascade effect that occurs with those players if they go into coaching, become regional development officers, analysts, or even if they become a solicitor and go on to start a children's section at their club. You can't measure that kind of thing financially.

But the MCC decided they were going to change it. They wanted to make the scheme more community-based. The ECB is panicking that participation numbers are going down, so that's what they're trying to work on, and the MCC has followed suit.

Going into mass participation is fine, and it's vital to get people interested, but you have to look after the good ones as well. Instead of just being about excellence, the person running the centre now has to look after all of the teams. Durham University has got three men's and two women's teams. How can you look after five teams? On top of that, the centre is also involved in running the development programme for women, which means getting girls started in the game, and running a community programme, when the ECB was doing all the cricket in the community stuff anyway.

I spent my whole time working with 20-odd players, trying to turn them into first-class cricketers. Now that very obviously isn't the case. Yes, the centres will still play first-class games – although it's open to question how long that will last – but the players aren't attending somewhere that is based purely on excellence. How can it be? By the time everything else has been covered, there won't be the time. To turn players into first-class country cricketers isn't something you do a couple of hours a week. It's time intensive. It's not just about a bit of training and practice, you need to get to know a player as a person; that was always very important to me. You can't treat all players the same, as one big lump; it doesn't work. Cricket is a mental game and you have to understand those you're working with to see what makes them tick. I built up very close relationships with my players – I'm still in touch with a lot of them, and I've been to their weddings. How can you possibly have that closeness, that vital understanding, now?

The MCC said that in their view they'd bolstered the scheme. What in fact they've done is changed it so that what I set up does not exist anymore. It's gone from excellence, which is one thing, to umpteen separate things. I didn't want to do that, and that's why I left. Once the MCC had announced the changes, that was it for me. The university had to say they agreed because otherwise the MCC would surely have cut their funding. Their hands were tied. What were they going to do?

It's been hard. I went through a prolonged period of depression after it happened. I've had to try not to dwell on it and instead dismiss it from my head. It's done. Gone. It's like when people ask me stupid questions: 'Do you still keep in contact with your first wife?' or 'Do you keep in contact with your first primary school teacher?' No. That's finished, move on. It's like when I finished playing; I didn't think one thing had ended, I thought something else was beginning. And I'm like that now. I know it has ended, but something else will open up.

I'm not sure how many great ideas I've had in life, but the centre of excellence was one. I know I've had a bigger influence as a coach than as a player. As a cricketer, they're just my runs, my catches. I helped win some games, but as an influence over the sport, that's bigger as a coach. You're in touch with people, helping them develop, and of that I'm proud. The real sadness is that for many young cricketers it's gone back to the situation I faced in 1975. Do I want to go to university or do I want to play cricket? Lads will have to make this choice again now.

A lot of young men would rush at that opportunity to join a county club, and a lot of counties pressurise them to do so, and I think that's bloody awful. They have a duty of care. How dare they limit someone's future? I've seen plenty of players, even successful ones, drift off at the end of their playing days and not know what to do. It almost ends their life. They've lost that kudos and status, they've stopped doing what they wanted to do, and they quickly realise the friends they thought were real were actually just fairweather. So what are they going to do? People leave and drive vans for a living, sell detergents. But what's going on inside their heads?

Mental health in cricketers is no better or worse than in the rest of the population, it's just more noticeable, and it's the first three years after a player's career has finished that are the most difficult. The PCA has produced a transition manual which helps guide players through the period from being professional cricketers back into, for want of a better expression, the real world. But it's a process that should start way before you finish. You shouldn't be sacked on Friday afternoon and then be thinking: 'What am I going to do now?' Some county clubs are looking into that and helping players do courses, and that's how it should be, but in earlier times there was nothing, which was why I went to university, to get a qualification to take the pressure off.

That foresight came from my dad. 'Get as much education as you can,' he told me. 'It doesn't matter how far you go, they can't take it off you. It will be useful.'

I decided to do a course I enjoyed, and went off to qualify to be a PE teacher. To have had the opportunity to go to Durham University, and to have turned it down for a cricket contract at Lancashire, my dad wouldn't have said anything but I know inside I would have deeply upset him. For me, though, it wasn't a quandary. I'd made up my mind to go to university to get some qualifications. In those three years my cricket didn't really progress, but I learnt a lot – how to use my brain, organise things and, by doing PE, the acquisition of skill, little bits of psychology. I loved it. It helped me organise my thoughts. It was absolutely central to how I lived the rest of my life.

And that's the thing, young people are not going to chuck their future away. So if you stop the centres of excellence, as they have done, the lads are still going to go to university, and in the meantime the game has lost all that talent. It might look from the outside that someone can still go to university, attend a centre of excellence, and go into first-class cricket, but that ignores how much everything has changed. The whole idea has been diluted so much that it can't possibly work anymore. The new system won't give them the same chance to be in a specific centre of excellence where they can advance their cricket alongside their education. Eventually, they'll disappear from the game. In ten years, the powers that be are going to be asking where that group of players has disappeared to.

Will Smith, aged 18, came to Durham University because of the centre of excellence. He never missed a session for three years, did microbiology and chemistry, got a high 2:1, and captained Durham to the county championship. If Will Smith was aged 18 now, he's not going to miss out on going to university, but his cricket is not going to progress like it did. In the end he might feel he hasn't got much future in this game, and head off to do something else.

At a centre of excellence we could do things that county cricket clubs didn't – devise proper fitness plans, get sports psychologists in, advise players on media, analyse them on videos. That was all part of the package. Andrew Strauss was starting his third year when the centre of excellence began and he said at the time that Durham University was more professional than Middlesex. By his own admission, what the centre of excellence did was start him thinking about his game, which is the most important thing. It kick-started him.

At Beefy's 60th birthday party, when I told former England selector Geoff Miller about the centres of excellence closing, he was gobsmacked. He hadn't realised. It's my bet Andrew Strauss didn't know either, because as England's director of cricket he'd have so many other things on his plate. It's sad more than anything else. When James Foster found out, he sent me a lovely text: 'Glad I was part of it, Fox. This is the end of an era.'

Will Smith once said to Sarah: 'Foxy's made me the man I am.' Admittedly, he was a bit drunk at the time, but it was a very nice thing to say, and even if only some of that is true, fine. Last year, I was asked to go down to London to meet some of the lads from down the years. I was expecting to meet a handful of them for a drink. There were literally dozens. They presented me with a book of memories. It was one of the most humbling moments of my life.

But now it's gone. Chucked away.

The awful thing is there'll be students at Durham now who have specifically gone there because I coach cricket. Essex used to encourage their batsmen to go to Durham, and their bowlers to go to Loughborough, because of the late Graham Dilley's involvement there. It's just so sad. I'm just hoping Andrew Strauss doesn't let it die.

CHAPTER 19

NO FUTURE?

The closure of the centres of excellence doesn't mean my brain has shut down, too. I've still got plenty of ideas how to take the game forward – because it needs to if it's to survive in a changing world with lots of different interests competing for our time and attention. It's no use saying cricket has been around for 300 years. If we're not careful, in a fraction of that time it could be gone.

Right up there for me is the belief that for the game to have a future, it has to become waterproof. It might sound odd, but there's strong evidence to say it rains more at weekends than it does during the week. Pollutants build up on weekdays and then, when there's less traffic on the roads at weekends, it rains. So for club cricketers, after being at work all week, when they turn up on Saturday it chucks it down. In a busy life they're soon going to get fed up with being sat in a dressing room all day. At the same time kids will come to the conclusion that there's no point in playing cricket because it rains all the time. Soon enough you're going to have no game to play.

But there is an answer. We have rubber crumb pitches for rugby, sand-based pitches for hockey, artificial pitches for football – we could do the same with cricket. My idea is you have an artificial outfield with a normal grass square. If it doesn't rain, you play on the grass wicket, but on some part of the square there's an artificial wicket too – if it's too wet to start, you play on there. I'm not saying players should switch halfway through, but if they turn up on a Saturday morning and it's raining we should have the technology and ability to make a surface they can play on, a ball they can grip in the wet, and a bat with a plastic coat. It would take a little bit of trial and error, but there are some bright people around. It's not beyond our abilities, is it? Pete Marron used to glue the wickets at Lancashire. They didn't deteriorate and you could play on them for ten days. So if you can glue them, you're not that far off being able to make one that's waterproof. I recognise there'd be a cost element to fitting all-weather pitches, but clubs pay a groundsman every week, so it's swings and roundabouts. And once you've got it, you've got it.

People might think playing in all conditions is a new idea – far from it. There was the Lambert & Butler competition in the early 1980s, six-a-side on artificial pitches at football grounds. Lancashire are still the holders of it, mainly because it was played only once. One of the rules was if it rained the teams carried on. It was a hoot. It did rain a couple of times, and it wasn't the horror show people thought it would be. We played at Stamford Bridge in the final and it was hammering down. We just carried on – nobody bothered. In fact, it actually made it a better wicket because it had more pace in it.

There's obviously limits, as you can't play in a thunderstorm, but how many times do people come off for ten minutes? They should be able to stay on. They don't stop football because it's raining. They don't stop rugby – and rugby is more dangerous than cricket. Hockey is played on an artificial pitch and that's improved the game. The same could happen with cricket. If it's flat and true, how good are your fielders going to have to be? I'm not saying players should wear actual waterproof clothes – it's easy enough to waterproof existing cricket shirts and trousers. I can buy a can of spray from the supermarket and when I put it on a T-shirt it's waterproof.

We have to start looking at this now, because if people are right about global warming, it's only going to get wetter. If we don't do something about it, there isn't going to be any club cricket. And if there's no club cricket, and no country cricket, what are we going to do? It just makes sense: you need to have a waterproof game.

Weather, as any lover of the game will know, is a recurring theme in cricket. It's one of the main ways the game insists on shooting itself in the foot. How can you have players going off for bad light, for example, when there are floodlights? That's a nonsense that has to stop. I don't understand how you play a one-day game under lights, play through the dusk, and yet in Test cricket come off. That doesn't hold true. You can see why it would infuriate the crowd. It would infuriate me.

What we also need to take the game forward is an

international Test schedule which acts like a league. You have one game at home and one away. Within that format you still have space for the Ashes, but the first Test of the series counts towards the league. You could do it all in two years and it would generate a lot of interest. But those who run cricket are obsessed with the Ashes and India. They're just narrowing the game down rather than broadening it. The fixture list is being organised by accountants not sportsmen. Professionally run teams are trapped in an archaic schedule. They need to stop and completely revamp it. You've got to have winners, second, third, fourth. How can you have international Test teams and no winner or runner-up? A ranking system just doesn't cut it. Tennis and golf have ranking systems, but they still have tournaments.

Can you imagine if in the Premier League they just had friendlies all the time and nobody won the league? Kids wouldn't be very interested, would they? And yet that's what's happening in cricket. There needs to be a one-day international league, every four years a World Cup, and a Twenty20 league. Instead, the schedule just aimlessly rolls round and round. Scrap it: we've got the ability to fly in and out. These days, everybody plays all over the world. You don't need the acclimatisation of old, as the wickets are not that different in other countries. Revamp the whole system and it all becomes more interesting, and it would be building towards a climax.

The ICC needs to remember what it's there for. It's an international governing body, so it needs to act like one to help people out. Like with DRS, I'm quite happy with the system so long as it's uniform across the game for every country in every series. There can't be countries opting out. If there's a cost implication for some countries, it's up to the ICC to help them out. There's enough money in the game, and it shouldn't all be channelled towards the stronger nations.

Currently England, Australia and India do the Egyptian breaststroke – they scoop it all in as they're going along. That's wrong. If the ICC wants the game to stop being a minority sport, which it is in global terms, they have to help it grow and develop. I wanted to set up a Chinese centre of excellence when I was at Durham University, the thinking being that those attending the English centre of excellence were going on to get good jobs and a lot of them would end up being quite influential people. You could do the same with Chinese students who come over. I had the green light to do that, but obviously I'm no longer at the university. But that type of thinking is where the future lies.

Cricket can be a global game and probably the best route in, especially in places such as America, is with women playing T20. Women led the way for soccer in America, and I think they can do the same with cricket. The same goes for China. Make the game a global one for women and then it can spread to men. I don't think cricket, nationally or globally, has sat down and worked out a vision for where it wants to be in 15 years. In this country, our focus is dominated by the Ashes, so the series seem to be happening more frequently. But the Ashes in 2015 was far from a great series, with every Test being one-sided. However, England's series against New Zealand provided great entertainment and yet was restricted to two Tests. That's just wrong, isn't it?

There are major decisions being made through very

short-sighted eyes. They seem to change the regulations of each format every year, tinkering with how many close catchers there are, power plays, how many fielders inside the circle. I'm not so much bothered about what the changes are as the fact it makes it impossible for the average spectator to look at the scoreboard and understand where the game is. Once upon a time, in a 50-over match, they used to say get to 30 overs and then, so long as you've got wickets in hand, you can expect to double your score by the end. Now all of a sudden we're told you can double it from 35 overs. That might be great for the scoreboard, but what about the fan who's paid his money and likes the game? If your team is 2-0 up in a football match with five minutes to go, you can be more or less certain you're going to win. But if they doubled the size of the goals for the rest of the match, you wouldn't know whether 2-0 was a good lead or not. That's effectively what they have been doing in cricket: the authorities have taken the ability to understand the game away from people.

Even when I played, I'd walk through the crowd at Old Trafford when there'd been some regulation change and people would ask me what a good score was under the new rules. That should never be the case. Spectators should never be wondering what's happening and who's winning. But if you mess about with the regulations all the time, people will never have a clue. And that's putting aside those coming to the game anew – they're not going to have the faintest idea what's going on. If they ask the person next to them, what are they going to say? 'Well, I knew what was going on last year, but I don't know much about this year. It's all been changed.' Confusion all round.

There's been an endless desire to keep tweaking the rules, trying to inject life into a game that doesn't need it. It's as if they're trying to achieve a win off the last ball of every game, but they've picked the wrong sport. Keep the formats the same, keep the regulations the same, and make it clear that for the next ten years they are not going to change. Then players would be able to get to understand it and develop systems and options. The spectators would understand it a lot better, and people would be able to go to a game and know what's a good score on that ground.

None of this is new. Historically, administrators have always tried to reinvent the game. At Durham, I set up a one-innings two-day competition between centres of excellence and based it on Australian grade cricket. It's a damned good system, because you actually have the ability to bat longer in that format than you do in the three-day format. You can bat into the second morning in the two-day format, whereas normally in the three-day format you would declare before the end of the first day and stick the other side in.

We'd been playing this for about seven years when somebody from Lord's suggested we changed the format, because it had been in place for that amount of time. I didn't agree with the idea. One, it works, so why mess about with it? And two, players only play it for three years because then they leave university, so what is the point of changing the format? It's like reinventing the wheel. You don't need to. Let the game develop, but let players develop within the game. Within the same game. If everybody knows what the format is, why change it?

The same goes for the county championship. They're

talking about going down to 14 county championship matches, so English players can improve at 'white ball' cricket. But changing down to 14 fixtures would create an uneven contest because not all the teams would play each other home and away.

I think a lot of tinkering, with the one-day game in particular, is due to the media, especially the visual media. They're forever inventing stats. Don't get me wrong, the Sky coverage is fantastic and it's progressed the game beyond belief, but occasionally you can't help thinking they're encouraging people to think a period of a game is dull, and it's not really, not if you go through the intricacies of what's going on.

There was the widely stated belief for a while that the middle overs of a 50-over game are boring. No, they're not; not if you appreciate cricket. They're the ones that really matter. If you lose your way in those middle overs, you've lost the game. To say those overs are boring is just not right. But what happens is people pick up on a particular school of thought, and it escalates. I'm not saying it started on television, but it started somewhere, and then all of a sudden there's a feeling everywhere – the spoken media, the written media, the visual – that it's true.

Constant analysis has changed how players are viewed, too. I heard someone say of Jos Buttler: 'He's a finisher – we only want him in in the last four overs.' Really? Can you imagine saying that about Viv Richards? I don't think so. You want him in as early as possible. Administrators and the media create all these little things rather than just letting the game speak for itself. Can you imagine if they had six weeks of boring

Premier League football and then decided to change the rules to make it more exciting? Suddenly, the penalty spot will be closer?

But cricket has a long, long history of this sort of decision. You watch the IPL and the commentators go nuts every time they hit a 'massive' six and then they show it has gone 71 yards. But that's not a six! It's just because they've brought the boundary in. Fair enough, when I played it wasn't unusual that behind the rope was a concrete fence. I saw Richard Ellison dive for a ball at Old Trafford and head-butt a bench that had old-fashioned cast iron legs. It split his head open. So the boundary needs to be in a bit so people can dive with an element of safety. But what they do is bring it in a safe distance and then take another five yards off, too. I see the ball going over somebody's head, but when I played that would have been out. They're putting them on postage stamps to make it more dynamic.

Add in the fact that modern bats are better; quite often the ball goes for six and they haven't even hit it that well. They're getting away with it. I was hitting catches with a new bat one day, and the ball was going ten yards further than before. It felt beautiful. You can't blame the bat manufacturers, but it has changed the game.

It doesn't even end with the on-field regulations. They mess about with things like the ages of players as well. The ECB has all sorts of regulations surrounding the ages of players and the amount of financial subsidy a county receives. But that again skews the game; it affects a county's thinking when selecting a team. An older player might potentially find their career over because it affects a county's income if they appear in the team. That's like a football team with experienced players winning the Premier League and being penalised for it. It doesn't make sense.

I know people question it when they see former players looking back and saying cricket was somehow better or harder when they played, but the only reason I use the phrase 'in my day' is to make comparisons. I loved playing in my era; I'd have loved playing in this one. I just want to make sure there's a game to be enjoyed for everyone in the future. Quite what that game will be lies in the hands of all those who surround it, and that includes the players as much as anyone. Regulations are one thing. The attitudes of those playing under them, and their willingness to cope with the demands of continually switching codes, entirely another.

In my view, there's essentially only two ways to bat. One, my approach, is that every ball is there to be scored off, but if it's a good ball you try to stop it. And the other is: occupy the crease and you'll pick up runs along the way. You can tell which one Boycott was, and you can tell which one Pietersen was. Now we see a situation where Test matches are over in three days, the reason being a lot of players aren't prepared to go and bat for six hours. Is that the influence of the one-day game? Or is it just the modern player has a different thought process?

Alastair Cook has scored so many Test runs and hundreds because he's prepared to grit it out. I keep saying he's one of our best Test players ever. Look at his attitude, determination and application when he's at the crease. It's described as 'old school', but it's old school because it worked. It's a skill learning to be patient. You learn to bat patiently by doing it. When that ball is on its way down, you've got the option of hitting it or defending it. If it's a short-format game, you're going to hit it, but if it's a Test match, you're three down and you're only 180, you're going to block it because you don't want the risk of getting out. You have to play higher percentage shots in Test cricket. But there are a lot of people not doing that. It may be we'll look back in five years and think of this as a blip. It does take time to learn Test cricket, after all, but at the moment few are willing to play the dour old school way. How often do we have five-day Tests? If we reduced the game to four days, would that produce more draws? I'm not sure it would.

Mentally, the short game is easier. In T20, if you have a good 35 balls as a batsman you've made a fifty and played well. After 35 balls in Test cricket you haven't even got in yet. In Test cricket you've got to prepare yourself to bat for five or six hours, maybe longer. In T20, if you're caught at long off third ball you're unlucky. There's no penalty because it's acceptable within the format. Whereas there is a penalty in Test cricket – you played a bad shot, you're out – in T20 few mind if you played a bad shot.

I once held the world record for being on the same score in a first-class match for the longest time – I was on 27 for 80-odd minutes. Lancashire were at Edgbaston, I didn't get a lot of the strike, and when I did, Anton Ferreira, a nice little seamer, was bowling most of the time. I was quite happy, no demons in my head, and I was quite content to stay there. Eventually I got a run, there was an ironic cheer from the crowd. I didn't realise the time I'd not scored was as long as it was. To me, I was happy to be in my office and was actually quite enjoying just being there.

There was something lovely about being comfortable at the crease: I'd find myself moving quite well, picking up the ball, everything going where I wanted it to, middling all my defensive shots, and just feeling really content. This was what I did for a living and I would be relaxed and enjoying it, being out in the middle playing this great game, blue skies, with one of my mates at the other end and other people I know in the opposition. If I played a rash shot I'd have to sit in the dressing room, so I wanted to be out there. That, in a way, restricted my shot selection. When I was playing well, I actually played fewer shots, because the ones I did I selected at the right time and executed them well.

Chris Tavaré had a reputation for being a blocker, not that it bothered me. In fact, when we broke the record for the first wicket against New Zealand at The Oval, he got his ton before me. I'd seen him in county cricket and he could smack a ball all over the place, but in Test matches he took it upon himself to be ultra-conservative. He got 66 not out all day at Perth in 1982-83, but he saved the game for us. Can you imagine if they had Chris Tavaré opening the batting for England now? He'd be a god, because they could rely on him. The opposition would hate it. And in Test matches, because they're five days, occupation is as valuable as runs. Without Tav at Old Trafford in 1981, Beefy said he wouldn't have got that massive hundred against Australia, like without Dilley at Headingley he wouldn't have got that massive hundred there, too. People would rather bowl at Clive Lloyd than Geoff Boycott, because Clive gave you a chance.

A lot of what we're seeing now is down to players being required to make constant transitions between formats. When

I played for Lancashire, we'd play a three-day championship match on Saturday, Monday and Tuesday, with a Sunday League game wedged in between. If you were not out on a Saturday night, and got runs on a Sunday, when you came back on Monday you'd try to smack it out the ground. Your head was still running in one-day mode. I was told by many bowlers: 'Eh, this is first-class. It's not Sunday!' The mentality goes with you, so if you're in a rich vein of form in T20, it must be incredibly difficult to adapt to a first-class match. That's a skill all in itself.

I don't think I'd like to do what they do at the moment, slipping between first-class and T20 then back to first-class again – that must bugger your head about. I can't imagine me being able to play at my best in all three formats. But that's just me. Probably the only person who could do it is someone like Kumar Sangakkara – but then he's one of the best players who's ever lived.

Making a transition wasn't always an option for me. I remember playing in one-day internationals against the West Indies and it wasn't any easier than opening the batting in a Test match. You still had three slips and a gulley, with Michael Holding, Joel Garner and Malcolm Marshall charging in. I remember being told in 1984 that Michael Holding was the 'weak link' in their attack: 'When he comes on, target him.' I was sitting there with Andy Lloyd and we looked at each other: 'Have we just heard that? When Holding comes on, he has to go?' Fucking hell!

T20 has changed the game for everyone – players, administrators, coaches. It's made it massively more complex. When I played, the Test team, with the exception of one or two, played the one-day internationals, and we didn't have T20. Now, do you have one coach for all three formats? One for each? One for Tests and one for limited overs? There's a lot to think about, because the difference between T20 and Test cricket is enormous. But whatever format you're playing, the basics are the basics. If you want to be a cricketer, you need to learn the mechanics of what you do. Once you have those mechanics, be it in a first-class match or a one-day game, how you implement them is up to you. If you look at the players who have thrived in T20 – such as Jos Buttler and Chris Gayle – they do actually have the basics. It's just the choices they make when the ball is on its way.

If I'd tried to play a reverse sweep in the mid-1980s, I'd have got sacked. Now it's something I'd have learnt to do because it would have been natural for me. But I'd still need the basics first. Most people won't succeed if they don't do that. The exception is David Warner, who's done it the other way. Credit to him, he's managed to go from being a T20 specialist to opening the batting for Australia in Test cricket. Even so, he's had to go away and work on the basics. If you went and played Test cricket with nothing but a T20 attitude, I'm not sure you'd last long. Joe Root is an exciting player, but he plays properly and positively. There's a difference between that and trying to smack it out of the ground. Sangakkara, if you watch him, in any form of the game, plays proper shots, he just plays them at a different rate.

In your performance, you have to work out whether you can expand your repertoire yet or not. Greg Chappell had a wonderful way of doing it. He used to hit the ball straight back, and as he batted over time his game, as he put it, 'widthened', until ultimately he could cut and pull. If I didn't know how the wicket was playing, I couldn't play cross-bat shots early on because I wasn't sure of the bounce. You have to work out what you can and can't do, and that might vary every day. The same applies to a Test team: if you decide you want to play a different style you have to be prepared to lose a few – because it is going to go wrong. Try smacking Pakistan's mystery spinners round the ground and you're not playing percentage cricket. You're playing high-risk shots that can bite you on the arse.

I don't look down on T20 – in fact, the way things are going, in 50 years there might not be anything else but T20 – but it isn't my favourite format. If you asked what I'd rather watch, a T20 or a Test match, I'd pick the Test match every time because I like the nuances, and how situations can build or change quickly. But I admire people who play T20. Some of the skills in it are phenomenal. You look on in sheer wonder sometimes. Watching Chris Gayle when he's on form, not only is it incredible to see, but it's world-class coordination at an amazing level. Seeing the very best at it, like Brendon McCullum, is great and it has its place within the game. Yes, there are times when I feel sorry for bowlers, but I know someone like Ian Austin at Lancashire would have been brilliant – he could bowl yorkers at will. In fact, I think our late-1980s Lancashire team would have been unbelievable at T20 – Neil Fairbrother, Mike Watkinson, Phillip DeFreitas, Wasim Akram, we'd have had one hell of a side.

I liked playing cricket, and I loved all the formats, so yes I'd love to have had a go – you grow up playing 20-over games, after all – but it wouldn't have been my preference. That was always for the longer game, because I believe over time you need more skill. That's the true test. First-class cricket will forever be the benchmark. That's where you see the game at its hardest and its best, especially as an opener. It's there where, as a cricketer, you find the ultimate challenge.

It's why my view has changed since I wrote my first book, a diary of a cricket season, 30 years ago. Back then, I said if I had my time again I wouldn't be an opener. I don't feel like that now. There's something about opening I like. I still think it's the hardest place to bat, but also, some days, it can be the best. It's rewarding to put on a good stand, see off the fastest bowlers when they've got a new ball. You might get only 30, but you've blunted the attack, leaving the way open for three and four, the likes of Atherton and Fairbrother, to come in and make the most of it.

It was Bumble who taught me that openers have to soften the ball so the glamour boys can cash in, and there is a truth in that, but there's something gratifying in knowing that you start the innings, and anything you achieve you've had to battle to get there. There's no such thing as an easy start. If you come in number four and its 220 for two and then you get 150, it's not quite the same, is it? When Gatt came in during my double ton in India, we were 178 for one, so it wasn't exactly fierce. A different challenge, admittedly, because it was turning, but not the same.

We had a situation at Old Trafford once where we needed only about 170 to win, but we knew the new ball was going to be a danger. If we didn't see it off, we were going to be absolutely knackered. Gehan Mendis and I just battled and battled. I got something like 25 in an hour-and-a-half – it was not glamorous, but by that time the new ball had gone. As I was walking off, some spectators in Stand D (where the blokes went who came on their bicycles in April and sat there whether there was a game on or not) shouted: 'Get off, Fowler, you're rubbish! We pay your wages.'

I looked at them and stopped: 'Pay my wages? I pay taxes. I pay yours.' They might not have appreciated it, but we knew the job was done and we ended up winning the game.

If you're an opening batsman, you're absolutely at the brunt of it, and that's even more so in Test cricket. There are times when you've been in the field for two days and you just want to sit down for an hour before going out to bat, but you've only got ten minutes between innings before Richard Hadlee comes steaming in.

When Richard Hadlee bowled at you in county cricket, he was brilliant and never gave you any rubbish, but even with him there was still a massive difference between how he bowled at you for Nottinghamshire and in international cricket. The same was true with the West Indians. I'd opened the batting against all their bowlers in county cricket, but when all four of them together went up a gear, Jesus!

No wonder people wanted to be a four or a five. You get to put your feet up, come in when the ball's a bit soft, but, on reflection, there's a certain pride in opening the batting. Also, I don't know how the hell I would have coped with waiting to go into bat. When I was in the middle order, I'd get in such a state I'd just want there to be a wicket so I could get in. And that's not really ideal in a dressing room or for your team-mates, so opening probably was the best place for me to bat, even if it was just so everyone else could get me out of their hair. But at the time, I didn't think about it – I just got on with it, despite having been a middle-order slogger up until Jack Bond moved me to the top of the order. And that's why I never batted like a traditional opening batsman, because my instinct was to hit the ball. Maybe, after all, I have a bit more in common with the modern cricketer than I realise!

CHAPTER 20

THE RHYTHM OF LIFE

'Hello, you don't know me. My name's Graeme Fowler. Although I play cricket for a living I'm a club drummer. You're an international drummer and a club cricketer.' It was the one and only time in my life I'd ever rung up someone out of the blue and relied on my name. Thankfully, right from the start the person on the other end of the line and I got on like a house on fire. John Keeble from Spandau Ballet is now one of my best friends. The musical connection doesn't end there. I've also spent time with Nick Mason out of Pink Floyd, got to know Bill Wyman, feature on a CD by Roy Harper, and have played with his son Nick a couple of times.

Sarah said it was a club, and when you analyse it, it is, because musicians and sportsmen are cut from the same cloth. What you do is all about timing, you're playing in front of an audience, you share the nerves, the performance element, the training, the practice, the rehearsals, the criticism. You're dealing with adrenalin, improvisation, the unexpected.

If I meet a musician, and he knows I've played international cricket, he automatically knows I understand half of what he does – and he understands what I do. Although the performances are different, a lot of the elements are the same. John Keeble, for instance, is a brilliant drummer and an average wicketkeeper. I, on the other hand, am an average drummer and a shit wicketkeeper.

The first set of drums I had I made myself out of biscuit tins and thick polythene. I was 12 and would use my mum's thick knitting needles she made string vests with for sticks. I liked bashing stuff, and as a kid it suited the amount of energy I had. Also, I didn't have the patience to sit in my bedroom and learn how to play the guitar.

I moved on from this rather basic set-up thanks to my mate Simon. He had a drum kit down at Cannon Street scouts and said I could go down and play them. So I did, and I could do it. I was then given a kit by Howard Riley's granddad, a big jazz kit, when I was 15. I'd drum along to whatever I was listening to – I still do now, except I've got my own kit, of course. It's permanently set up in the garage. I might not play it for months, but if it isn't there I miss it. Every now and again I have to go and play it. But I can't play the drums when I'm depressed – can't go near them. I can't listen to music when I'm depressed either. If I'm struggling with my mental health, music is so intrusive it messes my head up – it's too fiddly and painful. And yet when I'm well I love fiddly music.

That side of depression is hard, because music has always been massively important to me, a huge part of my life. I grew up in a house full of music; unfortunately it was opera – Paul Robeson, Kathleen Ferrier. There was just so much of it, and I can't stand it. Instead, the first single I bought was 'I Want To Hold Your Hand', by The Beatles, and the first album was *Goodbye Cream.* I didn't understand it the first time I heard it, but it cost me £2.15, and it was the only album I had, so I just played it again and again. Over time I came to love it. The second LP I bought was *Meddle* by Pink Floyd. Side two contains just one track, 'Echoes'. The first time I heard it I was in heaven. I actually remember thinking: 'This is my classical music. This is fantastic.' I still love listening to it now.

I liked Yes because vocalist Jon Anderson used to be our milkman. He and his brother used to come round in a van with big bull horns on it, and I'd jump in the back and help them. I liked the instrumentation; it took me somewhere. I'd close my eyes, turn the lights off in my bedroom, and get so involved. I didn't have a great stereo system – in fact it wasn't stereo – but I managed to get inside it somehow. It's the closest I've ever been to deep meditation. And then my mum would burst in and ask what I was doing. The funny thing was she used to be a semi-professional singer.

I'd rather have been a musician than a cricketer, I'm sure I would. And it's nice to have that thought, otherwise I wouldn't have a retrospective dream. That's how I see it – not a regret, a retrospective dream. It's been with me all my life, so I'm not going to let it go now.

I did manage to make that retrospective dream a bit of a

reality. John Keeble and I actually played together during one of the PCA dinners at the Royal Albert Hall. If you get to dip into that other world, the buzz is amazing. Playing drums at the Royal Albert Hall was one of the highlights of my life. I had nerves, of course I did, just the same as when I was a cricketer, but there was a slight difference in that I was supposed to be good at cricket, and I really, really, really didn't want to find out I was a shit drummer. That would have spoiled the fantasies I've had all my life.

I'm glad I've tested myself in areas off the pitch. Not that I've always had much choice. When I finished as a player at Durham it was a tight time for Sarah and me. She'd finished at the club, and I was speaking at dinners, and that was all we had, so there wasn't a lot coming in. The following summer I started writing for the *Sunday Telegraph* and doing commentary. Vic Marks, Jonathan Agnew and I had been doing a once-a-month lunchtime slot on *Test Match Special* (*TMS*) called 'County Talk' where we chatted about various cricketing issues. I wasn't earning a fortune, but was getting credibility from it.

It wasn't the first time I'd been on radio. That came when I was walking round the ground at the WACA in 1986 when England were playing in Australia and I bumped into Peter Baxter, the *TMS* producer. 'Come up to the box,' he said. 'You don't mind doing five minutes, do you?' I went in, sat down next to Christopher Martin-Jenkins, put the headphones on, and next thing I knew it was the drinks break.

'We'll just have a few words from Graeme "Foxy" Fowler,' said CMJ, 'and then it'll be Neville Oliver.' At which point he got up and went. I analysed the position England were in, tried to project what would happen, talked and talked, and after two minutes I was wondering 'Where the hell is Neville Oliver?' I turned round and they were all at the back of the box waving at me – they'd stuffed me out of sight. So I carried on and, just as the drinks cart was leaving, Neville came and sat down and thanked me.

I laughed, because I knew what they'd done, and asked Peter Baxter who I'd been talking to, and whether it was just those in Australia or in England as well. He had these little flick boards which told them which networks they were on. We counted them up and it came to anything between 135 and 175 million people. It was going all round the world, Asia and everywhere. If I'd known that beforehand I probably would have panicked, but now I'd done it I knew I could do it again. Whenever I did radio from then on, I didn't care how many people were listening, I just pictured in my head that I was talking to a friend and explaining the game to them, as if I was talking to my mates in the pub.

In the end *TMS* started asking me back on a regular basis, the person I most enjoyed broadcasting with being Henry Blofeld. I just loved Blowers, although there was a famous occasion where I refused to talk to him on air because he'd insulted my trousers: 'Do you not like my trousers? Right, well, I'm not talking to you.' Half an hour passed and I said nothing.

Sartorially, I'd taken the individuality I was known for in cricket and taken it into the commentary box. I remember interviewing John Keeble for the 'View From The Boundary' slot one lunchtime. To look the part, I'd put on a pair of black leather trousers, black leather T-shirt and black Wrangler leather jacket. I also had a pair of Doc Martens which had mirrors on the top and a pair of black Ray-Bans. I hate being late, so I walked into the box quite early and there was CMJ, standing there with a big broadsheet – he always read his articles every morning to make sure they hadn't been incorrectly edited. 'Morning, CMJ!' He turned round: 'Fuck me!' That was the only time I ever heard him swear.

Those big characters of *TMS* were brilliant, but the whole artistry of it, the whole flavour of the programme, came from Peter Baxter. He allowed and encouraged the mischief, but only up to a point. If there was a feeling it was getting too much, he'd make a little movement with his hand. There were always going to be double entendres and innuendo, but he managed to keep it so it wasn't smutty. You knew what you could play with and what you couldn't, although there were some things he had little control over, like Brian Johnston mentioning the groundsman at Lord's: 'Here he comes, Mike Hunt!' After that, Mike had to be called Mick. But Johnners wasn't told off – it was Johnners, that was what he was like.

Another time I was on with Blowers. It was a Saturday, which after the excitement and settling-in period of the first couple of days of a Test match is often when the game can quieten down a little and the mischief starts. In this case, Bumble had written a letter to Blowers and gave it to Aggers. The way Blowers worked was he looked out the window and talked about what he could see; he hardly ever looked at the monitors. If he couldn't see what he wanted, he made it up. Butterflies, pigeons, buses, they weren't even there half the time. If he wanted you to join in he'd look at you, but at the end of the over I had to speak whatever. At the start of the next over he'd usually say: 'Well, quite right, my dear old thing,' which meant he hadn't fully listened to you, and carried on.

So I was sitting there with Blowers in the old commentary box at Edgbaston and Aggers came across and leant over with this letter. He was smiling, so already I was thinking: 'I don't know what he's given to Blowers, but this can't be right.' What I expected to happen was we'd get to the end of the over, Blowers would look at me, I'd start talking, he'd look at the letter, realise it was rubbish, and throw it away. He didn't. He got to the end of the over and just started reading it.

'Dear Blowers,' it read, 'may I take this opportunity to thank you and the rest of the team for all the wonderful commentary and entertainment you have given us through the years. On this occasion, could you please do me a favour. Every Saturday of the Test match at Edgbaston, our uncle comes and sits in the Eric Hollies Stand with his Radio 4 headset and score-book. Unfortunately, our scorer today has been taken ill and we need him back. If you read this out, we'll know he'll get the message. Thanks again for all the entertainment. PS: Our uncle is affectionately known as Shy Ted.'

Aggers ran out the back of the box pissing himself. Blowers hadn't even realised what he'd said. He just carried on. 'So if you hear me, Shy Ted, give me a wave.' He looked out the box. Everyone was waving.

'Foxy, there appear to be a lot of Shy Teds in the ground.'

'There will be,' I said, 'We're in Birmingham.'

And Peter Baxter told me off for saying that! Looking back, either Blowers had no idea what he was doing or knew exactly what was going on.

Right back to being a boy, I was aware of the history of *TMS*, the nature of it being an institution and the fact it revolved around big characters. In the summer holidays I used to have a glass of water on the windowsill outside the house. When I came back for a drink, *TMS* always seemed to be on the radio. We were also one of those households who had the radio commentary on when the cricket was on the telly, because commentary on telly was incredibly minimal. In fact, it wasn't just the commentary – there was only a camera at one end. I once played a video of me batting to some of the students at the centre of excellence. 'Turn it up,' said one of the lads. 'The volume's on,' I told him, 'there's just no commentary!'

So I was well aware of the likes of Blowers long before I started working on *TMS*. In fact, I'd had an encounter with him on the Ashes tour of 1982-83. I was rooming with Chris Tavaré in Newcastle, New South Wales, and Tav had just made 150, his first hundred of the tour. Tav was out when there was a knock at the door; it was Blowers with one of those big old tape-recording machines and a microphone. 'Hello Blowers, have you come to interview me?' He just looked at me – I was averaging 14 at the time. 'My dear old thing,' he said, 'if you ever get to thirty I'll interview you.' I thought, 'You bastard!'

A month later, in the second Test, I got 80-odd in the second innings after a long run of low scores, so I went and found Blowers: 'I'm here. Ready when you are.'

'What are you talking about?'

'You said if I ever got to thirty you'd interview me. I got eighty-odd.'

Years later, when we worked together, I reminded him of the story. We had an absolute scream about it. Even now I'm really close to Blowers. When he was unwell and needed a heart operation we hugged, and both of us nearly cried.

I knew I had a different relationship with each of the broadcasters. When I was on with CMJ, I had to be a bit more analytical and serious, because that's how he was and he would ask thosc kind of questions, whereas with Blowers it was just open season. Anything could happen. Aggers would cross both boundaries. Then there were the Australians Neville Oliver and Jim Maxwell, West Indians Tony Cozier and Donna Simmons, a barrister with a beautiful voice and the first woman on *TMS*. Peter spotted the dynamic and seemed to know who would work well together. He knew there were some combinations that were far better than others. He knew the programme inside out.

For years, Fred Trueman and Trevor Bailey were the only two summarisers. Fred, as everyone says, was a one-off. I was standing in the corner of the box one day and it was raining so they'd put a repeat of the 1963 England v West Indies Test series on the telly. Fred just came out with it: 'Isn't it funny how black and white television makes you look slow?'

As Fred and Trevor were getting older, it was Peter's view the programme needed broadening. He wanted to inject something a little bit new and different. He was a master at it and I could see where he was coming from. You have a shelf life on radio. If you do it day in day out, you become a broadcaster, like Athers, Paul Allott, Charles Colvile and Beefy, but if you only dip in and out, like I did, one day a little kid is going to ask who's talking and the dad won't know. That's what you don't want. You don't want someone on a radio or television programme you don't know.

I don't think I'd have been good enough to do broadcasting seven days a week. I think I'd have got bored, and you have to take it seriously. You have to do research, you need a good memory for things, and I haven't got that. Peter Baxter once said to me, 'You are a cricketer who now broadcasts, but Jonathan Agnew is a broadcaster who used to play cricket.' I got that instantly – he was absolutely spot on. Aggers cares passionately about cricket, about his broadcasting, and about the BBC as well.

It's strange looking back. *TMS* is a wonderful programme, the most listened-to in the world, but there was always an impression the BBC put it under pressure. It was almost as if they didn't like the fact it was so successful. You got the impression it always had to fight to be on air. Peter, though, to me was a genius. I feel a pride about being part of the institution. I look back on it with great memories.

I did 19 years at the BBC, just dipping in and out. However, at Sky, where I was a roaming summariser, I might do ten days out of 14. I would do a one-day game at Nottingham, then head down to Hove the next day, and then go back to Nottingham the next for *TMS*. I was doing an incredible amount of miles. It was just ridiculous. Eventually, Sky got a bigger contract and needed more people. They questioned why they were dragging me round the country when they could use someone more local. That was fine by me. I admire what Paul Allott did, banging on the door of Sky and ending up working for them, and I take my hat off to him for that, but it wasn't what I wanted to do.

When it came to writing for the *Sunday Telegraph*, that wasn't quite so simple. For a start, I wasn't really welcomed in the press box by some people. There was an attitude from certain individuals that I was taking a journalist's job, as in those days there were far fewer former players working for the papers. The first game I did was at Harrogate and I didn't know what the hell I was doing, where the press box was, anything. Eventually, I found it, went in and sat down. 'Get out of that seat,' a voice snapped, 'that's mine.' It was the county cricket writer Martin Searby.

The following day, my piece was in the paper, but I looked at his article as well. Half of what I'd been saying in the press box was in there. I thought, 'You're having a go at me because I'm nicking your job, but actually it's lucky for you I was there or else you wouldn't have a piece.' So, often I wouldn't go in the press box and would sit somewhere else.

After a one-day final, I'd written my piece and phoned it in. Right at the end, Ian Austin had gone berserk and won man of the match for Lancashire. I was in the pub when the sports editor rang and asked me for 500 words on Austin – immediately. I sat in an emergency exit across the road. Somebody must have spotted me because they brought me a pint. I managed to do it and ring it in. That was the first time I felt massively under pressure, but weirdly enough I always felt more nervous before writing a piece than I ever did before standing up to speak, going on radio, or going on telly, because there's something in me that says once the word is written it lasts forever. There's nothing more permanent, more precious, than the written word, and because I knew my grammar wasn't that good, I didn't have a lot of confidence. I used to say, 'Can you pass me them shoes?' and I didn't know that was wrong, because I was brought up in Lancashire and our English teacher didn't correct me. It was only Sarah who corrected me. 'It's *those* shoes,' she said.

I might not be writing for newspapers or be on the radio any more, but these days there are other ways to communicate. Social media has been an amazing outlet for me, not so much for cricket, more for when it comes to talking about mental health.

Initially, I was drawn to Facebook, basically to see what my lads at university were getting up to, but I never really got a handle on it. I kept getting requests from people to be my friends. I'm quite a sceptical bloke at the best of times, so I'd think, 'You're not my friend.' It's for the same reason I hate people calling me 'mate'. I've lost my cool on a couple of occasions because of people who don't know me calling me 'mate'. It was the same with Facebook. So I didn't use it a great deal, and then, to make matters worse, another bloke called Graeme Fowler, from America, kept posting college photographs that somehow ended up going to all my friends who wondered what I was up to. I had no idea what was happening, so in the end I thought 'Bollocks to this' and deleted it. It was just an annoyance.

A bit later I heard about this Twitter thing, but I didn't know what it was, so I asked George, who told me she had a page. That changed things. I wondered what my 14-year-old daughter was doing on Twitter and was it an evil place.

She set up a page for me. I had a look at it, couldn't fathom it, didn't know what it was, and so I didn't touch it for a while, but then came the winter I had a really bad cough and ended up being really depressed. I was sleeping on the settee downstairs. One night there was bugger all on telly so I went on Twitter and, in a way, just started shouting into the dark. One of the things I put out was a quote from a Marillion song called 'Afraid Of Sunlight'. The line is: 'I'm already dead, it's just a matter of time.' I posted that and got quite a reaction, but that reaction was things like: 'Keep going, you'll be fine' and 'Hope you're OK'. All of a sudden I realised: 'Wow, I don't know these people and they're wishing me well.'

Over the months, my understanding of Twitter developed. I basically have three topics. One is cricket, one is mental health, and the other is bollocks. I love just tweeting rubbish. Like when Eurovision's on I'll just commentate on it. I love doing that. Another time I had a rant on a train, as if really I was talking to Sarah, because this bloke had sat next to me and he wouldn't shut up. He was talking shit to everybody, and I was on Twitter: 'I wish this fucking bloke would be quiet.' I don't know what happened but I got dozens of followers because of that. People were retweeting things. I actually took a picture of him and posted it.

The thing I also like about Twitter, which is different from Facebook, is you're not equals. If I follow somebody, I am a follower, therefore I am subservient to them; I respect their views and I am polite. So if somebody follows me, we're not equals either. They're subservient to me. I'm not saying they're less of a human being, I'm just saying on this form of social media these are the rules of the game. So anybody who has a go at me – and I've had a few, although not like Beefy, who gets death threats and all that sort of crap – I will block. I'm not going to reply to give them the satisfaction of a response. Beefy will say something like: 'See you, numpty!' Well, I'm not even going to do that. I've even blocked people just because they're boring. Oddly, the thing most people have a go about is cricket, and that's the thing I know most about.

I remember one bloke had a go at me about something to do with mental health. I looked and he didn't follow me. He must have seen a tweet, got the wrong end of the stick, and had a go at me because he thought I was having a go at somebody about mental-health issues, which obviously I wasn't. All I did was retweet it so all my followers saw it, and it unleashed fury on this poor bloke. I don't know how many people dived into him saying: 'If you knew what Foxy had gone through . . .' I never said a thing to him but he got this tirade, so much so he deleted all his tweets. For me, that was amazing. I could see by then that Twitter can be quite a powerful thing.

I have some wonderful people I follow, and I have some wonderful followers, and I keep it lovely because I've found that if I'm down, when I say I'm down, when my MH is below ten, I get unbelievable support. It's not always what they say, it's the fact they're saying something. There's one woman I follow in Holland and if I'm down she just tweets, and if I'm really down she messages me so nobody else can see, little things like a smile, or a wave. At the start I said to her: 'Sorry, I'm not always going to reply, because I'm not always able. But just to let you know that what you send to me really helps.' It's such a lovely and incredible thing.

So I get an enormous amount of support from Twitter, and, because I also say things, I get feedback from people thanking me for helping them by saying what I do. Out of Twitter has grown lots of really good stuff. When I'm depressed, because I can't communicate through speech, I find it so much easier to type something. The support you get back, and the thanks from people, is incredible. I'm never going to meet 99 per cent of them, but I can't imagine what my struggle with MH would have been like without it.

That people find what I say helpful is not born out of me being an expert on mental health, it's born out of me being honest and talking about it, and people finding their own solace in it. It's not me standing up as a clinician and telling them what they need to do, it's simply about me sharing what happens to me and how I feel. I welcome such open discussion about depression in society. I think there's a long way to go, but it's definitely progress. If one in four people will suffer with mental-health issues in their life, how can you keep quiet about that?

It's not shameful to have mental-health issues. Neither is it a tick in the box that everybody needs, to make them a man or a woman. There seemed to be a thing in the 1980s where actors, actresses, rock stars and all sorts of people were revealing 'My Drink And Drugs Hell'. It was almost like a rite of passage. What a load of shit that is. Having a mental-health issue is not a rite of passage. It's just something we need to talk about, something we need to help people with, and the more we talk, the more it becomes acceptable to say, 'Well, actually I have a bit of that as well, but don't worry about it, we can deal with it.'

I was at the Emma Bridgewater factory in Stoke-on-Trent to meet Alastair Campbell, another who has experience of mental-health issues, who was giving a talk at the city's literary festival based at the pottery. In the gents, there was a poster specifically referring to mental health, advising staff, if they felt affected, what to do and where to seek help. I thought that was brilliant. It was just so refreshing that a place of employment was not only open about the fact some of its workers may have mental-health issues, but also had the attitude of caring about their staff, not hiding from the issue, and being available to help out. How many workplaces are there where that exists? That was such a lovely thing to see, messages dotted around everywhere looking after the welfare of the workforce. But if you think about it in a logical way, it makes so much sense. The more you look after your staff, the more they're going to enjoy working there, the atmosphere is good, it's going to be productive. Surely you'd like them to come into work knowing they've got support?

Let's just pretend I was working at Emma Bridgewater and my MH was under ten and I was not feeling good, but they knew about it, because I'd been open about it, and I went in one day and I just really sank. If I went up to my boss and asked if I could have half an hour off because I was absolutely struggling, my guess is the answer would be: 'Yes. Go and sit yourself down somewhere.' Knowing that would actually give me the ability to go into work in the first place, but if I didn't feel I was going to be supported when I got there, I'd probably have stayed at home and not bothered.

And yet still there's a lot of places where the attitude is to pretend it doesn't happen, because they don't know how to handle it. And that can never be acceptable; they've got their heads in the sand. In the past, people might have said someone was a moody bugger, but now they might ask themselves if that was it, or did he have MH issues? I'm sure there are still moody buggers who don't have MH issues. It's really hard to tell the difference sometimes, even for the person who is suffering, but if there's an openness about mental health, they can feel encouraged to talk about their problems, find out, and maybe get help.

CHAPTER 21

CRICKET'S FAULT?

There's a question I'm often asked, be it on Twitter or elsewhere, about depression in cricketers – is it the game's fault? My view is that I don't think cricket attracts depressive people, but it is a sport based on failure. It can be a mentally stressful place if you're not playing well, especially as a batsman. If you're having a bad trot, it can play havoc with your head. It's difficult to get away from it. It preys on you somehow, nagging at the back of your mind, as you consider trying this or doing that to solve a technical problem. But that's not the same as having a mental-health issue.

It is also a very mentally confusing game because of its outcomes. Bowlers can bowl unbelievable spells, only to see catches dropped and decisions not given; the next day they'll bowl some terrible dross and get four wickets, and that's hard to reconcile.

As a cricketer, you're living on the edge, putting everything in, and you can't do that without going over the top sometimes. It's a fraught business, a hell of a mix-up. Professional sport is not a nice jolly place, because the whole point of it is to win and to be massively competitive, and if you think somebody is not doing the right thing, they get shouted at. It's not a cakewalk or 'let's turn up and have a nice game'. If something needs to be done, it has to be done immediately because you're playing a game. You can't get rid of that desire and competitiveness, because it's part of human nature.

Let's put it this way: if somebody explained the environment to you, and didn't reveal it was cricket, and said, 'This is where you'll be working, what do you think?' you'd most likely reply: 'I'm not doing that. Where's that? I'm not going anywhere near that place.'

A cricket career is life in concentrated form: you're a junior, you're a good player, you're a young pro, you're a mature pro, you're a senior pro, you're finished. And all that happens in about 12 or 15 years. Sarah once asked me if I thought I'd have a midlife crisis. I said: 'I had my midlife crisis in my mid-thirties. I was finishing playing cricket. That was my midlife crisis right there.' It was as if I'd had a life and somebody had taken it off me. If I was a musician, or an actor, or even a golfer, I could keep going. If I'd been a footballer to the same level I was a cricketer, I wouldn't have needed to work again. But as a cricketer, here I am. Somebody's taken my life off me and I have to find a new one. That's a sadness. Something that you love doing, all of a sudden you can't do it anymore, you have to stop. I knew that was going to happen, but a lot don't. That must have an effect on some people.

Whether, when you put all these elements together, you

can justifiably say cricket can cause mental-health issues, I would imagine in some people it possibly can. It didn't do with me – mine came ten years after I'd finished. But either way, we don't do enough mental training. You can actually make people mentally tougher. If you couldn't, you wouldn't be able to create a good soldier.

How many times do you hear people say cricket is a mental game? And yet 90 per cent of what we do is physical training. Where are the mental practices? How much are we actually doing to help people mentally prepare for the game? We spend more time grooving the physical than we ever do with anything in the mind. And yet you can learn toughness. You can improve it. I've never had a fight in my life, but my dad always told me when I was a kid playing football: 'If there's a fifty-fifty ball, don't back out – you'll get hurt. Get stuck in and you'll be OK.'

He was right, and I took that mentality into my cricket. If I was playing against somebody absolutely rapid on a pitch I didn't like, I was going to get stuck in. If I flinched away, I thought I would get hit and be hurt. Basically, I didn't want to get hit. In some ways, I was almost brave because I was a coward. But it doesn't matter which way you approach it. As long as you don't back out, it's fine.

I took the mental side of the game into my coaching. I'd say to my lads: 'If you don't have a lot of confidence against the short-pitched ball, you've got to practise it.' I'd feed stuff from a bowling machine designed to hit them, but I'd do it slowly at first, so they got to track the ball down and get out of the way. I found the best way to put the danger into context for them was to tell them to put their bat down, watch one delivery, then stand in the way and catch the next one. They'd be amazed that it didn't appear too fast. I'd wind it up a little bit, let them catch four or five, and then I'd say: 'Right, pick up your bat. You know how fast it is, you know what height it's coming at you – what is there to worry about?'

Over a period of time I'd increase the speed, and then eventually they'd go in to bat one day and I'd tell them I was going to give them four bouncers to start with. And they'd be straight out the way, no problem. That mental toughness had come from a confidence and a realisation that the ball isn't that fast, but also from a belief that they could handle it.

I'd had that same training in a slightly more unorthodox way that first time I went to Australia. As soon as they found out I was a Pom, they bombed the shit out of me. Everywhere I went I got abuse and bouncers. But I came back from that winter and I didn't care who bowled at me, what length, or what they said because I knew I could deal with it. I'd learnt that mental toughness and become mentally stronger. So you can teach it, but you have to know what you're doing.

However, making someone mentally tougher to play cricket does not make them immune to having mental-health issues – they're two separate entities. You can't stop depression by rationalising things. That doesn't work. Sarah made a good point. 'If I won the lottery,' she said, 'that would lift my spirits, but if you were depressed it wouldn't make any difference to your mental health.' And she's right, it wouldn't. Just as being rich doesn't make you immune to flu.

So where's that mental wellbeing in cricket going to come from? And what's being done about it? Because something needs to be done. If you've got a twelfth man, that means, statistically, three people in your side, at some stage, are going to have issues, so you can't ignore it. However, it's only in the last ten years that people have started talking about mental health in any sector. Cricket, thankfully, is leading the way in sport. The PCA has been an incredible driver in that. I've contributed videos about my own experience to their website, as have Sarah and George, and I'm sitting down with PCA assistant chief executive Jason Ratcliffe to help put together a mental-health charter. It's not an easy thing to do as I'm not medically qualified, but one thing I do have is experience.

One of the first things to do is to help people know how to recognise symptoms. The more you can get the information out there, the more people can self-analyse and so realise if they've got certain traits. But perhaps more important is the question of seeing it in those around us. It's not just how do I recognise them in me, but how do I recognise them in my mates. Because they may not realise they are suffering, as happened with me.

You have to understand that everybody is different. I've never personally been one to seek counselling. When I'm depressed I can't talk to people. I don't have any words, so sitting in a counselling session would have no point. There's also the fact that I would worry that a counsellor wouldn't know me when I'm well, so what they're seeing when I'm depressed is only half of me. So I'd be very mistrustful of them. I've never really shared my problems with people. I always go inside my own head and sort them out. If, on my scale, I'm a nine, I can deal with it. If I'm a five, I can't talk to anyone. And if I'm a 15, I don't need to. But I know that's not how everyone in my position would see it.

That's not to say there is no point in talking about any issues. For example, I'd use a sports psychologist to help with my cricket, but that's not about who I am, rather it's about what I do. However, seeing a psychologist is about who I am, and I don't want anybody to tinker with that. I don't want someone to take the lid off, because there are a lot of worms underneath. I'm worried there might be more worms than I thought. I might be more screwed up than I think I am, and I'd rather suppress it. I'm sure a lot of psychologists would say that's the worst thing I could do, but I'm 59, it's too late now. I reckon I would get worse the more I found out before I started getting better, and I don't know how long that process might take. It might take years and I have a fear of how awful it could be. It might really tip me over the edge. That's just me, though. Others might find it hugely helpful. I would never dismiss counselling from that point of view.

One thing we can agree on is the fact that Marcus Trescothick, Michael Yardy and Jonathan Trott have all talked about their issues has undoubtedly helped shift boundaries, opened eyes to problems, and encouraged others to seek help. There remain others stuck in the Dark Ages though. I thought David Warner's comment about Trott being weak in Australia was crass and ignorant. He thought he was being hard and clever. He wasn't; he was being an idiot. I wasn't surprised, though. He played at Durham University once and at that stage he was known for one thing and one thing alone – hitting the biggest six ever. You'd have thought he was Don Bradman the way he strutted up and down.

Thankfully, the likes of Warner are an exception. Cricket generally is very receptive to the issue. It's worth players remembering that in cricket you might have been at a club since you were 17 or 18. They've invested a lot of time in you and seen you grow up into a man; they like you and get on with you. They're not just going to chuck you out, are they? Perhaps they might have done in my day, but not now.

Cricket nowadays is dealing with mental health in different ways. It is putting itself ahead of other sports. I was sat next to a very well-respected football manager at a dinner once and we got talking about mental health. 'What did you do with players who might have had any issues?' I asked him. 'Would you send them to talk to someone, sit down with them yourself, have a chat, try to work things out?'

He looked at me. 'No,' he said. 'I just got rid of them.'

Incredible. That should never be the case. Nobody, professional sportsman or otherwise, should ever be treated like that. Cricket is trying to ensure that never happens. And if by adding my voice and experience to the debate I can help to change attitudes, reinforce the fact there should never be stigma attached to mental health, then I can take some satisfaction.

CHAPTER 22

NOT OUT

The summer I have written this book has been my first without cricket for 47 years. It's been weird, firstly not to be involved, and secondly not having so much to do. But that's not been a problem. I'm actually enjoying this period of my life. I don't care about a lot of things. This settee I'm sat on is 35 years old – I'm not bothered. A lot of things that seem to matter to other people are just irrelevant to me.

I'm not bereft that I've finished at Durham University. There's lots of things that need doing, I'll just potter along and do them. I've been like this all my life, when something starts I know it's going to finish, and when it finishes I do something else. Whatever has happened in my life, I've always rather moved forward then dwelt on it. When I separated from my first wife, I just thought: 'She can have the house, she can have everything she wants really, because all I need is me, I can make my way again.'

And that's what I've done – twice. I suppose there's an arrogance in that, but that's always been my viewpoint. I've got me, that's all I need – me. When I stopped playing, I never missed it. So now I'm not thinking my coaching has ended and my life has ended with it. I'm actually seeing it as an opportunity. 'Right, what am I going to do now?' I've enjoyed writing this book, and I'll enjoy other things that come my way, like working with the PCA about depression. My life has never been quiet, and I don't see why that should change. I'm a granddad now, there'll be more grandchildren, and my own children will be doing new things. Who'll be taking the grandkids to school, doing all that stuff? It'll be me.

When I played cricket I was unbelievably selfish. I was the main person in my life. I'm not anymore, and I enjoy not being. It's actually quite nice not being the focus of attention. I love going places and nobody knows, not who I am – why would they? – but what I've done, because if they knew they'd want to talk to me.

When the village had a pub, I used to like going in at tea-time. I rolled up one day and there was a bloke I knew in there with a friend over from New Zealand. The Kiwi started talking about cricket and I just gently joined in, bit by bit. After about ten minutes, he said: 'You seem to know a fair amount about the game.' At which point the other chap piped up: 'Before we go any further, I'd just better tell him who you used to be.' Who I used to be! I'm quite happy with that.

When I went to Beefy's 60th, there were people I'd played with for years who didn't even recognise me. The beard might have had something to do with it.

'Hello, I'm Vivian.'

'Hello, I'm Graeme Fowler.'

'What!?'

I loved playing cricket. I had a great time and that ended. It's like going to school: I had a great time at school and I left. It's the same with travelling. I really enjoy being in this country now. I've been to Australia 16 times. God knows how many times I've been round the world. When I finished playing there was an element of, 'Thank Christ, I don't have to go anywhere anymore!'

It's one of the reasons why, whatever happens, wherever life takes me from here, I don't think I'll be getting depressed simply because I'm getting older. I don't have any great worries on that score. I know there's a chance of another bad episode of depression, but if I have to go through a storm I'll ride it. My brain will make up its own mind, like it always does. All you can do is keep taking the pills – and keep breathing.

Life makes your glass half empty sometimes, so you've got to push against it. You've got to keep going. I don't feel sorry for myself even when I've got depression. It's a bastard. It robs you of your life. It steals your head, your time. But I'm not thinking: 'Woe is me! "My Depression Hell!"' Bollocks. It's just a thing. Let's deal with it. And let's try to help other people by talking about it.

When my doctor described the winter of 2014 as my second episode of medium depression, I thought: 'Thank God it's only medium!' I also thought: 'Once every ten years? I can live with that.' If it takes me another ten years to have another major episode then I'm happy. Make no mistake, there's a lot of people who have a far, far tougher life than me. I only have to say one word – 'refugee'. They might be able-bodied, highly intelligent, and have great mental health, but they're displaced, with everything that comes with it.

I think I'm incredibly lucky. I've had a very lucky life. I've never had to sit in an office doing something I didn't like, waiting for the weekend, desperate to go out with my friends on a Friday night. Basically, all I've done is be me, and at the end of the month the bills have got paid. I've never woken up and thought: 'I hate going to work. I've got to sit behind that desk, go to this meeting.' I'm very thankful to the game of cricket because it's given me my life.

When I finished at the university, I sat down with Sarah and said: 'I'm fifty-eight, and I've never really had a proper job.' I said that in a flippant way, because cricket is a job whether you're playing or coaching, but it's not really, is it? I'm just doing something I love. To get to 58 doing that? Christ! Am I a millionaire? No, I'm not. Have I lived like a millionaire? Course I have. Have I had a privileged life? Yes, I have.

When it came to writing this book, I didn't want to change people's opinions, but I did want to say: 'Look, I have had some fun, but it's not always been how you've thought.' It was also important to me to be open about mental-health issues. Make of it what you want. I don't have some burning desire to tell society about my life and I'm certainly not saying: 'You should all be living like this!' I just want people to share in the fun I've had, and the experiences, be they good or bad.

I look at pictures of myself when I was playing and see the same me, but different – a person living for then. A person living in that time. What I feel inside are echoes. Echoes of my earlier self. These days my focus is within these four walls, with my family. I love to be with them, to hear them laughing. What I have here is everything.

I love everything about life. I just want to go and live it.

AFTERWORD

by Alastair Campbell

It says something about his fine reputation as a cricketer that Graeme Fowler asked Ian Botham to write the Foreword to his book, and that Botham, one of the greatest players of all time, agreed. I hope it says something about Graeme's determination to help change the national conversation on mental health and mental illness that he asked me to write the Afterword.

As an ambassador for Time to Change, the campaign to change attitudes to mental illness, I hope that Graeme's book finds an audience well beyond the cricket fan. First, because the sport as a whole has played something of a leadership role with regards to mental health; and second, because Graeme is someone who has been there, knows what mental illness is all about, writes and talks about it with enormous honesty and humanity. Honesty and humanity – two qualities we require in large quantities if we are to make the steps needed to deliver what any civilised society should have – parity of esteem, understanding and services between physical and mental health.

I know all about Graeme's struggles with depression, because he and I, a fellow sufferer, have discussed them in the past. But it is only on reading his account in full that I have realised just how many similarities there are between us. Born just a month apart, him in Lancashire, me in Yorkshire. Both of us resistant at first to medication and to therapy, even when we knew there was a problem. Both atheists. Both of us finding that writing about our depression helps, and finding that humour, even the darkest kind, helps too. I also learned that we both have a similar recording system for how we feel, though he marks his moods out of 20 – one is suicidal, 20 is ecstatic (though he never gets above 16 so that's OK!) – whereas I mark mine out of ten.

But perhaps where his account resonates most with me is when he writes about how he puts so much energy into what he has to do – like play cricket, or talk about it on the TV – that by the time he gets home he has literally no energy left to do the things he should do, like be nice to his wife and children. I have also got to know his wife Sarah, a huge and positive figure in this story, and the role of the family is so important when mental illness strikes. Graeme and I have both been lucky in the partners and the families and the doctors we have had. Not everyone can say the same.

By coincidence, I am writing this, having just read Graeme's written account on his depression, on the day NHS England are setting out a new strategy for mental health. A representative of one of the leading mental-health charities has just been on the radio, saying that this report is a massive opportunity for the country to take a step change in attitudes, backed by proper government funding for the services we need. Let's hope so. The government has talked the talk on mental health, but not always walked the walk. And of course government must take a lead in all this. But when it comes to changing attitudes, which in some ways is just as important as the money, then stories like Graeme's have a huge role to play. For it is outmoded attitudes which create the walls of stigma and taboo that we are trying to break down.

He writes about some of the other names in cricket who have led the way, notably Marcus Trescothick and Michael Yardy. But then there are those who took their own lives, such as David Bairstow, who I used to watch as a young Yorkshire fan, and whose entrance into the game – he took an A-level on the morning of his debut in 1970 – was one of those sporting facts I just loved and have told others hundreds of times since. He always seemed such a lively and happy character when I watched him play. But do we ever really know what is going on inside the mind of another? As Graeme points out, most people with a public profile spend an awful lot of their time 'acting'.

Graeme is reluctant to 'blame the game' for the seeming high prevalence of mental-health problems among cricketers. But any rational analysis of the modern game at the top level – weeks and months spent away from home, including Christmas, missing so many key moments in your children's development; the macho culture of professional sport in which to think 'man up' or 'pull yourself together' was the right response to someone struggling; the reality of failure for all players (as Graeme points out, for every innings Australian great Don Bradman hit a century, he had twice as many when he didn't) – is not naturally conducive to good mental health, even if the fitness requirements may be.

Attitudes are changing and cricket, including ruling bodies and perhaps especially Players' Associations, deserves a lot of credit for the openness it encourages, and the support given to players who are struggling. But it is always the human stories that connect, and will bring those walls of stigma and taboo tumbling down. Graeme was a great team player on the field, and a genuine talent with the bat. He is now part of another team, the one that is fighting for better understanding of illnesses that can strike anyone, rich or poor, successful or not, surrounded by a loving family or living alone.

When I wrote a novel about depression, *All in the Mind*, the response that touched me most came from a friend and colleague, Charlie Falconer, who had been in the Blair government as Lord Chancellor. As happy-go-lucky a character as anyone could want to meet, he said after reading the novel that he 'finally understood what it must be like to have depression'. I think a lot of people reading Graeme's book will say the same thing. He tells it like it is. No two people are the same. No two depressive episodes are the same. But I defy anyone to read this book and not come away with a better understanding that depression just is. There does not have to be a trigger. There is not always an explanation. Some people get it, some people don't. Like cancer or diabetes or asthma. People who get it get it sometimes, but not all the time, and we all have to find our own ways of dealing with it, and the more we share those, the better.

Graeme's is a very human story, and he tells it in a very human way. And in doing so, I hope it helps him find a peace that has often been missing. But more important, in sharing his story as he has, he will send a message to people struggling right now that they are not alone, that the debate on mental health is becoming normalised, and one day we will look back and wonder why it took so long.

Oh, I forgot ... he was also a bloody good batsman. But Beefy has told you all about that.

ACKNOWLEDGEMENTS

I would like to thank Ian Marshall for giving me the opportunity to write this book. Sir Ian Botham OBE and Alastair Campbell for their kind words, I admire them both, and am humbled by their comments. I would also like to thank Mark Stoker for the wonderful cover photo.

Most of all I'd like to thank John Woodhouse. He made the writing of this book a joy. Without his direction, care and humour, this book would not be as it is. My thanks also go to Steph, his wife, who has put up with him working all hours.

It also has to be said that Sarah and I have become firm friends with both of them and we are grateful for that.

Finally, I could not have done this without the support of Mrs F, my favourite drinking partner.